Dining Tables

of

Indonesia

Valensia Harumi Edgina

To Edhie Dellarosa and Juliati Soehalim,
my biggest influences on appreciating the simplicity of life.

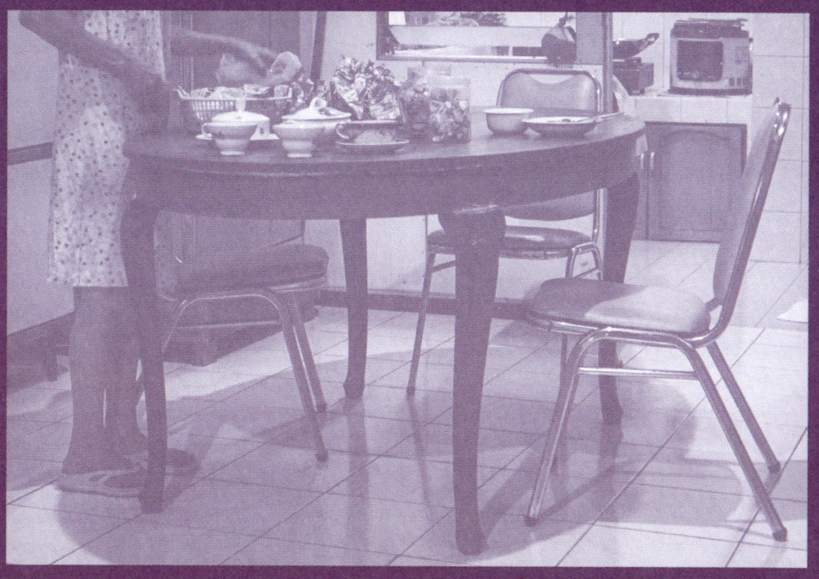

Home in Pontianak, 2024

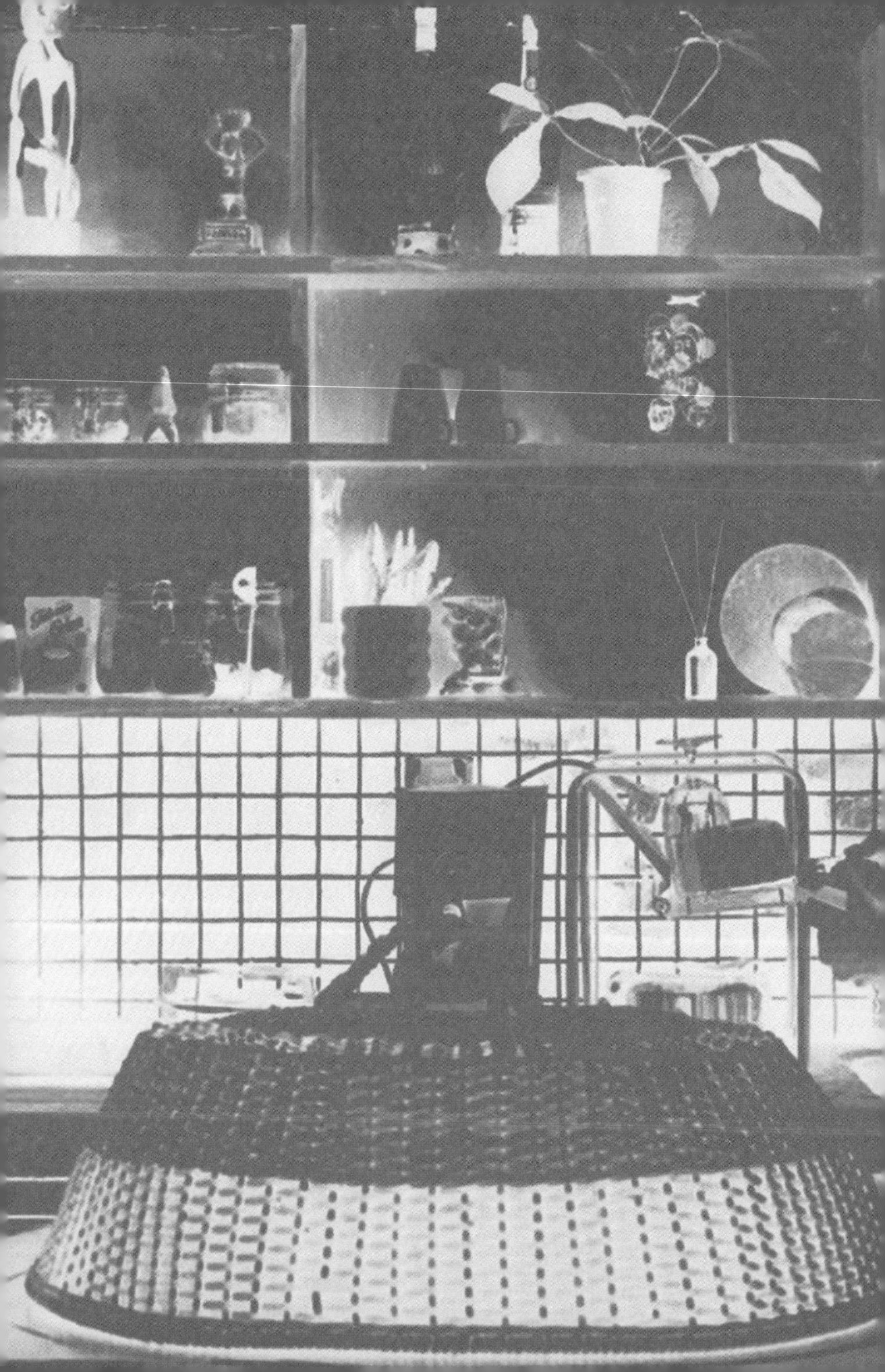

contents

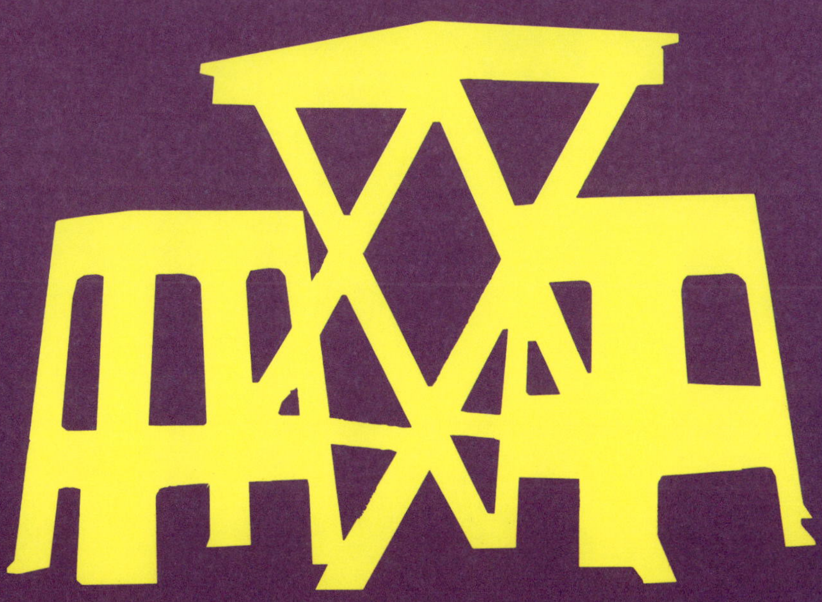

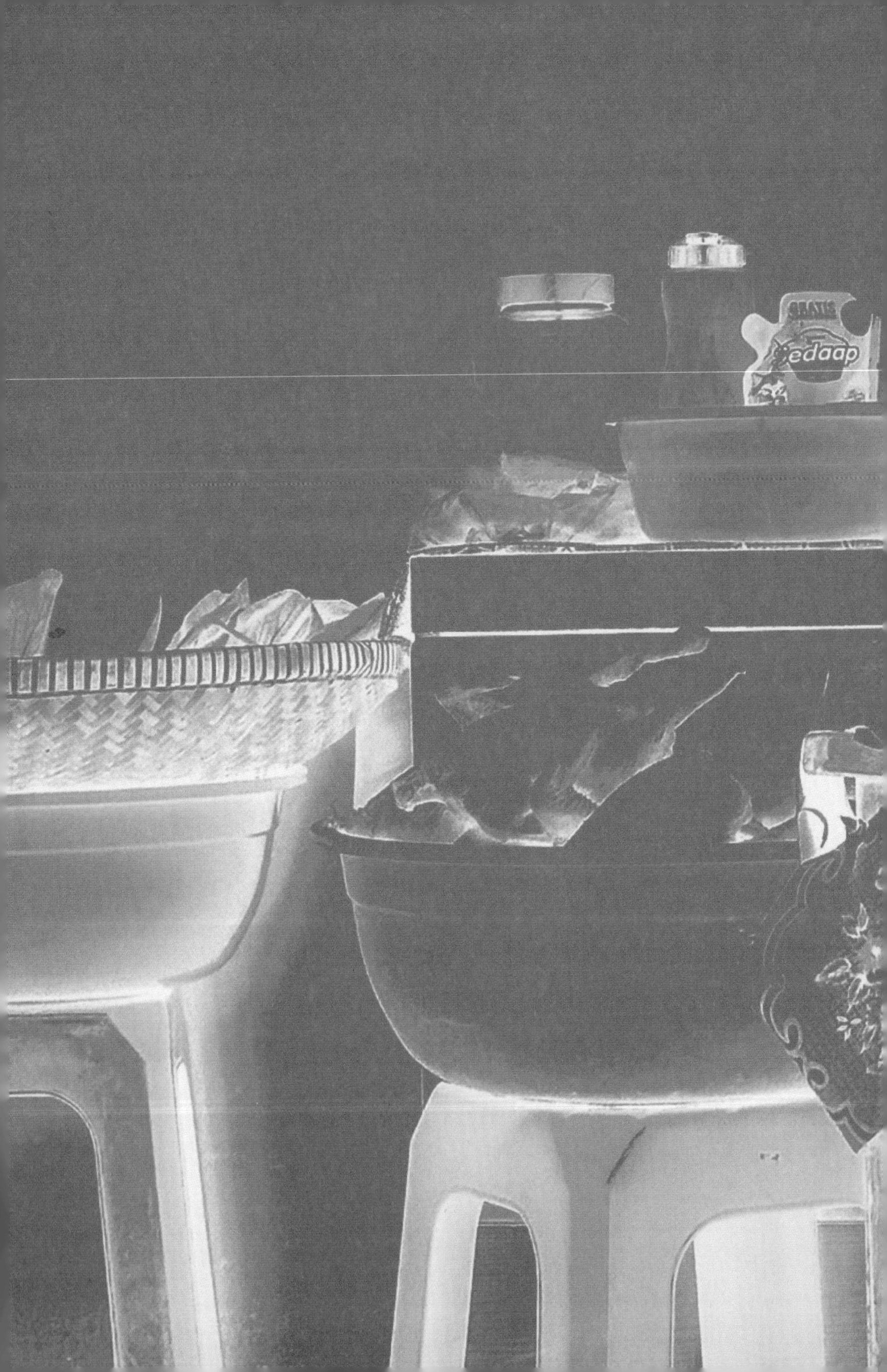
Sedaap

preface

It's truly fascinating how much can happen at a dining table. From simply sharing meals that introduce us to new cultures, to the pivotal moments of diplomacy and decision—making that have altered the course of nations, the dining table embodies the essence of human connection and possibility, all within the most ordinary setting.

Across cultures and centuries, tables play a central role in private houses and public eating establishments. Specifically in Indonesia, they symbolize a meeting point where socio-cultural norms intertwine with relationships, non-formal education, local wisdom, and the creation of collective memories. In some traditions, dining tables serve as more than just surfaces for eating, they are spaces for ritual, celebration, and transmission of cultural heritage.

For me personally, the dining table has always been a quiet anchor. I remember one Christmas Eve, when our parents were away caring for our father's recovery—I invited my sisters to sit and share a meal together. I must've been in primary school, but something in me just knew: we needed to gather. There was no feast, but I believed that being at the table together could bring us closer, especially when everything else felt uncertain. From small joys to the hardest conversations, many turning points in my life have happened right there—around a dining table.

However, the shapes of dining 'tables' may not always include a flat, tall surface for placing food and beverages on. Indonesian sometimes eat with '*lesehan*' style, a term for traditional dining style where people sit on the floor or on low benches around a low table or mat, sometimes on the ground, or even with hands as the surface.

Through my lens, you will find that in Indonesia anything can serve as a table as long as it fulfills the expected function:
to share meals and often times — stories.

Dining Tables of Indonesia is an attempt to document and share culture featuring tables of various public eating establishment types around Indonesia from 2019 – 2024 through photography as a medium.

May this piece serve as a window into
the cultural abundance of Indonesia.

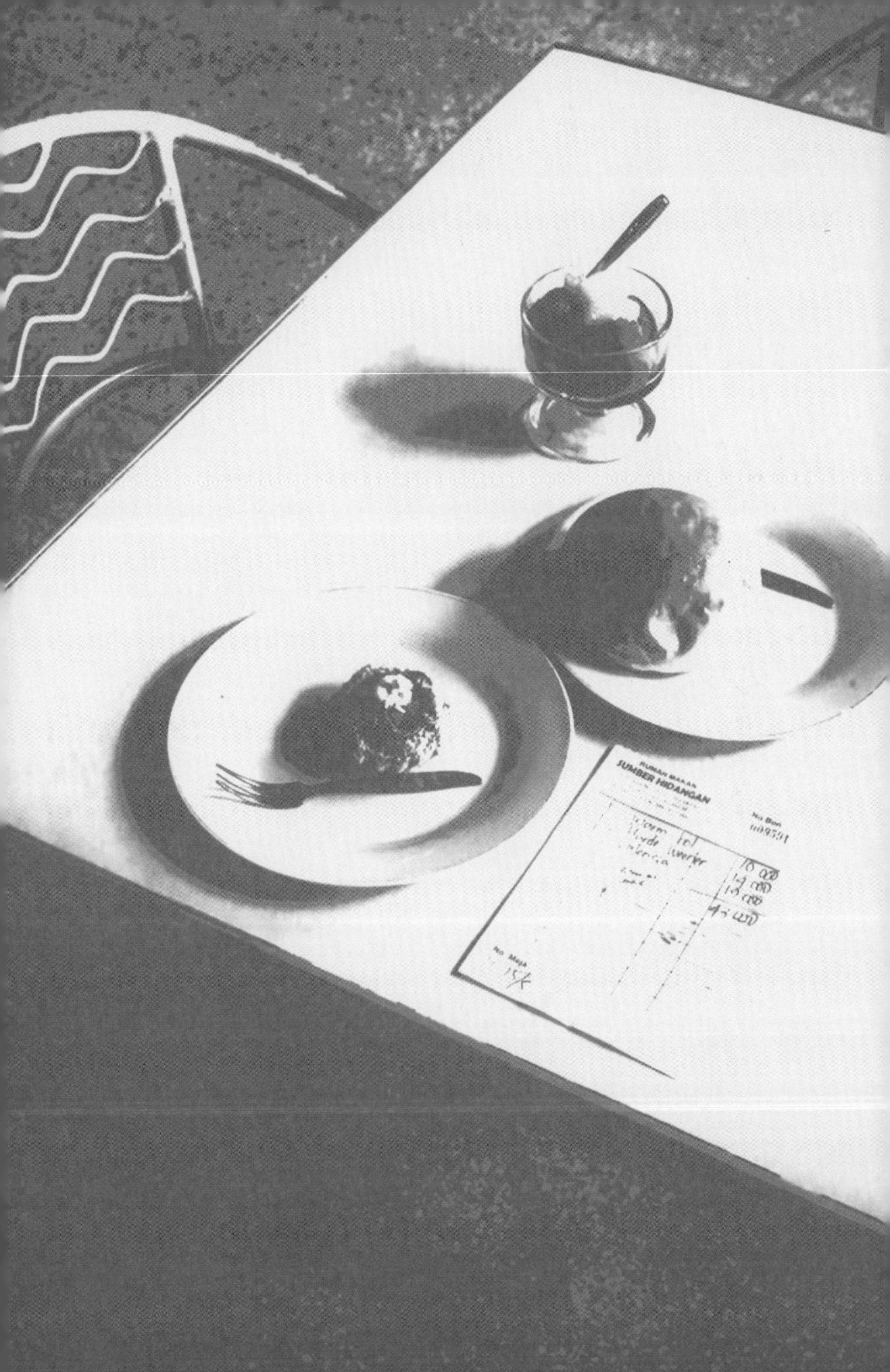
RUMAH MAKAN
SUMBER HIDANGAN
No Bon
No Meja

dining table and sharing

Across generations, dining traditions have been passed down in diverse ways. Each table, with its unique shape and history, embodies the lives of different people. Its significance in personal and family life is profound, as many Indonesian families make important decisions at the dinner table. As a community that values collective over individual interests, the dining table plays a pivotal role in facilitating these decisions.

According to Professor Murdijati Gardjito, an admirable professor and maestro of food education from Gadjah Mada University, dining tables also teach tolerance and mutual respect in the society.

Not only decisions of small families around the archipelago, dining table also played a significant role in the creation of Indonesia as a nation back in 1945, where the nation's leaders gathered to dine and decide on Indonesia's Independence Day.

Whether choosing something as trivial as school holiday destinations or debating ideological deliverances, countless pivotal decisions have been made around these tables.

In daily life, the act of sharing food continues to reinforce a sense of togetherness. Many Indonesians are raised with the habit of offering what's on their plate before serving themselves. This practice, whether it's offering the last piece of *gorengan* or inviting a guest to eat with the familiar phrase *"mari makan"* reflects the deeper values of generosity and collective care embedded in our food culture. These shared spaces are not always harmonious, but they remain constant, a witness to the everyday negotiations of love, duty, and belonging.

While the photos in this chapter aren't exclusively taken at home, the spirit of togetherness lives on. Whether captured at roadside stalls, school canteens, or humble warungs, these tables still hold the same intimacy—where strangers become companions, and meals turn into memory.

The settings may vary, but the essence remains: food as a bridge, and the table as its meeting point.

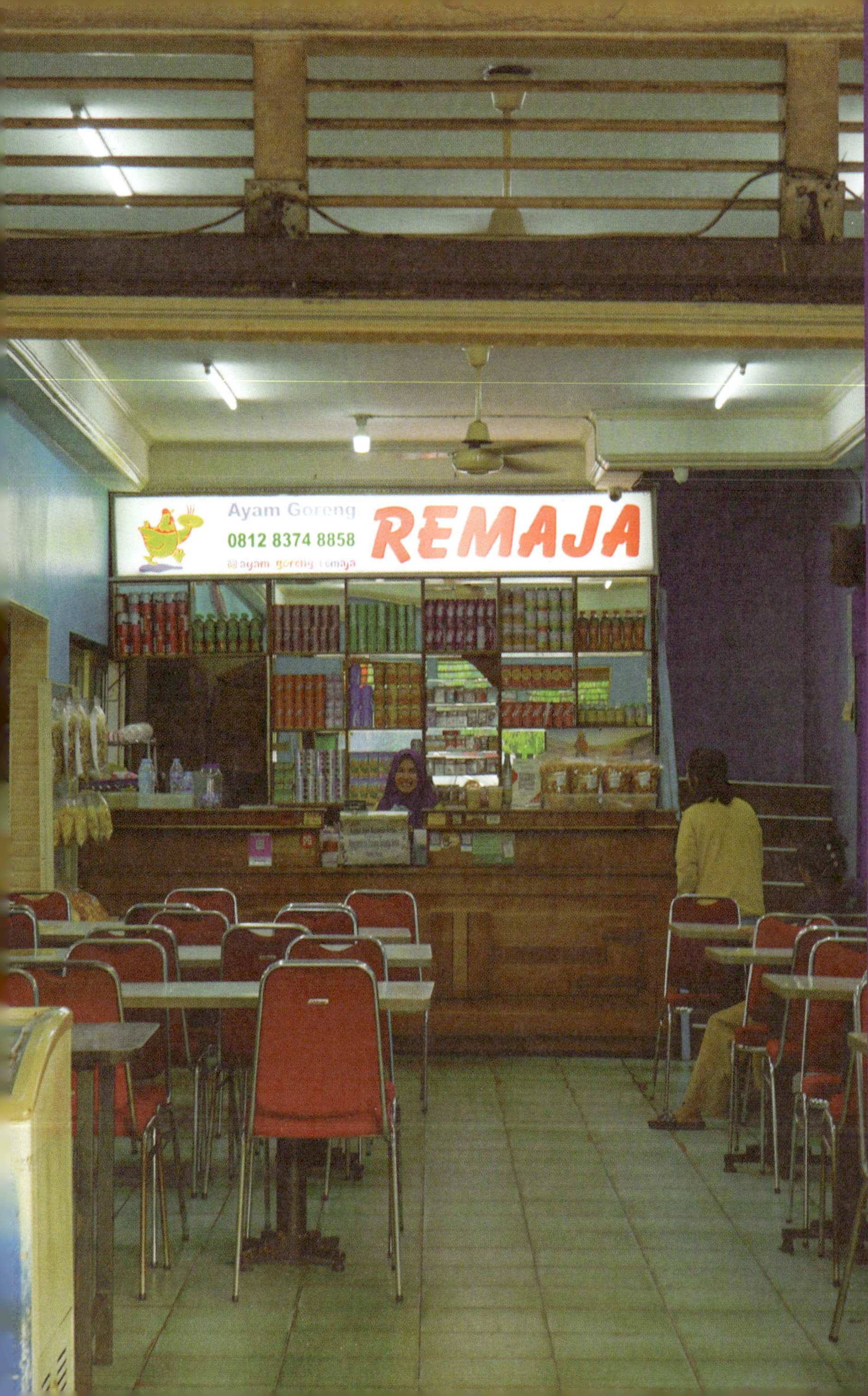
Ayam Goreng
0812 8374 8858
@ayam_goreng_remaja
REMAJA

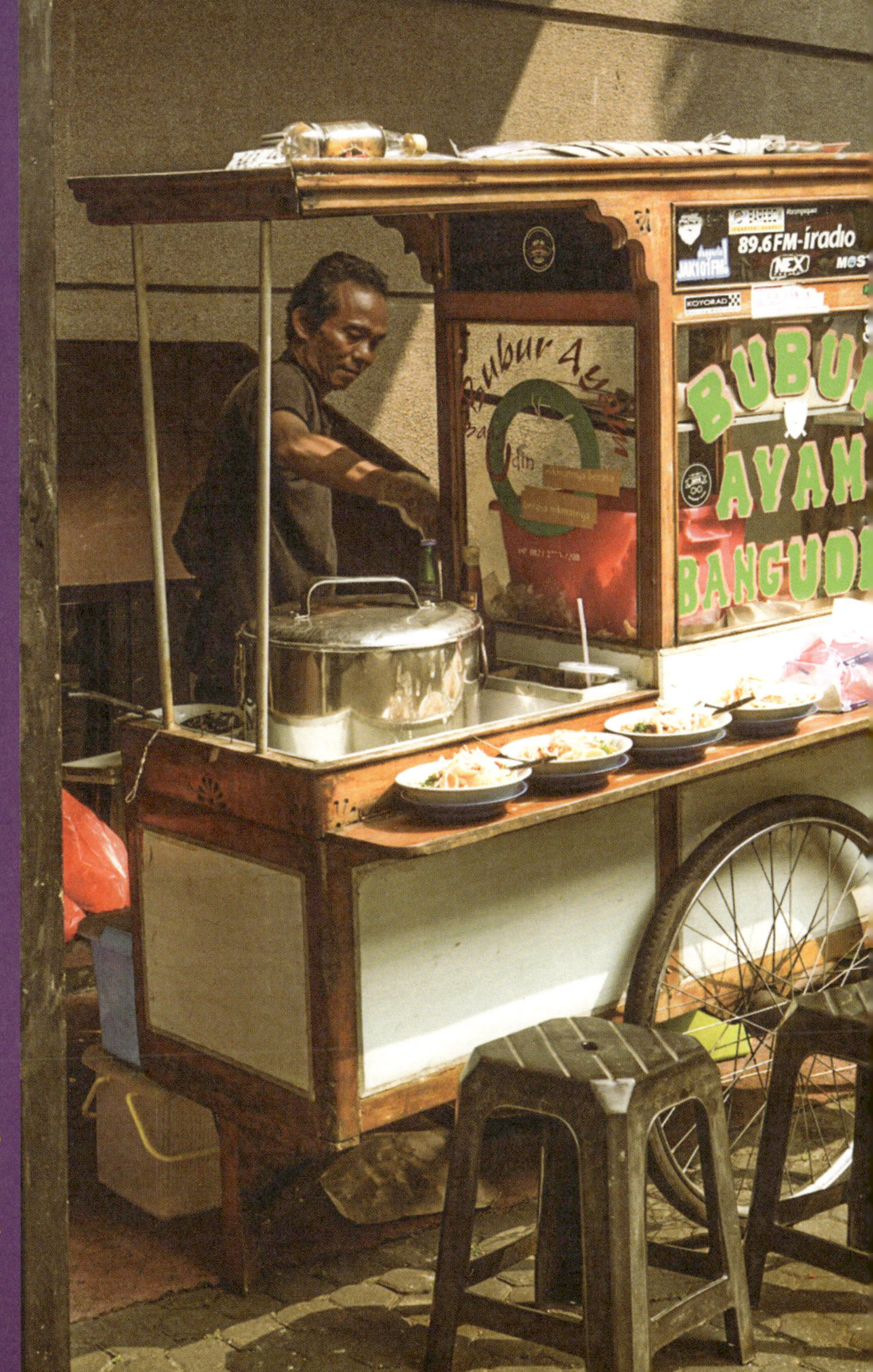

Bubur Ayam Bang Udin, Jakarta, 2023

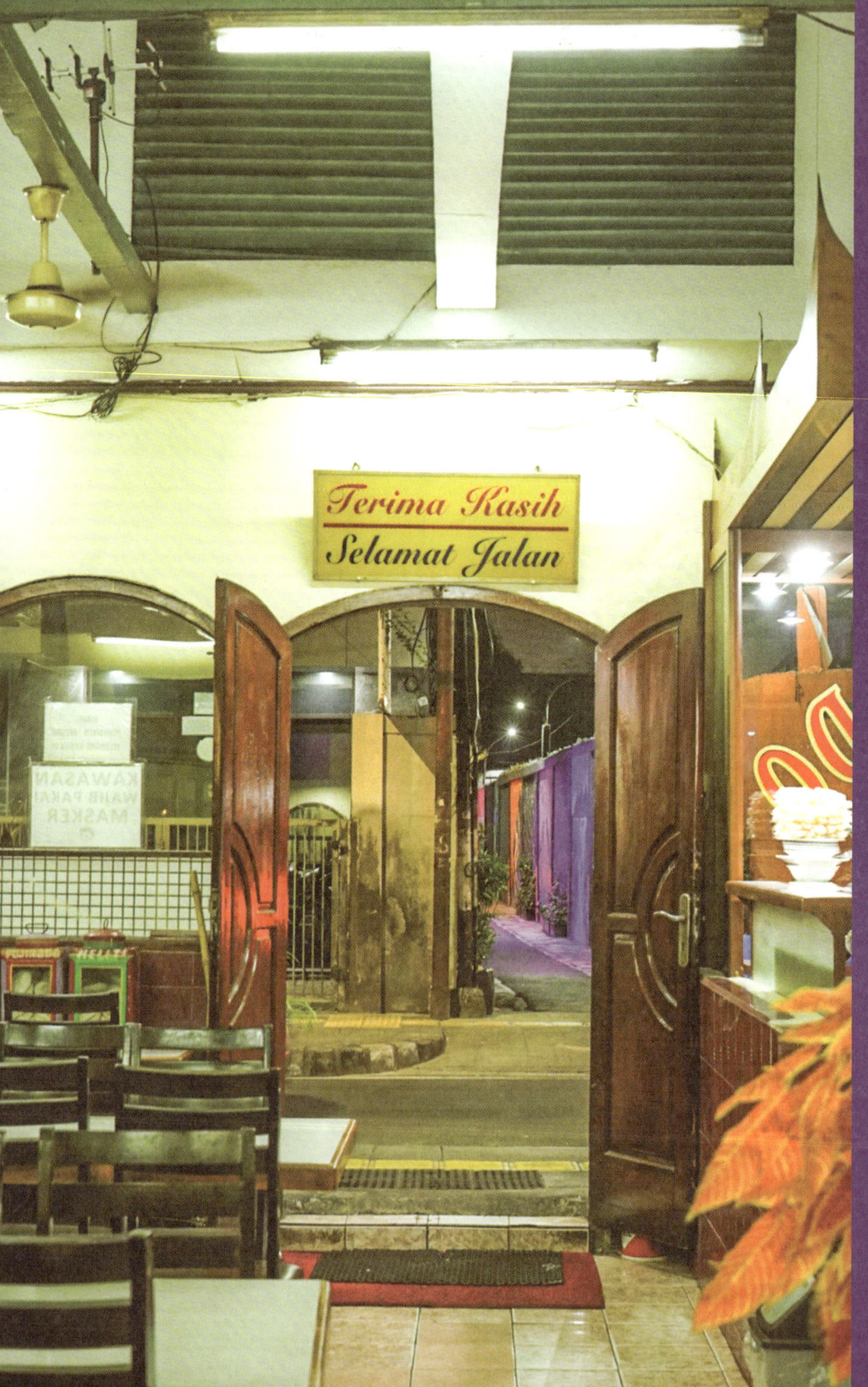

Rumah Makan Jasa Bundo, Jakarta, 2022

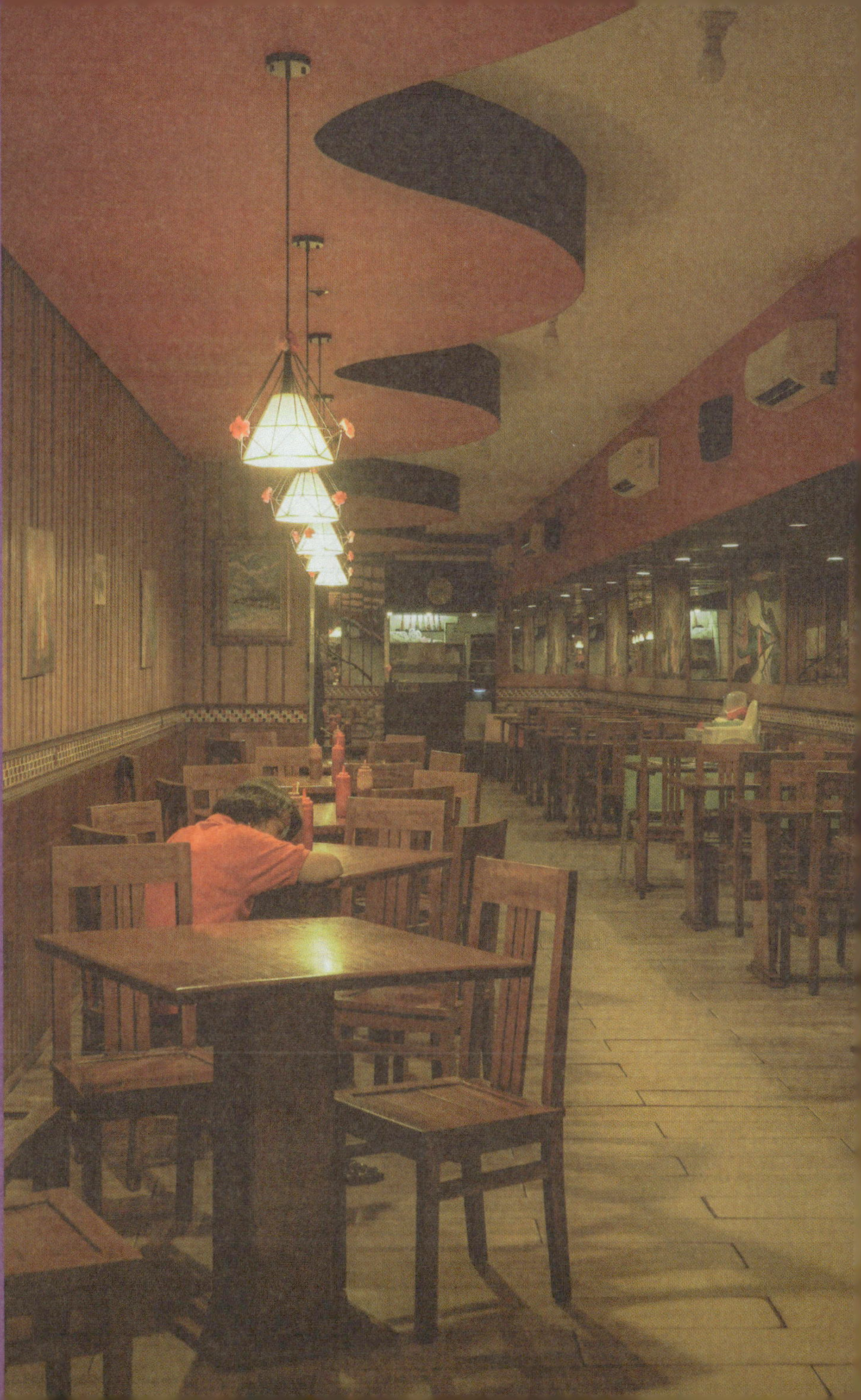

American Chicken, Pontianak, 2024

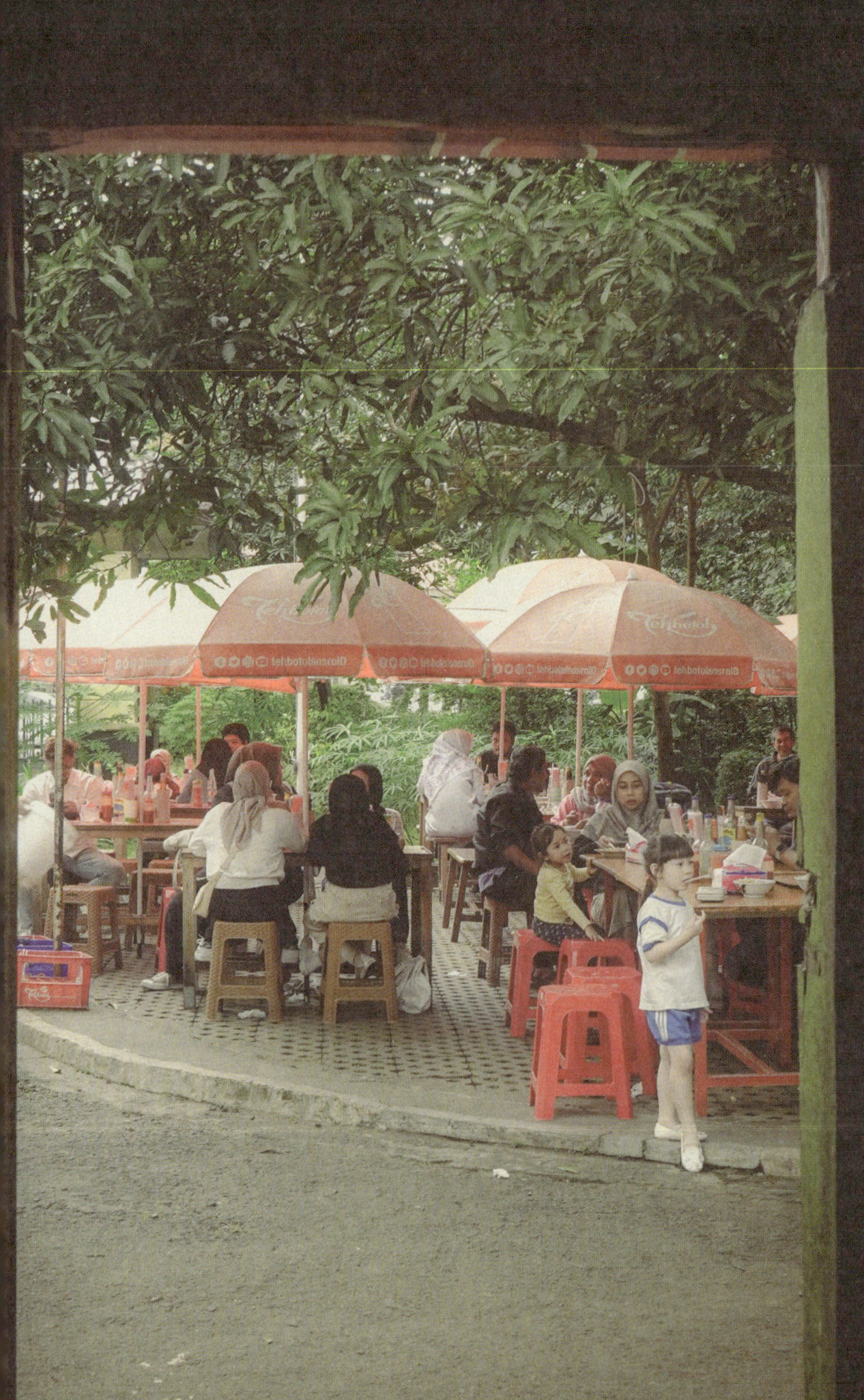

Cuanki Serayu, Bandung, 2024

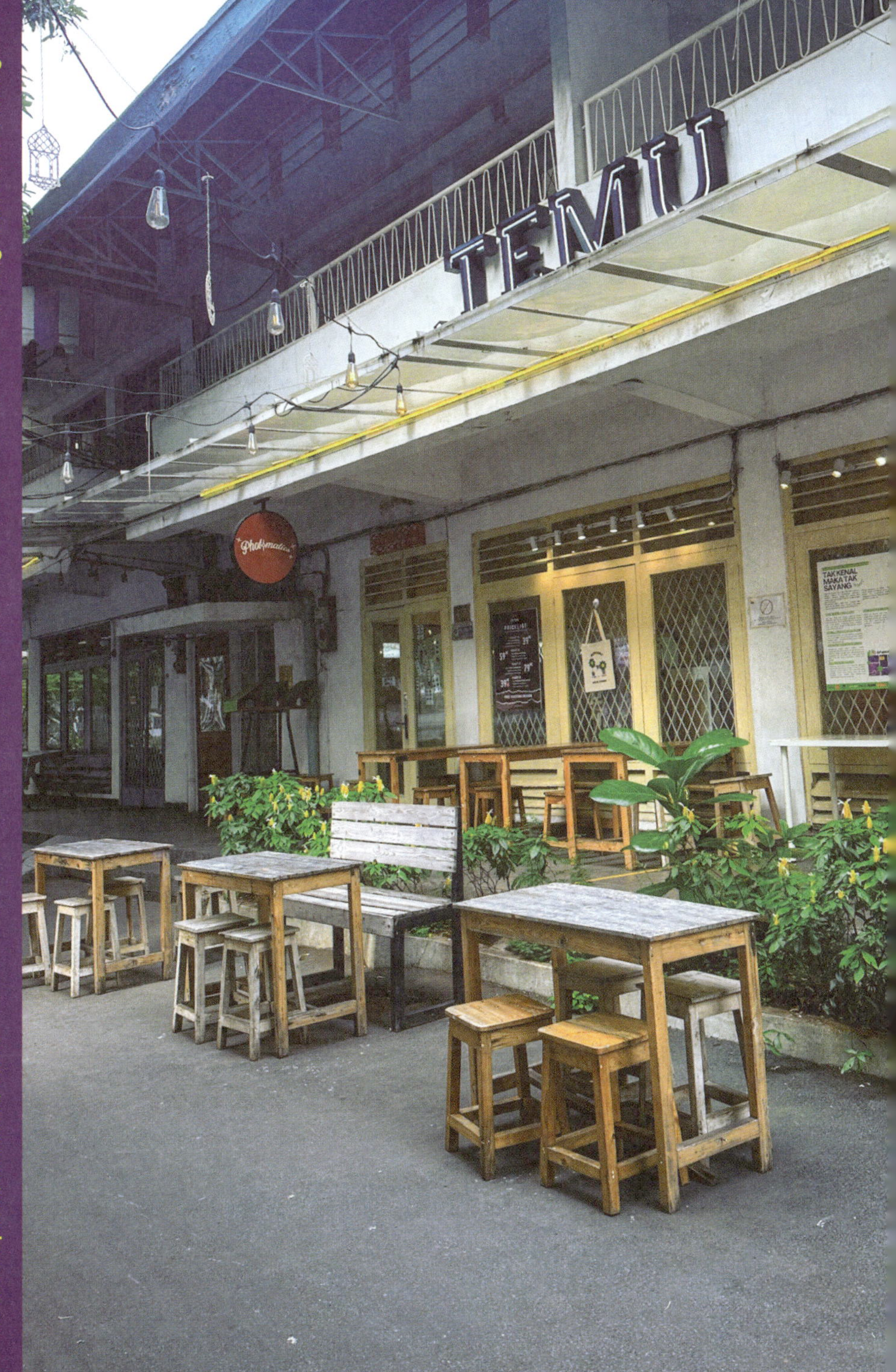

M Bloc Space, Jakarta, 2023

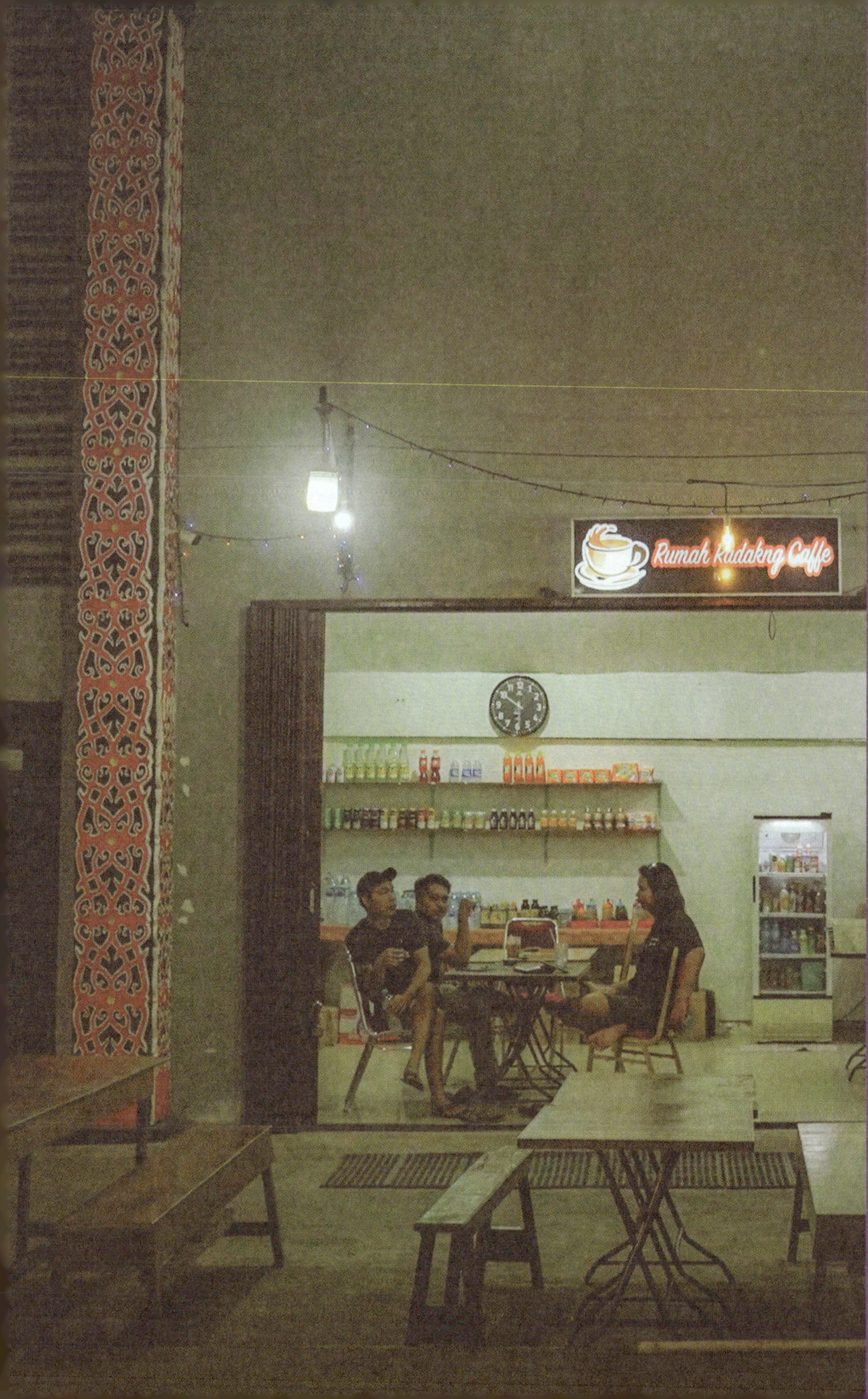

Rumah Radakng Cafe, Pontianak, 2024

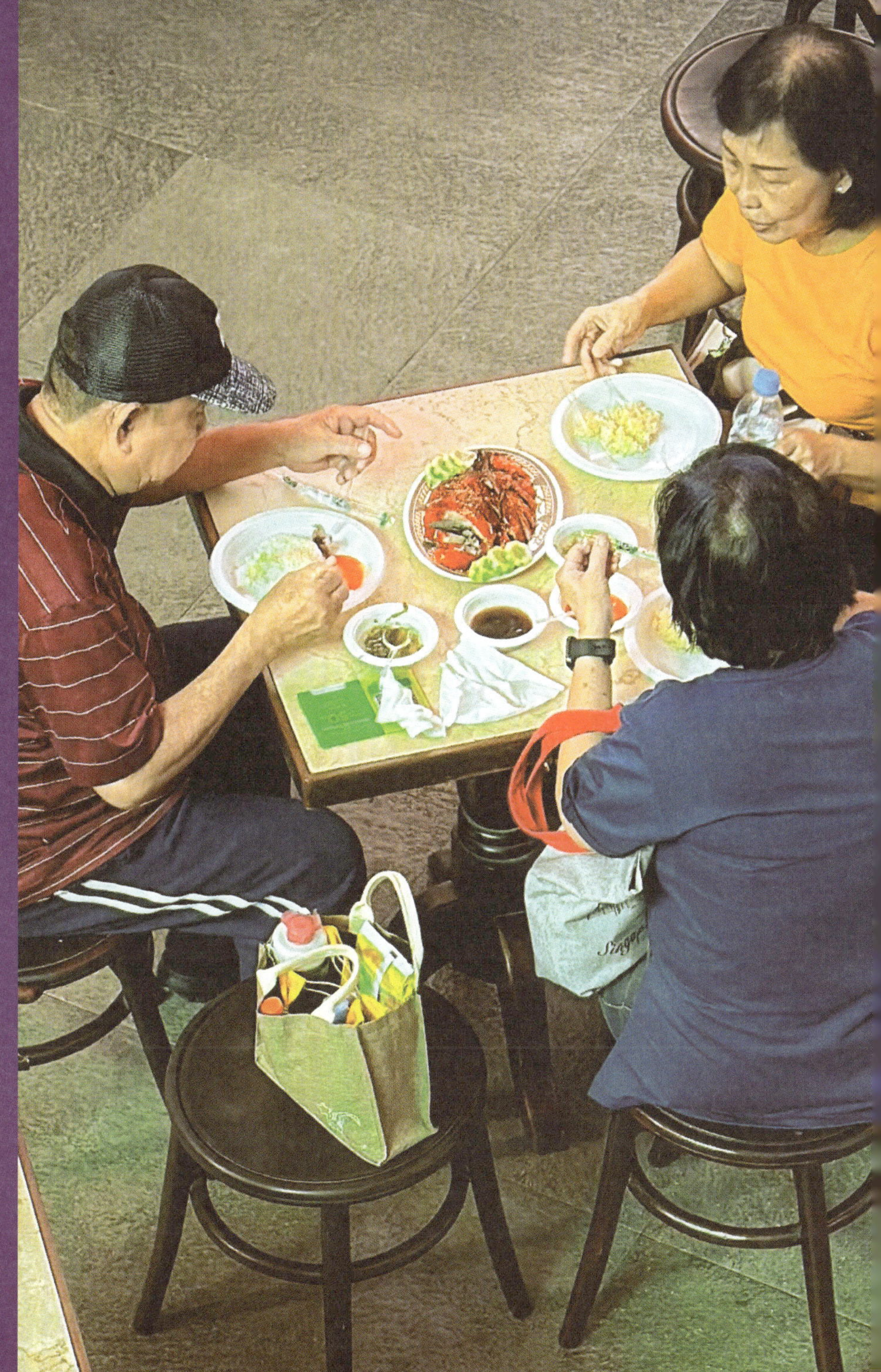

Petak Enam, Jakarta, 2024

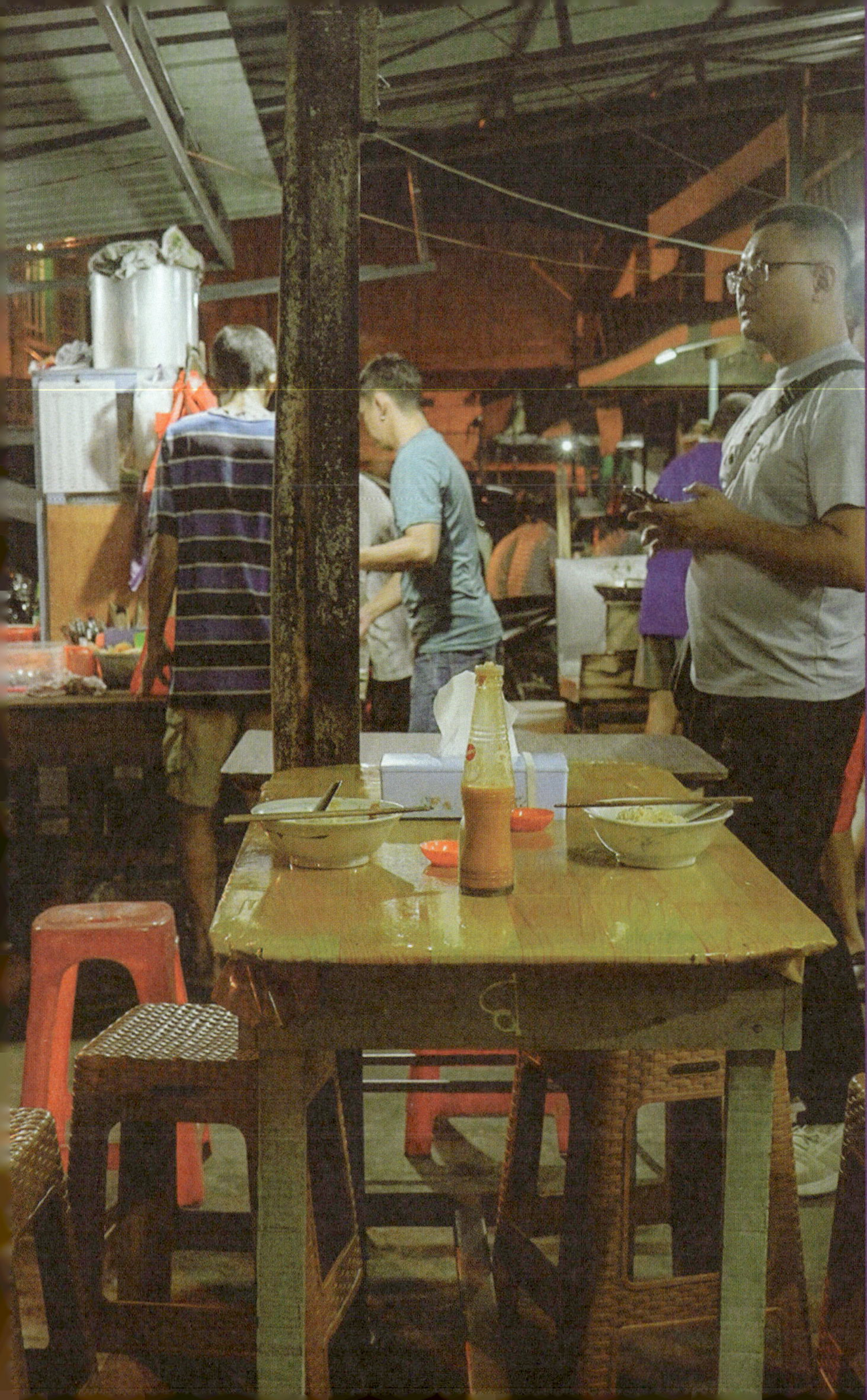

Bakmi Tunggu Tauke, Pontianak, 2024

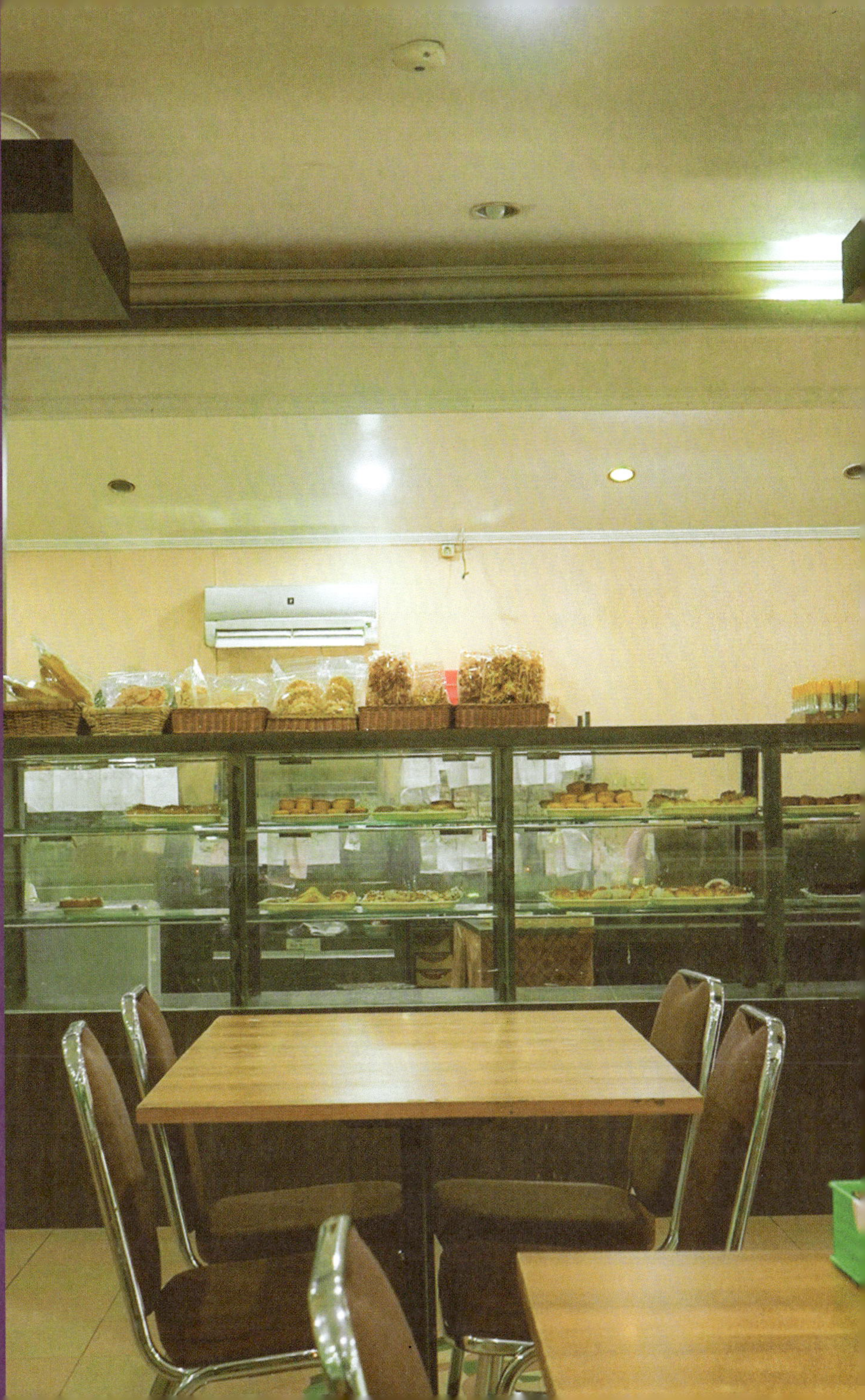

Cita Rasa Restaurant & Cake, Pontianak, 2024

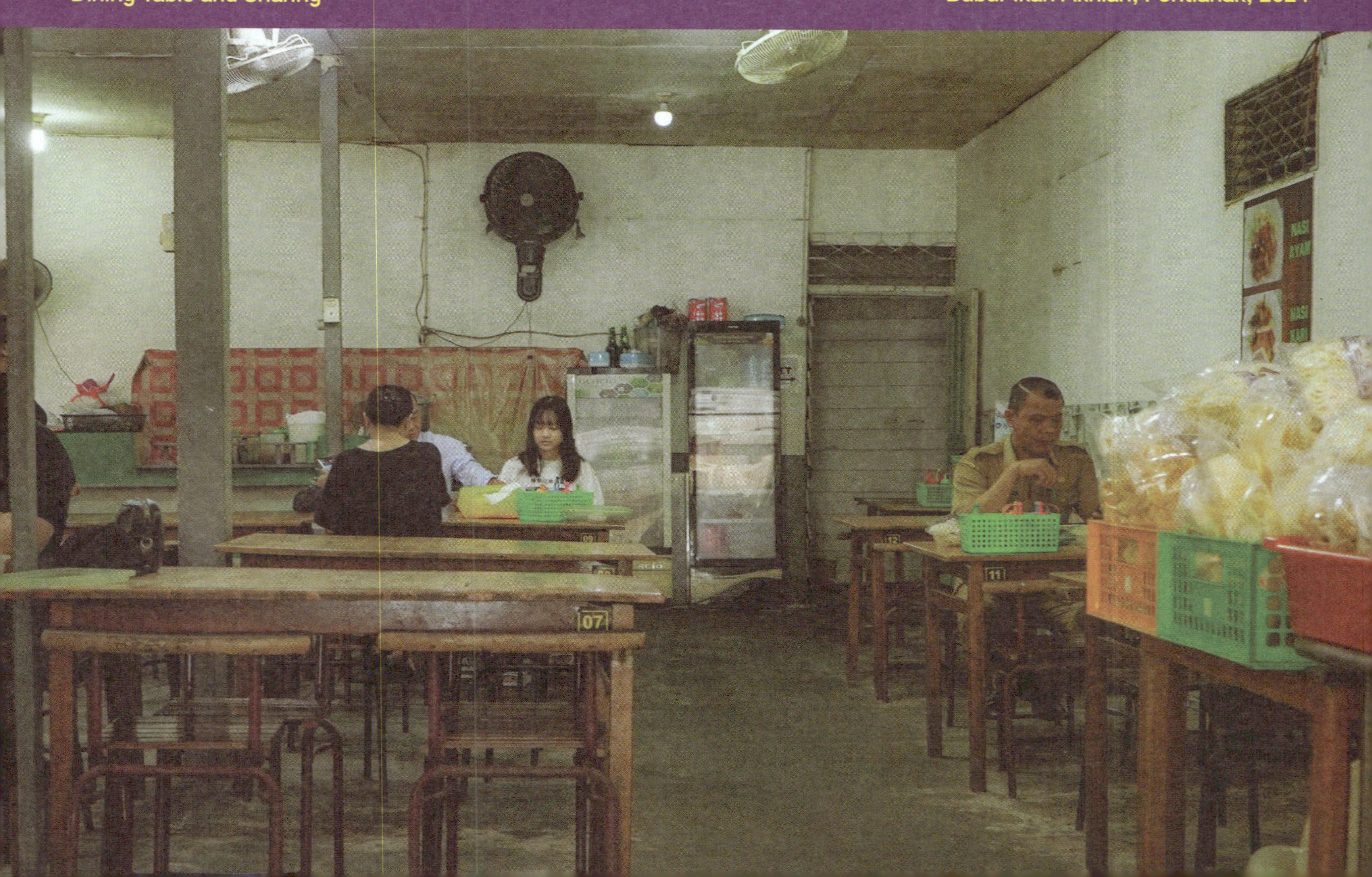

Bubur Ikan Akhian, Pontianak, 2024

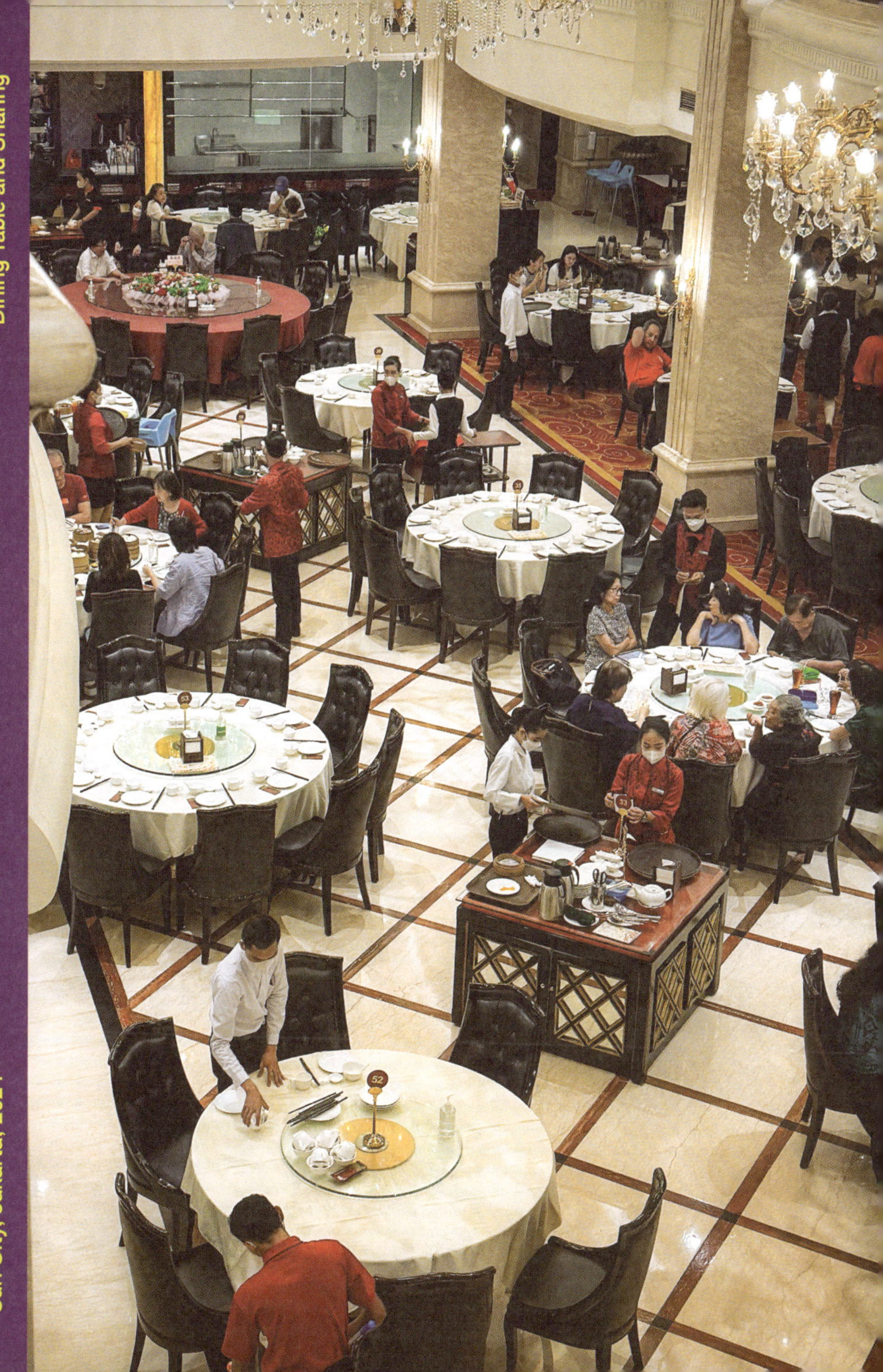

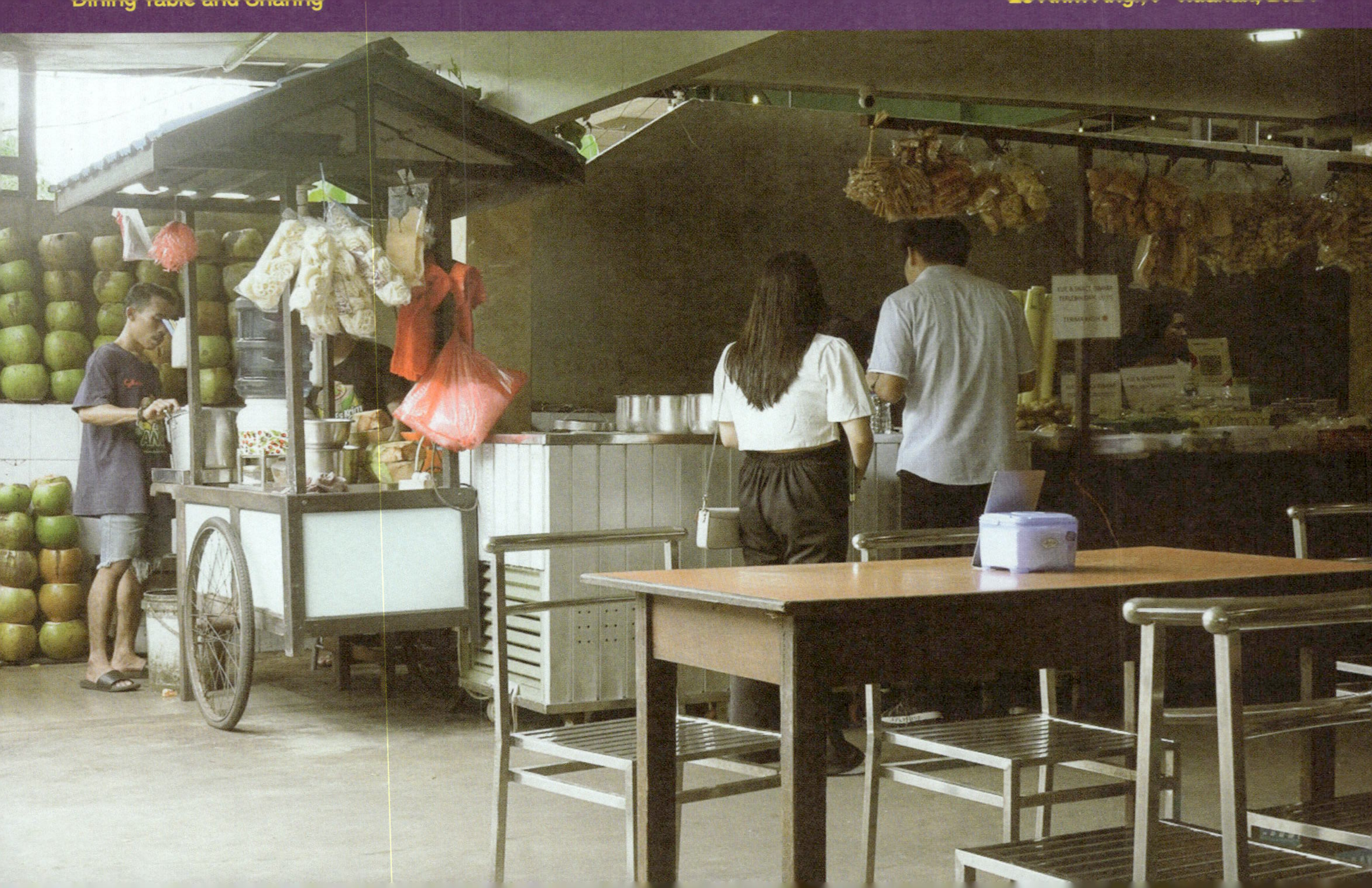

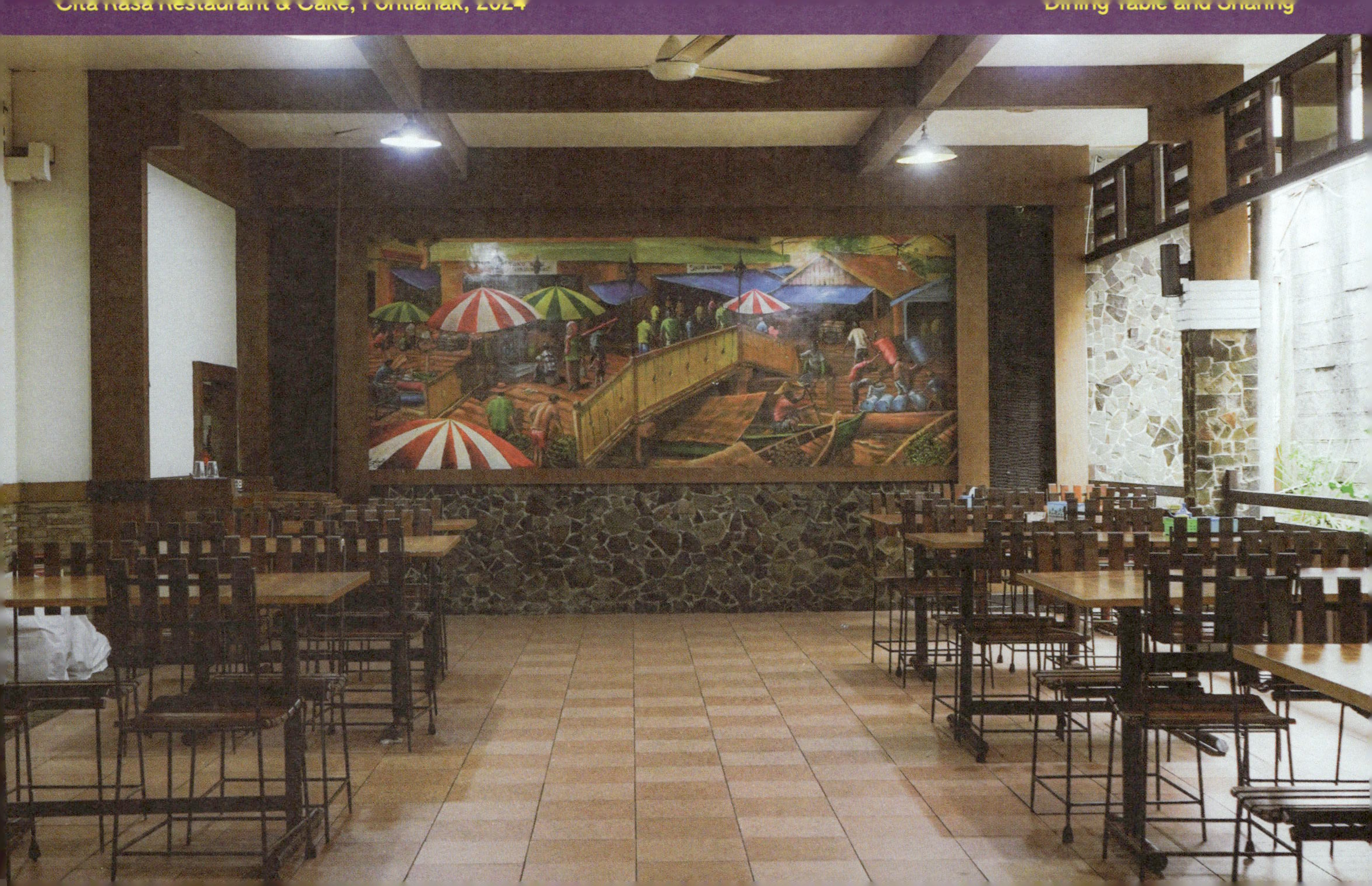
Cita Rasa Restaurant & Cake, Pontianak, 2024

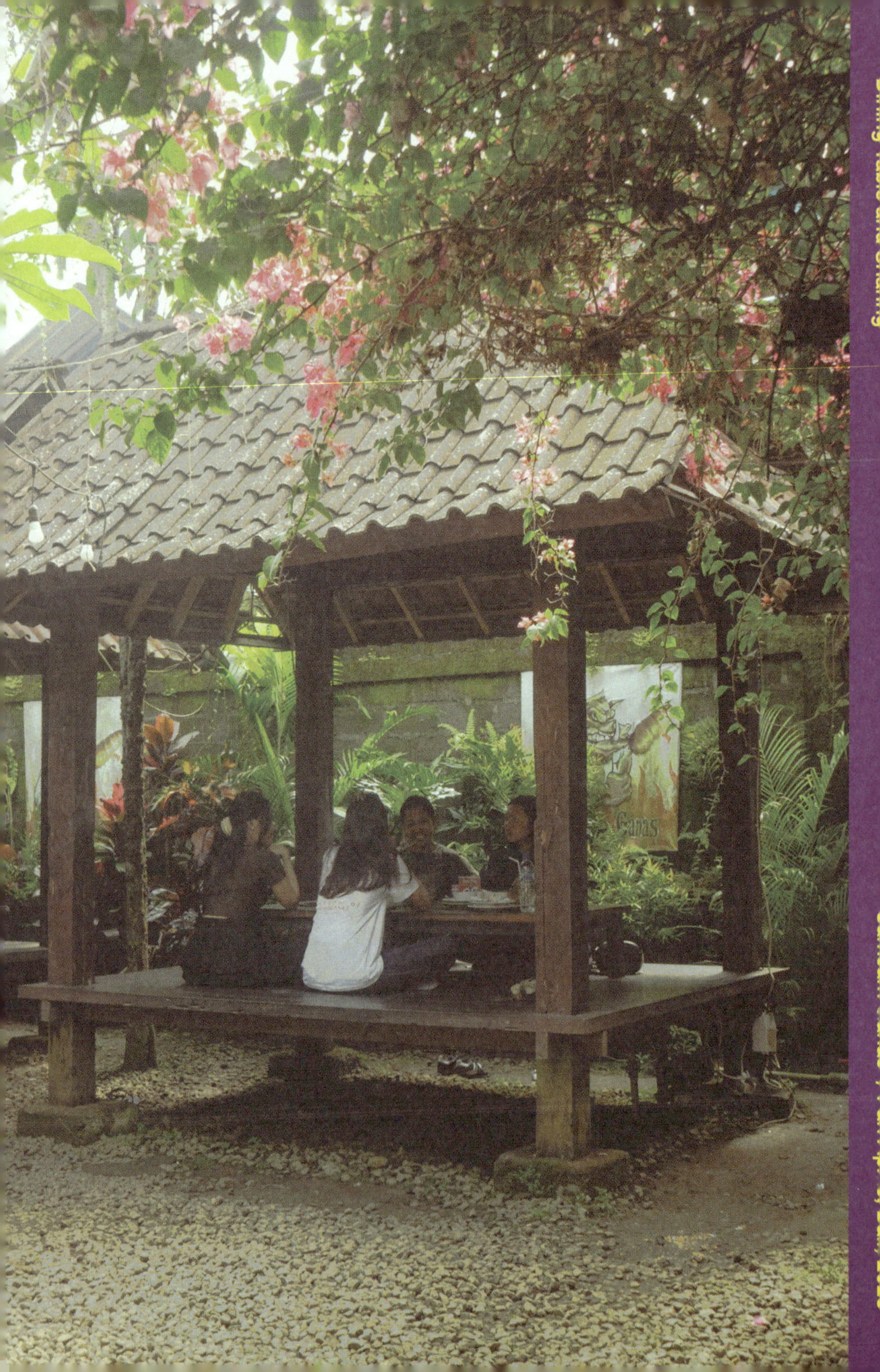
Ganas

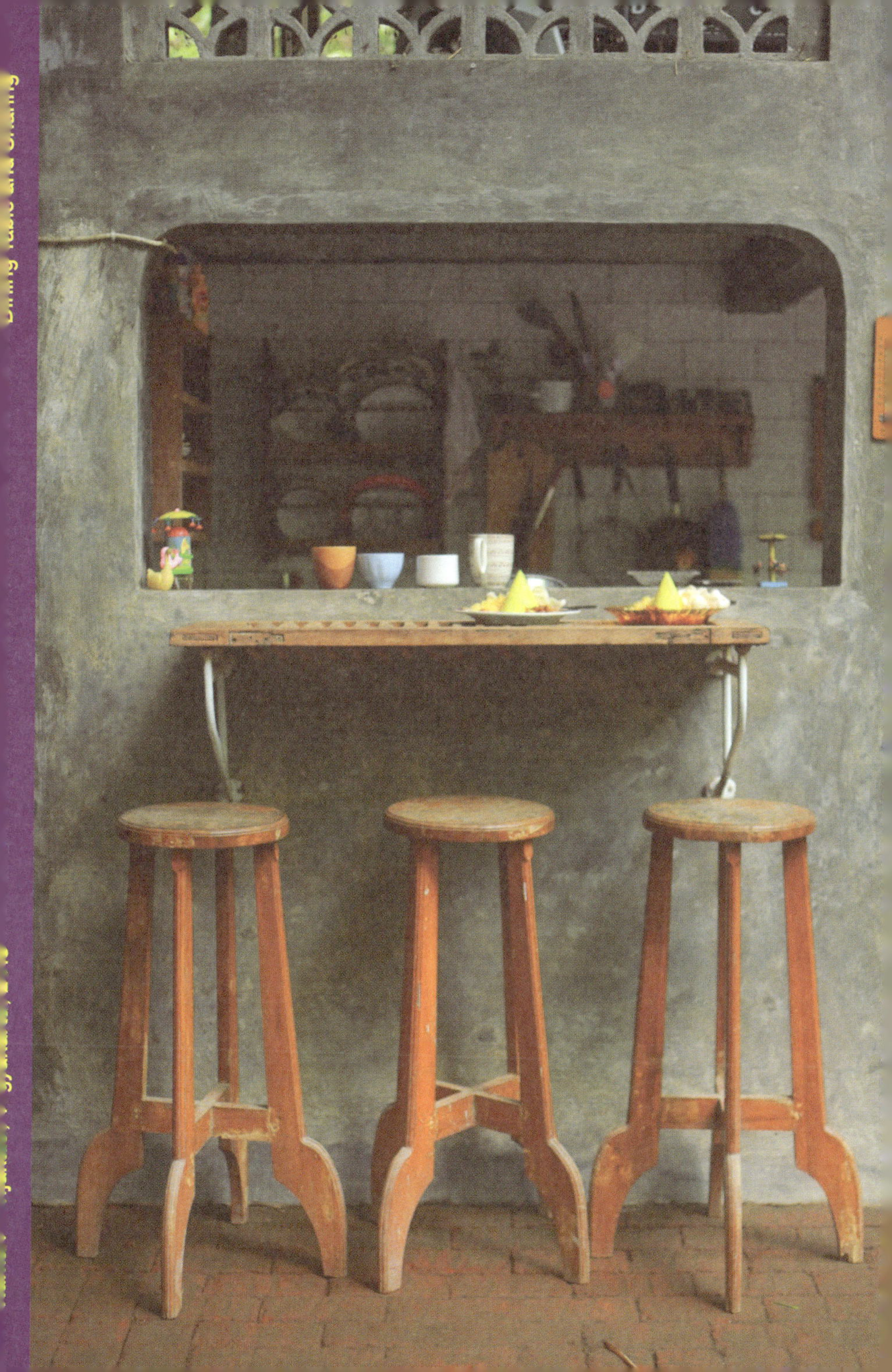

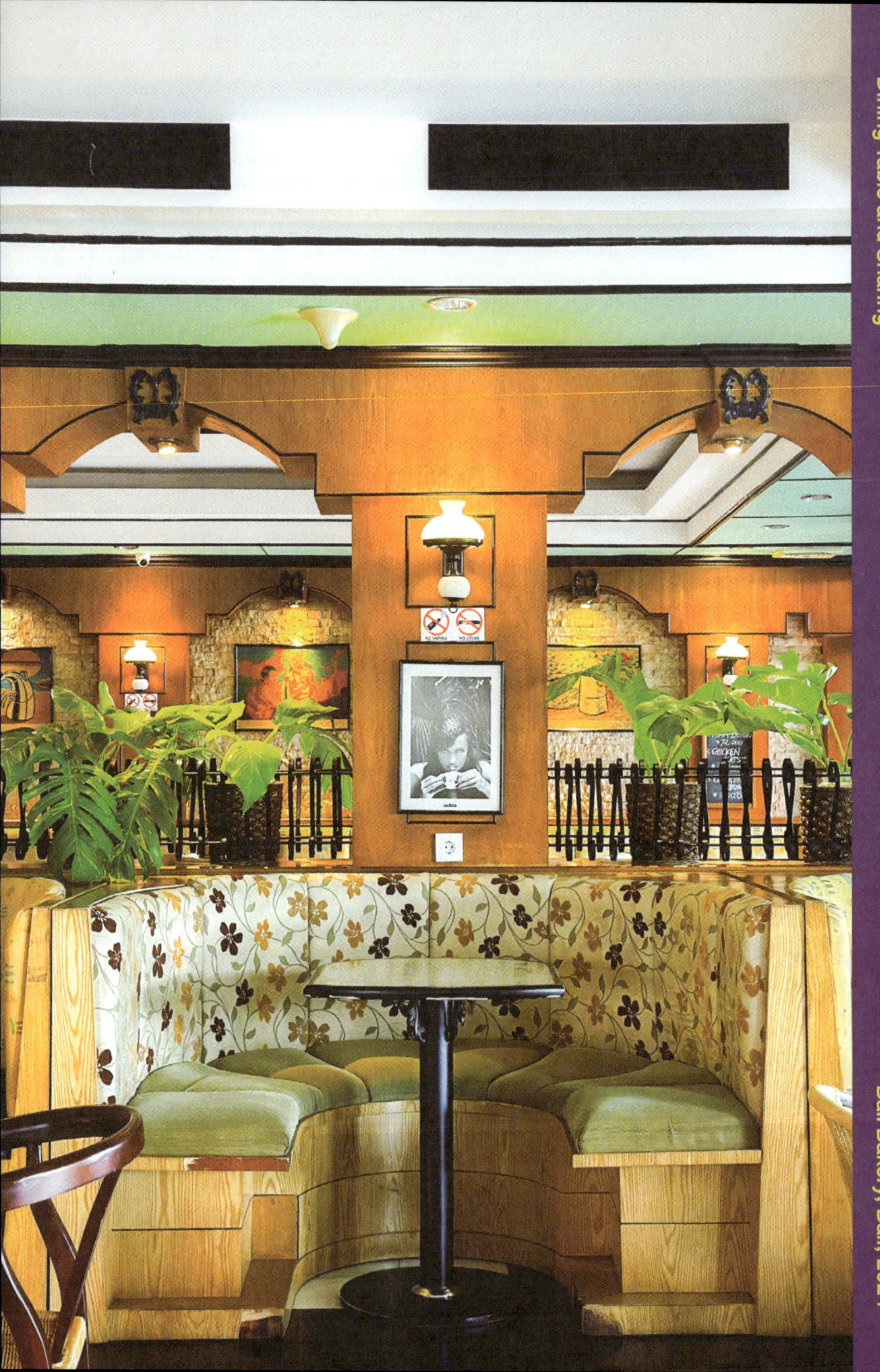

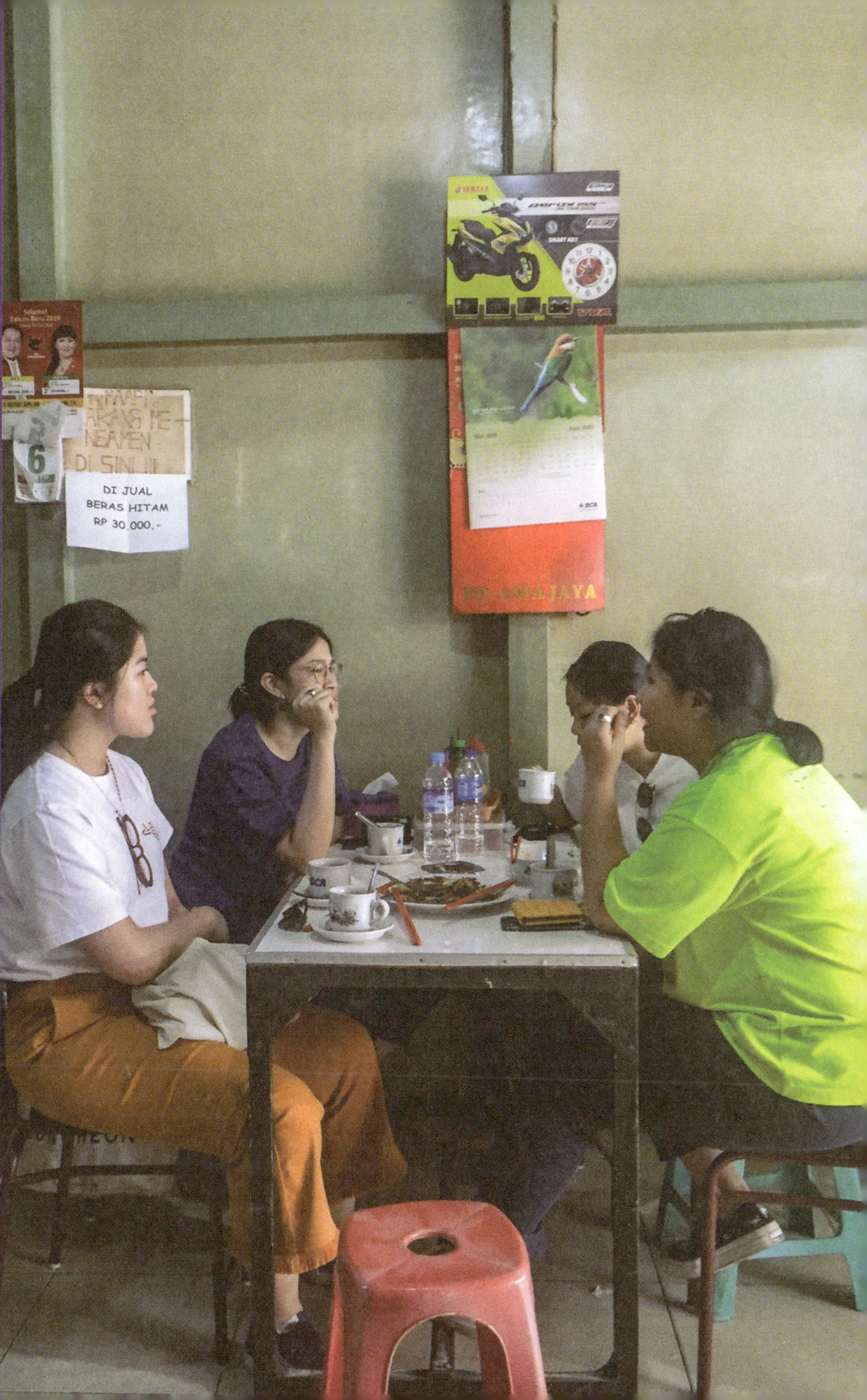

DI JUAL
BERAS HITAM
RP 30.000,-
PD. ASIA JAYA

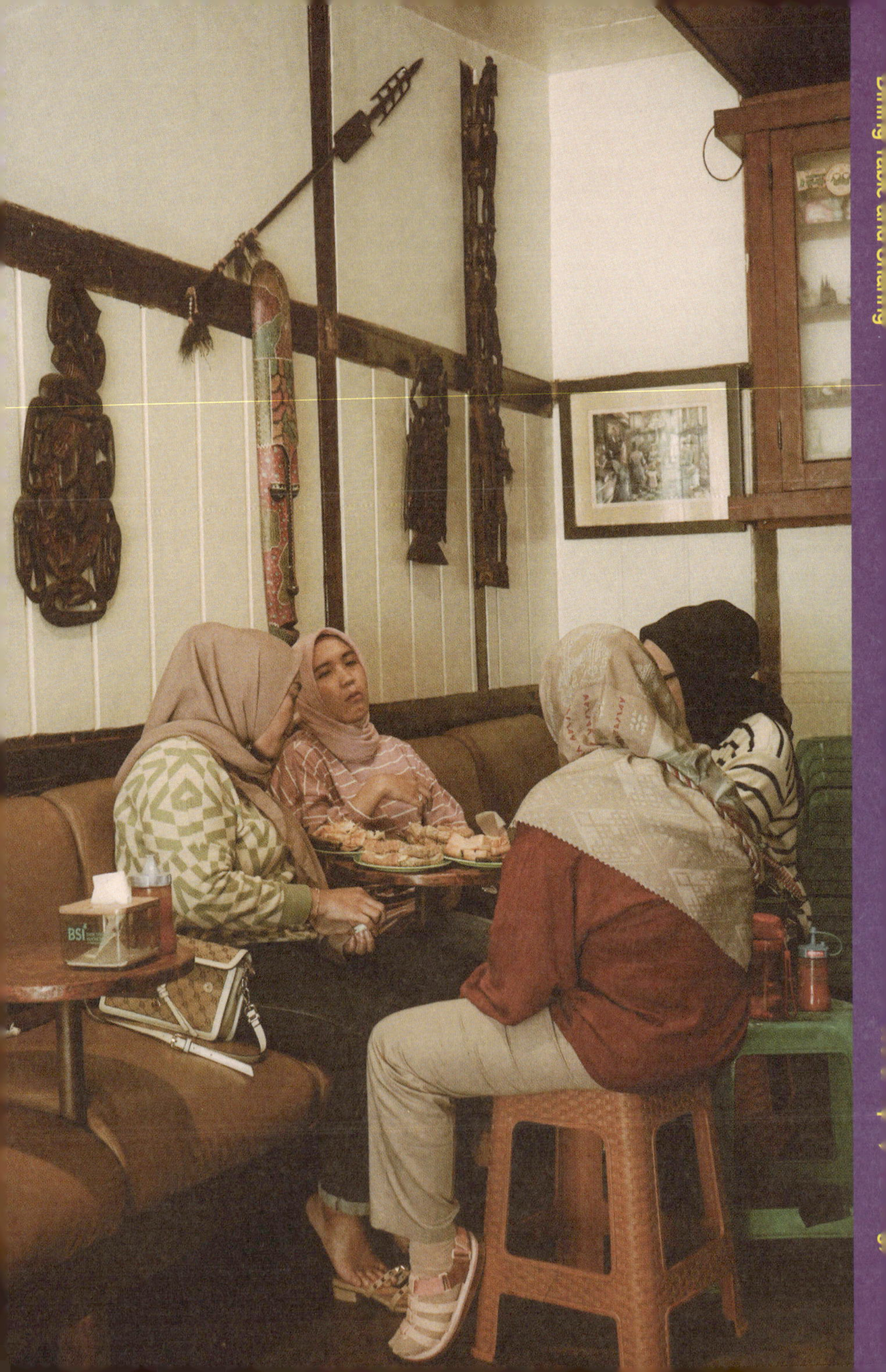

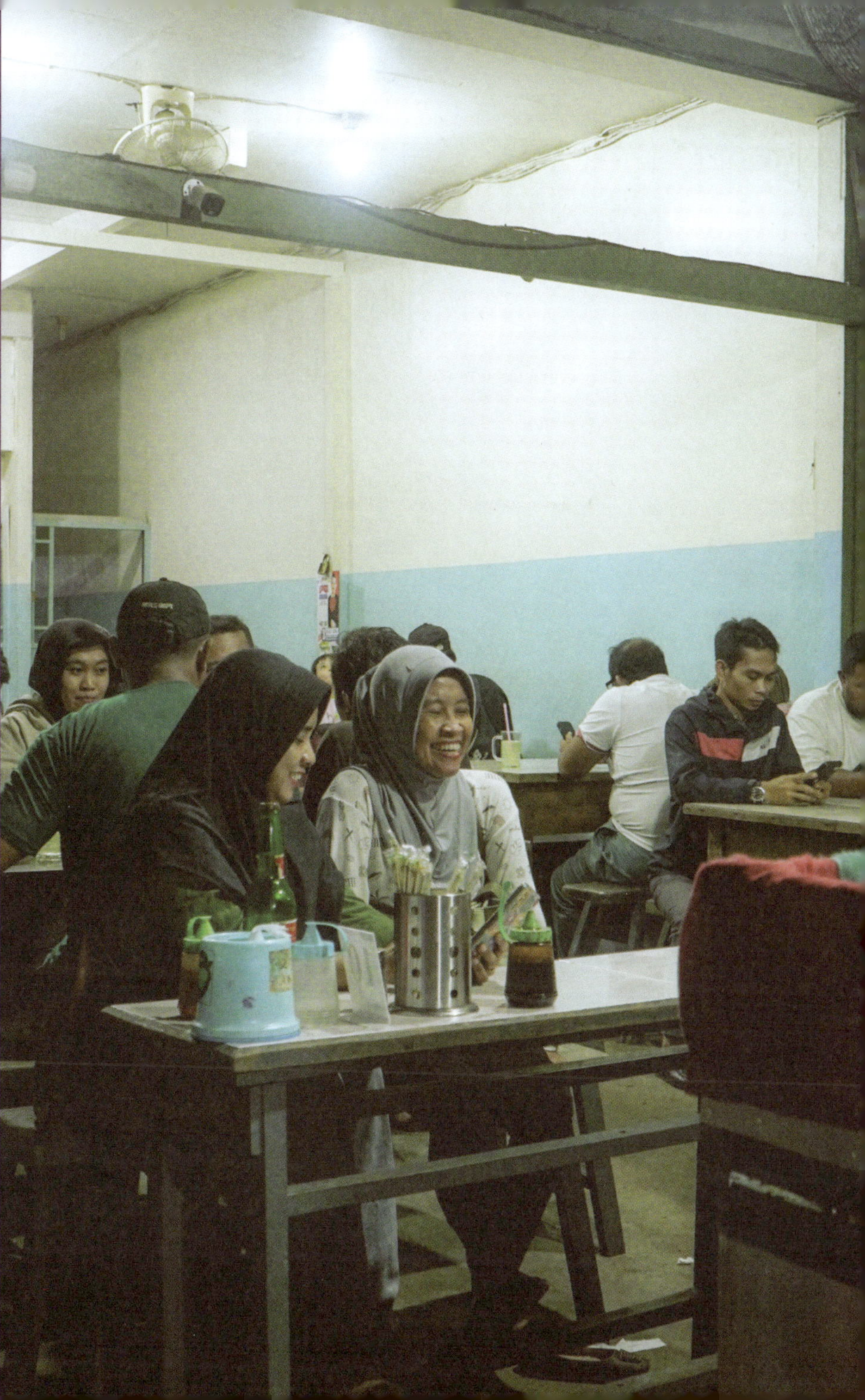

RM 999 Ayong, Pontianak, 2024

Dining Table and Sharing

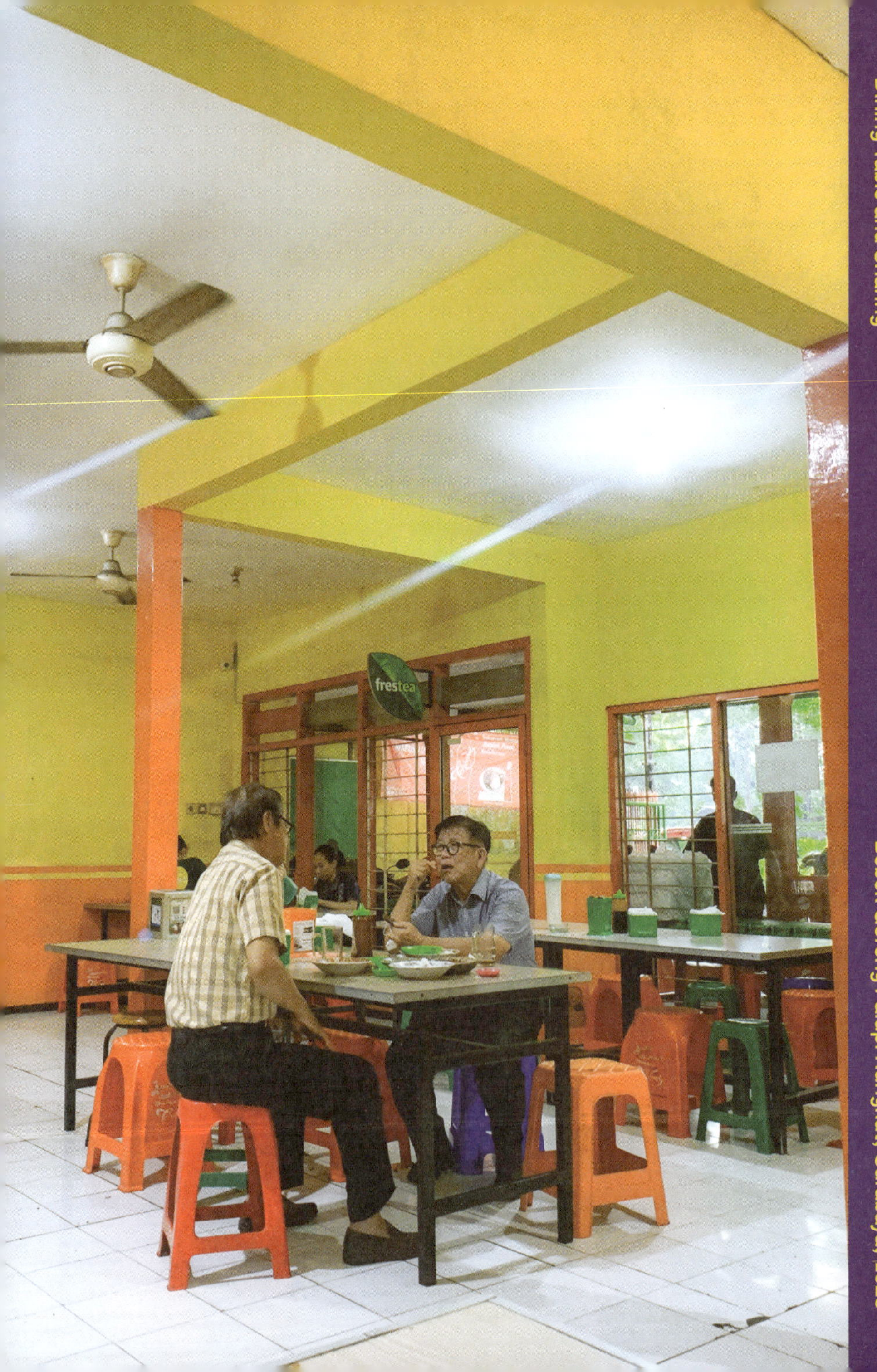

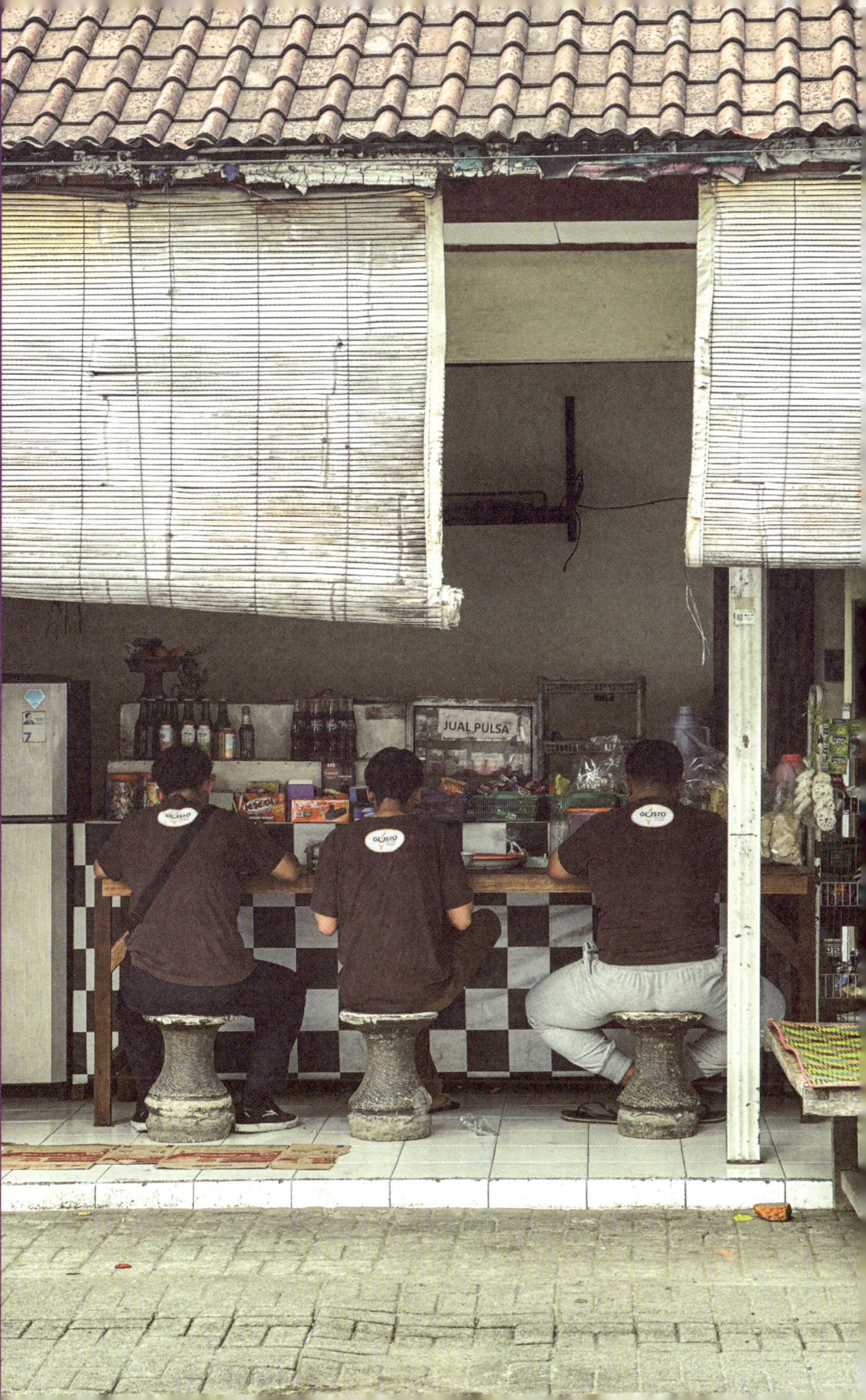

Nasi Jinggo Kerobokan, Bali, 2024

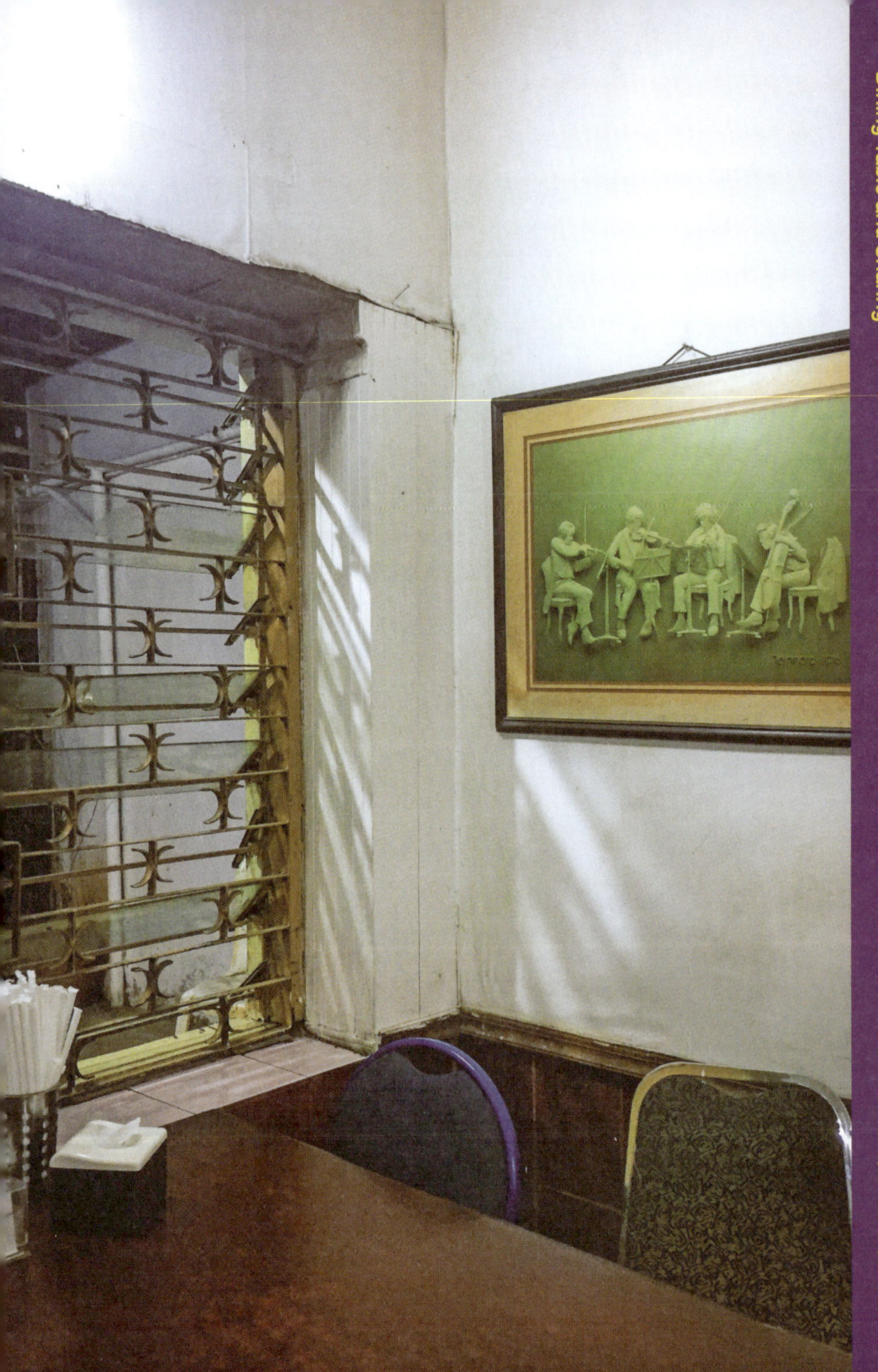

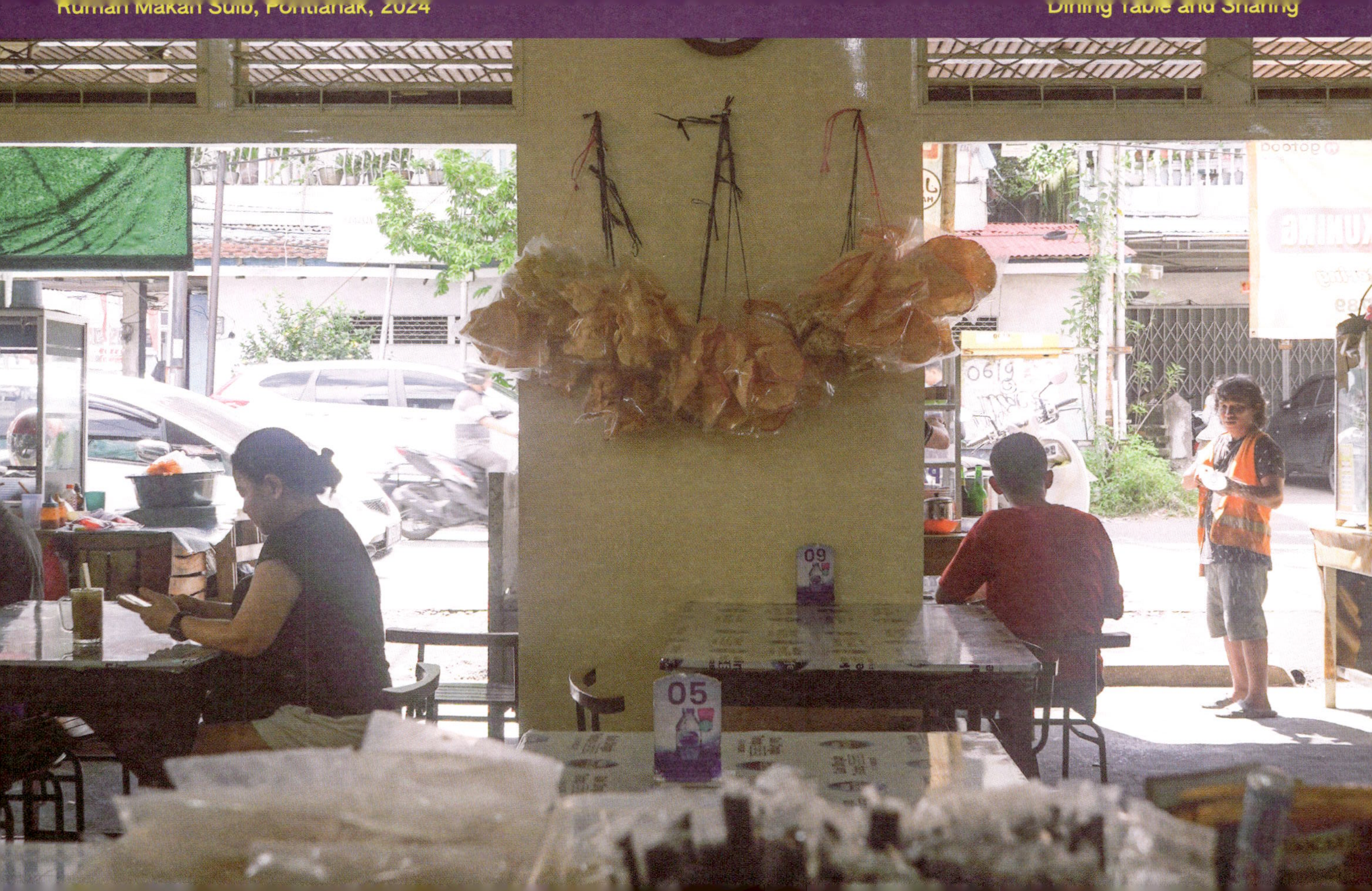

Rumah Makan Suib, Pontianak, 2024

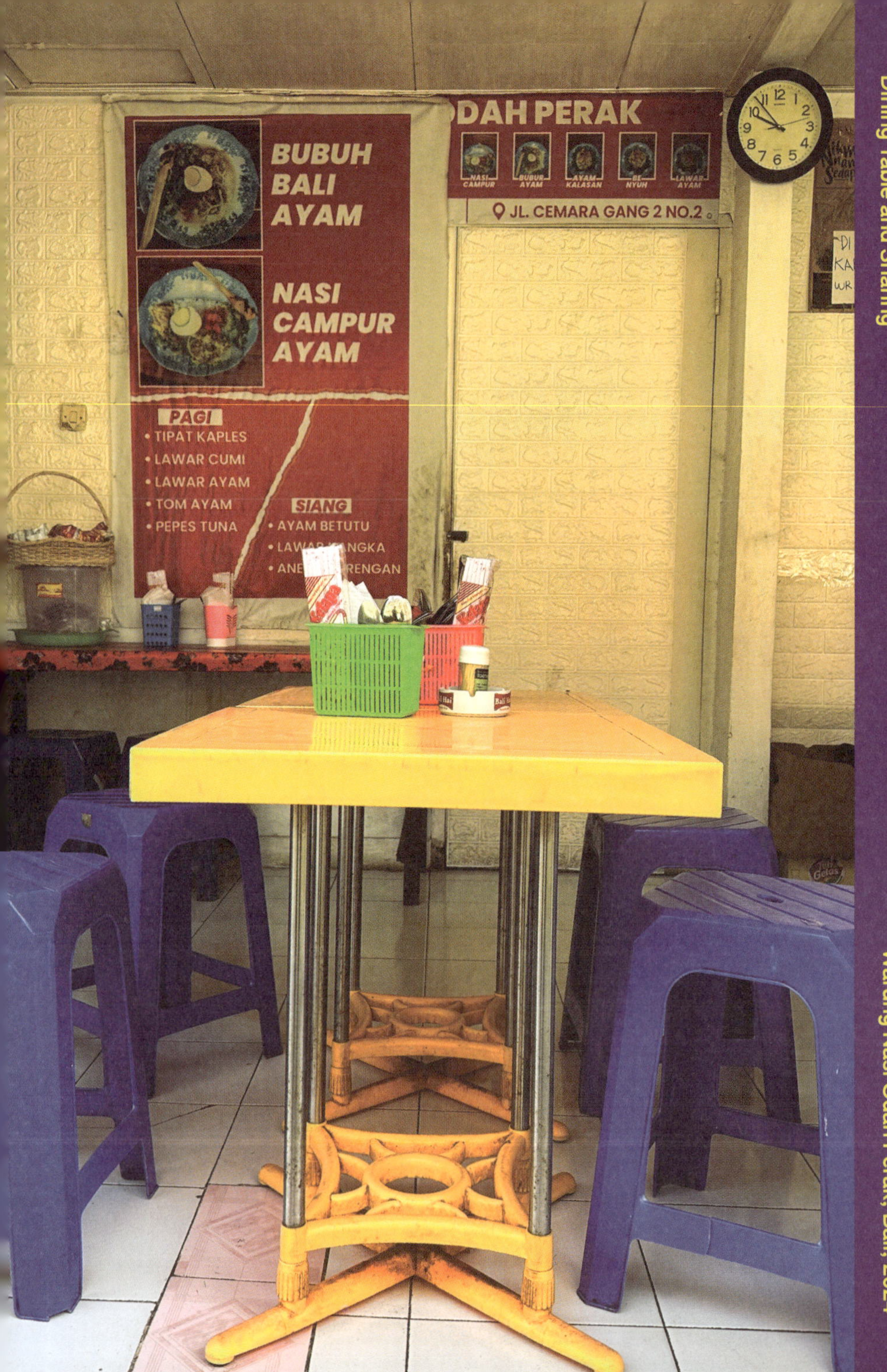

DAH PERAK
NASI CAMPUR
BUBUR AYAM
AYAM KALASAN
BE NYUH
LAWAR AYAM
JL. CEMARA GANG 2 NO.2
BUBUH BALI AYAM
NASI CAMPUR AYAM
PAGI
• TIPAT KAPLES
• LAWAR CUMI
• LAWAR AYAM
• TOM AYAM
• PEPES TUNA
SIANG
• AYAM BETUTU

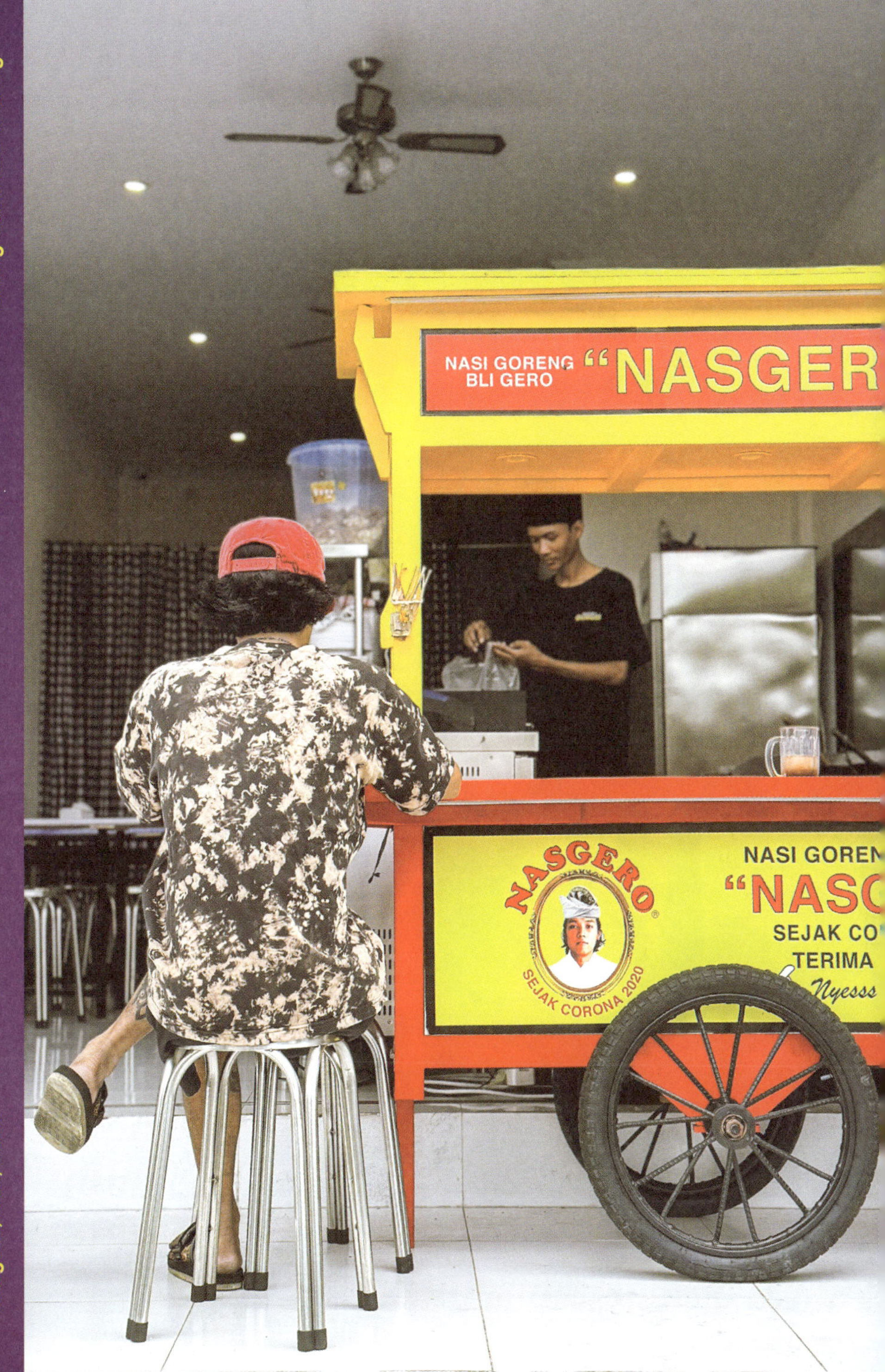

Nasgero, Bali, 2024

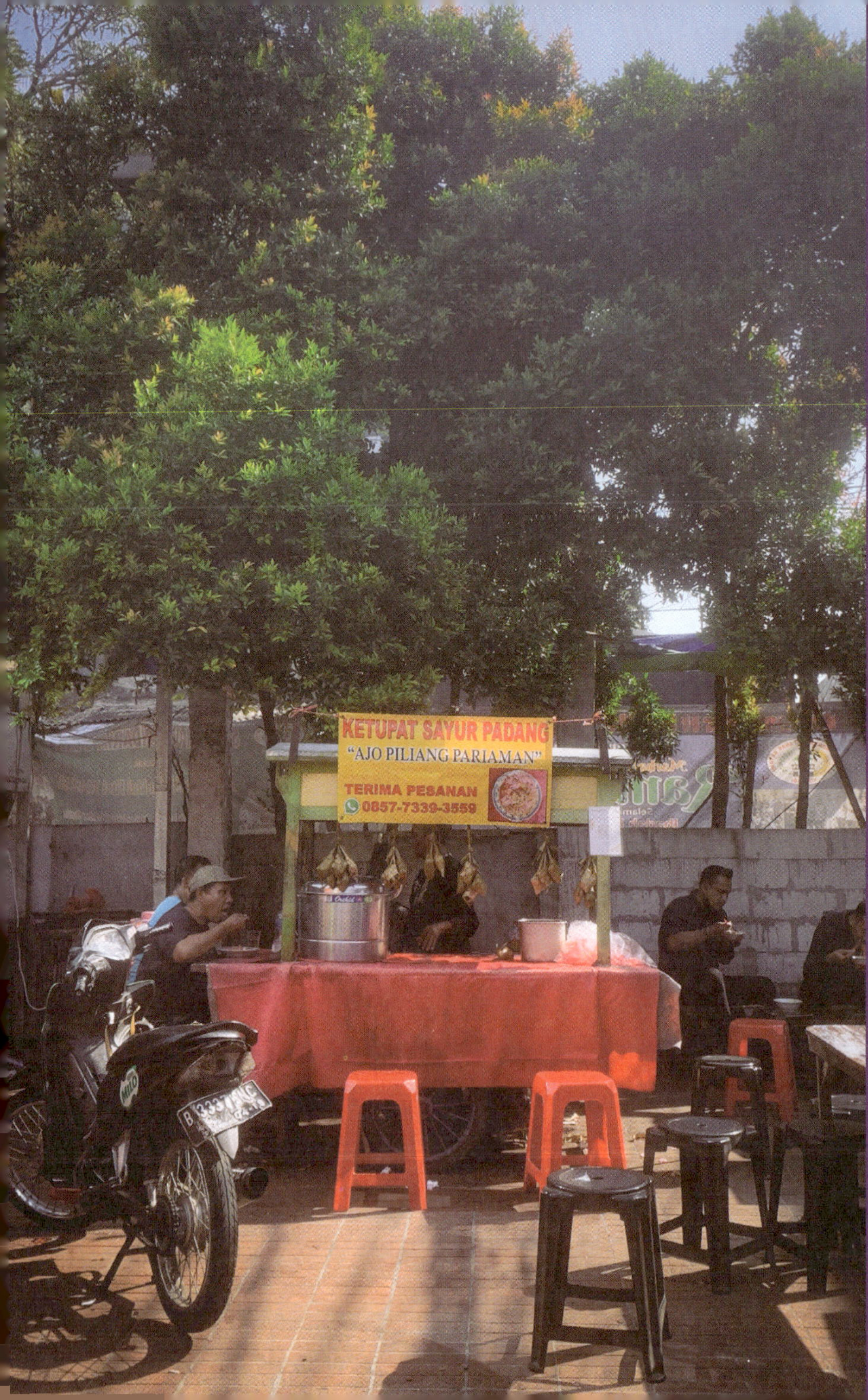

Ajo Piliang Pariaman, Jakarta, 2022

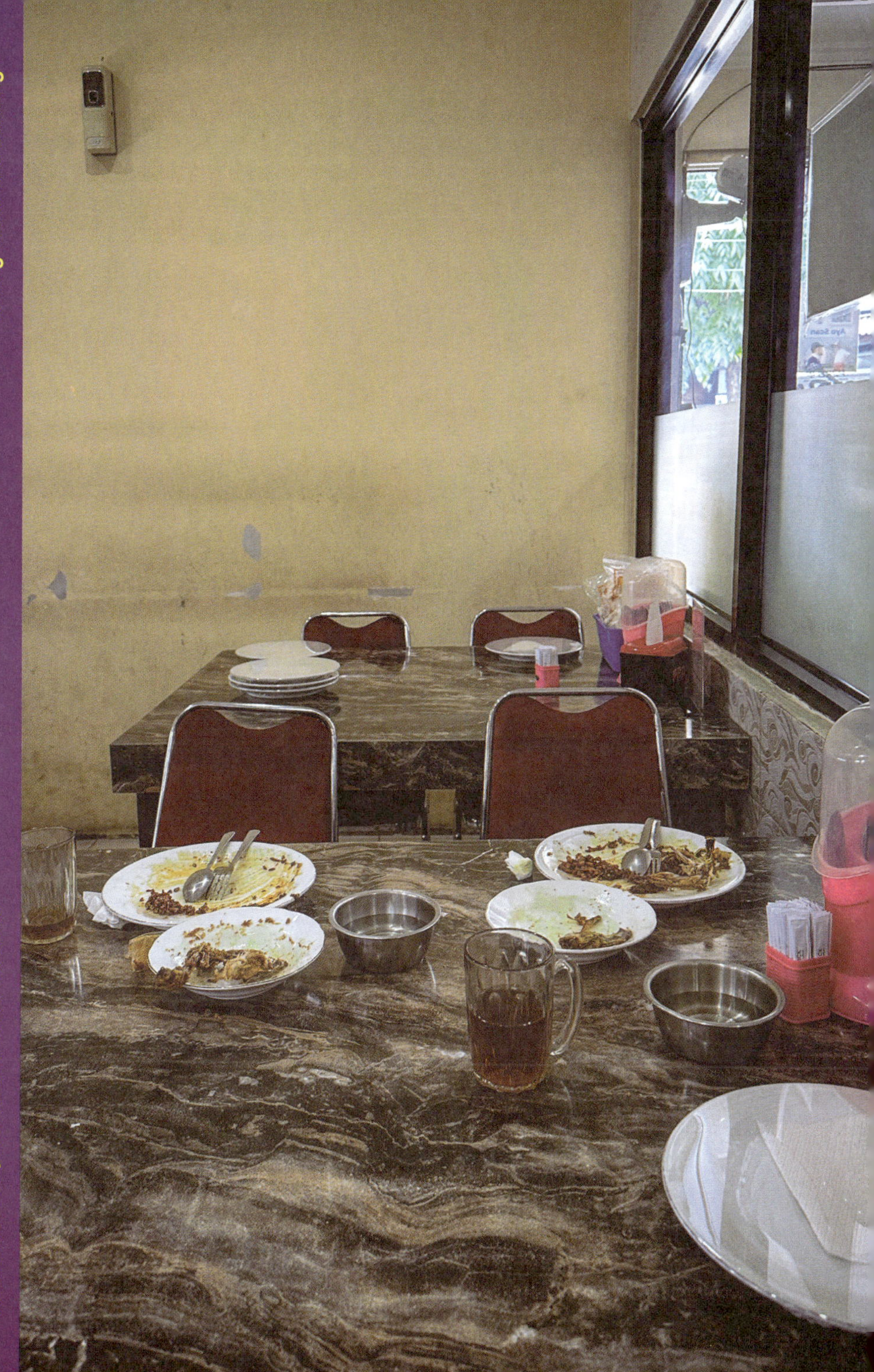

Restoran Kebayoran Baru, Jakarta, 2023

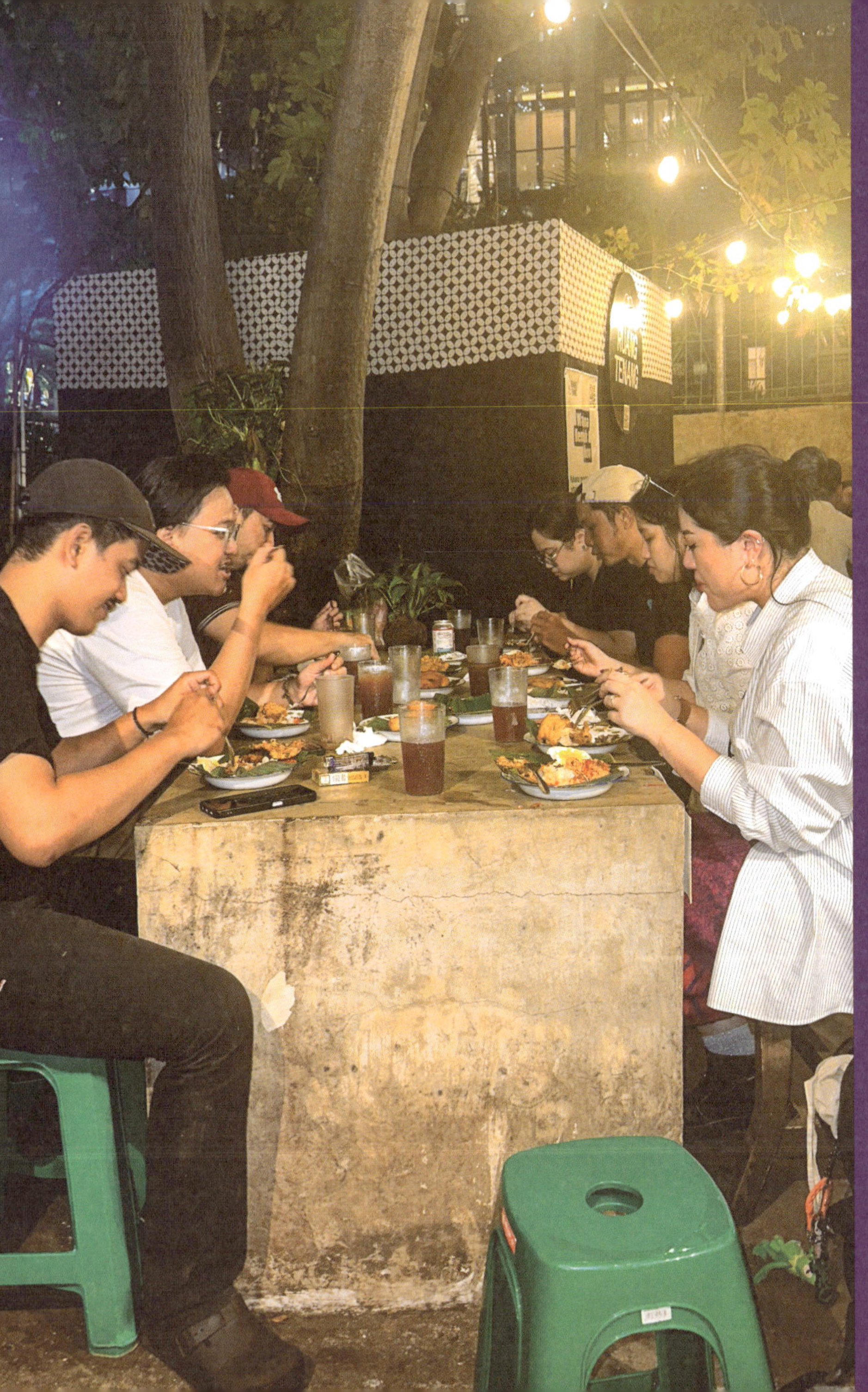

Roku-Roku, Jakarta, 2023

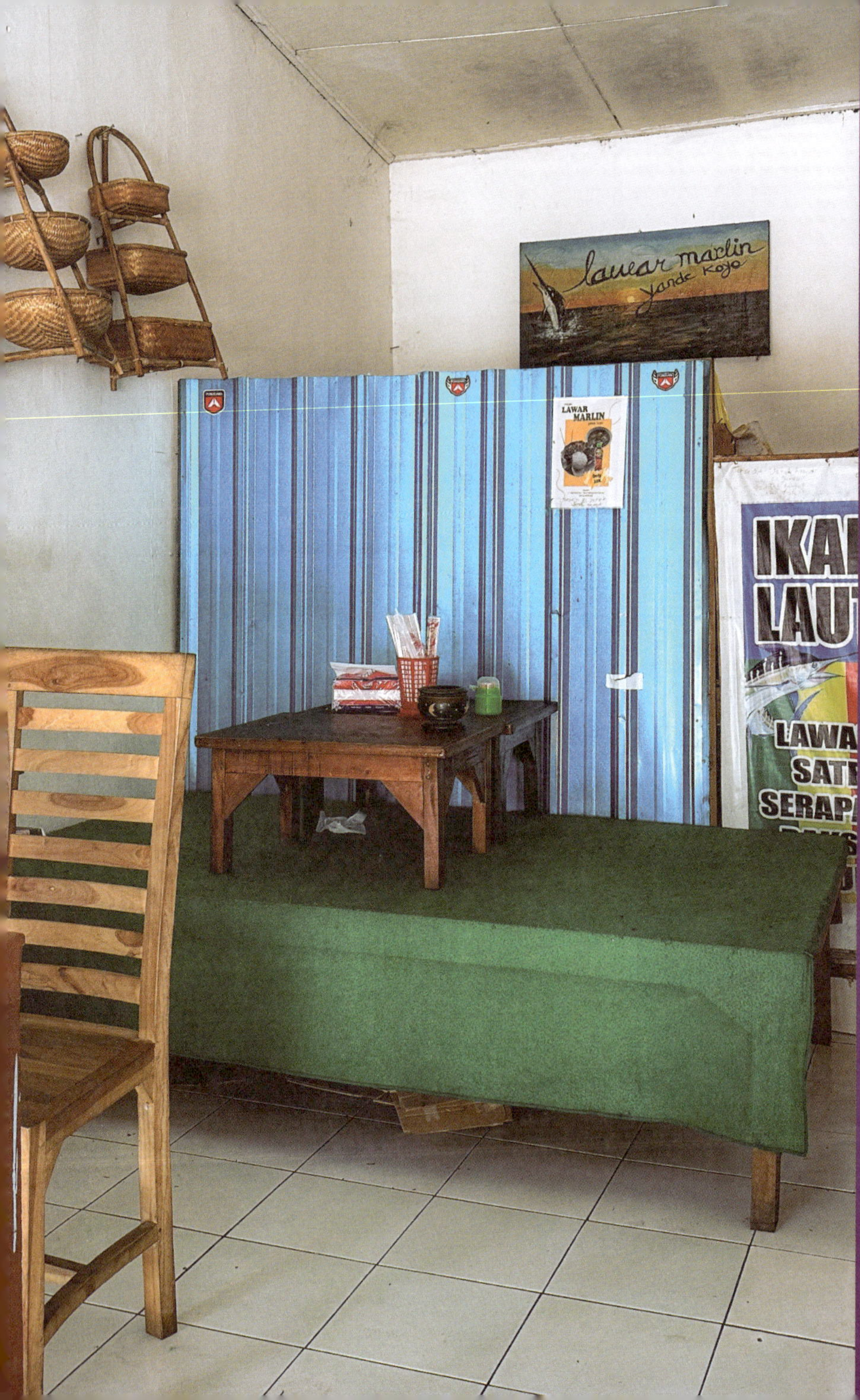

Dining Table and Sharing

Warung Lawar Marlin Made, Bali, 2024

RM Bu Ugi, Tawangmangu, 2025

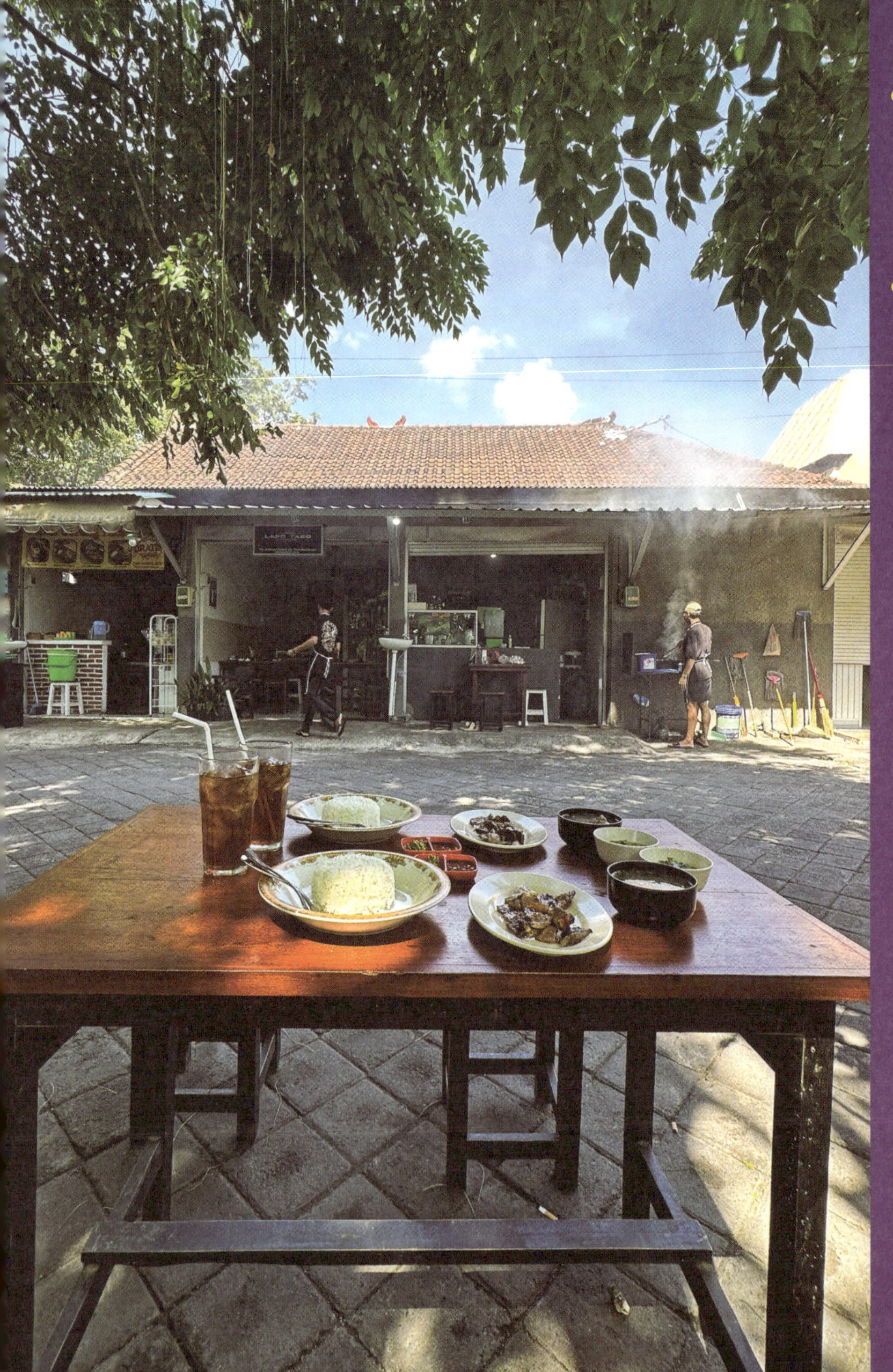

Lapo Tabo, Bali, 2024

Kate Jeanne, Solo, 2023

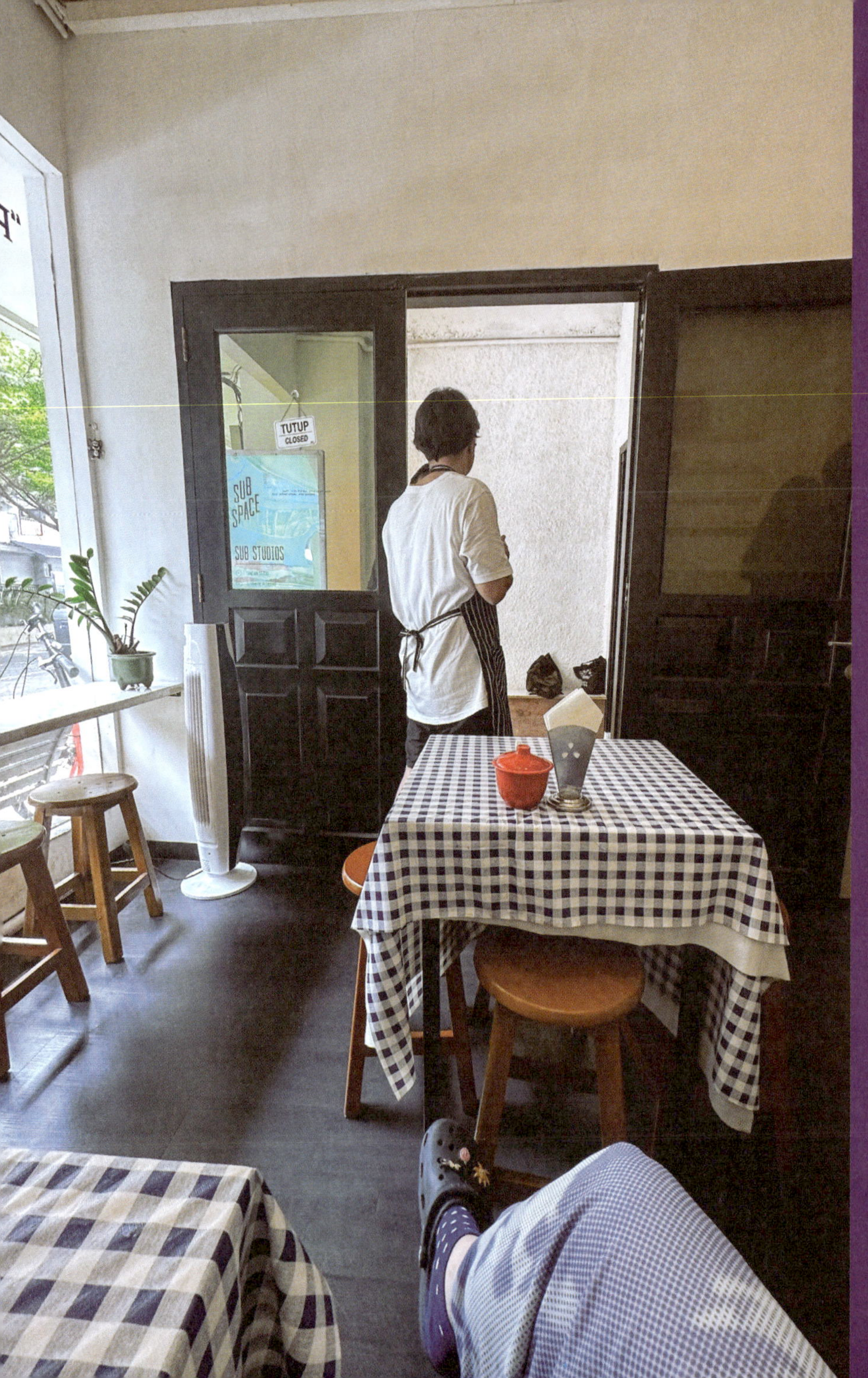

Dining Table and Sharing

Warung Pak Chandra, Jakarta, 2023

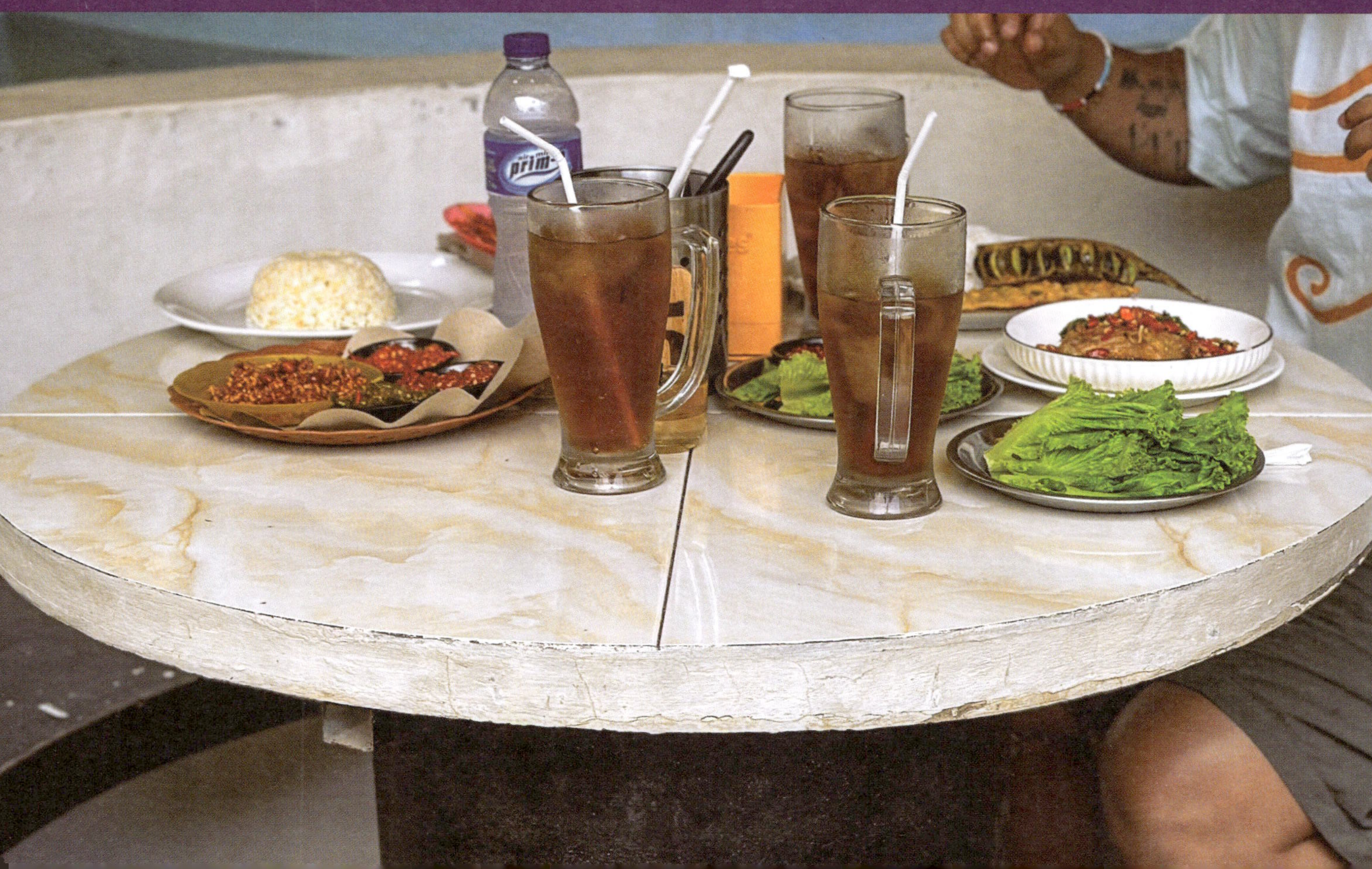

Kembang Wangi, Bandung, 2024

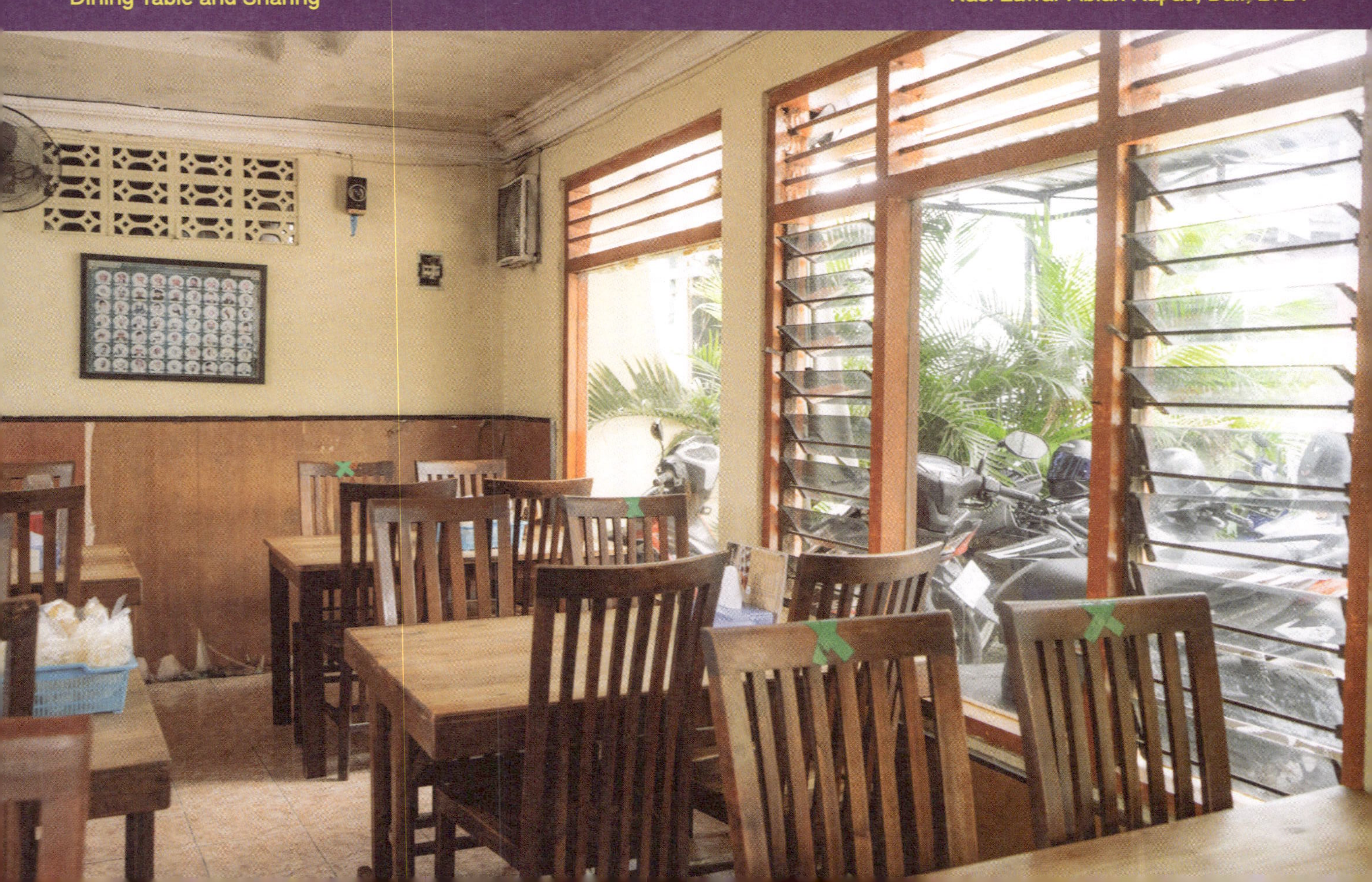

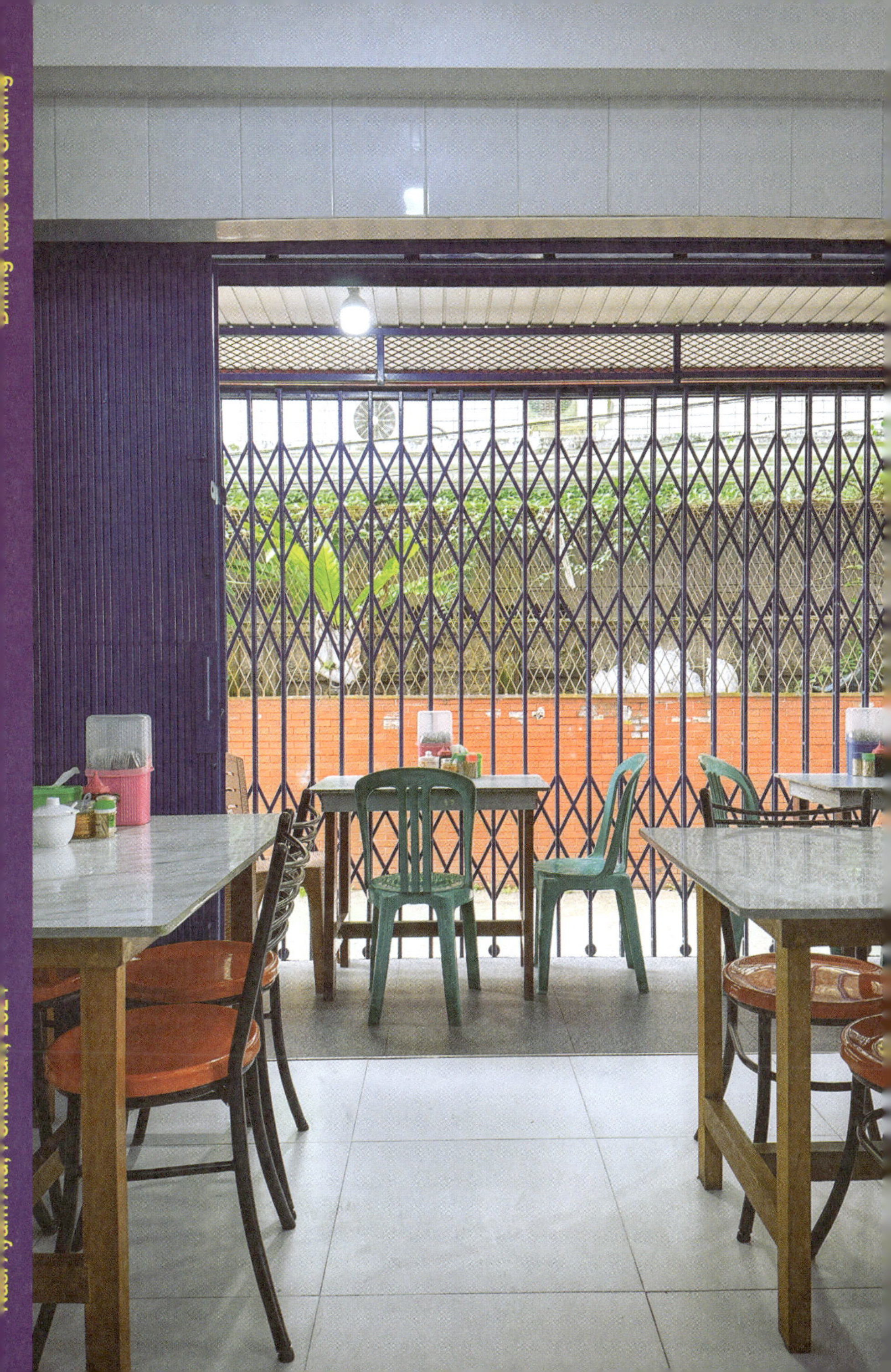

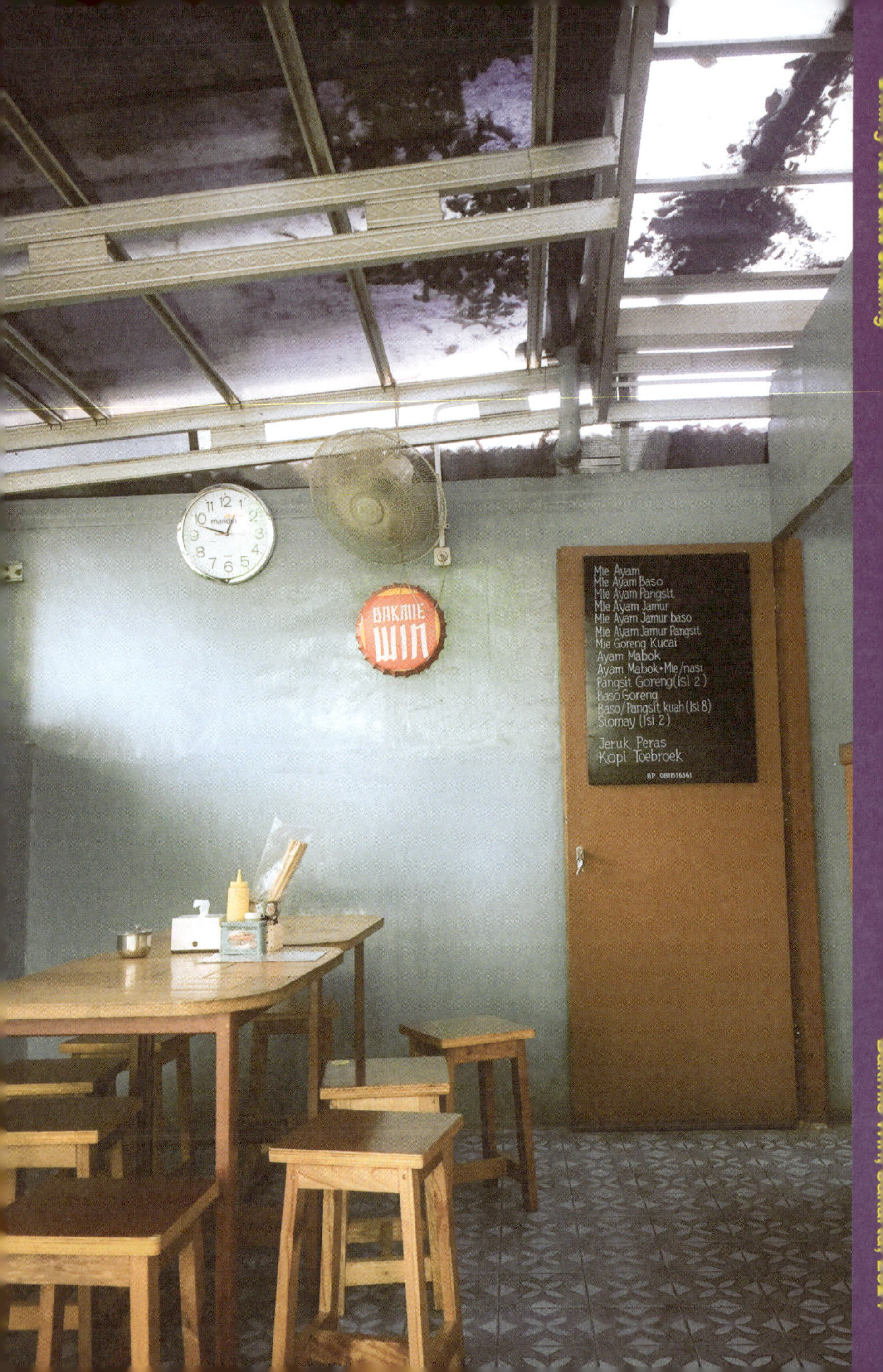
BAKMIE
WIN
Mie Ayam
Mie Ayam Baso
Mie Ayam Pangsit
Mie Ayam Jamur
Mie Ayam Jamur baso
Mie Ayam Jamur Pangsit
Mie Goreng Kucai
Ayam Mabok
Ayam Mabok+Mie/nasi
Pangsit Goreng(isi 2)
Baso Goreng
Baso/Pangsit kuah (isi 8)
Siomay (isi 2)
Jeruk Peras
Kopi Toebroek

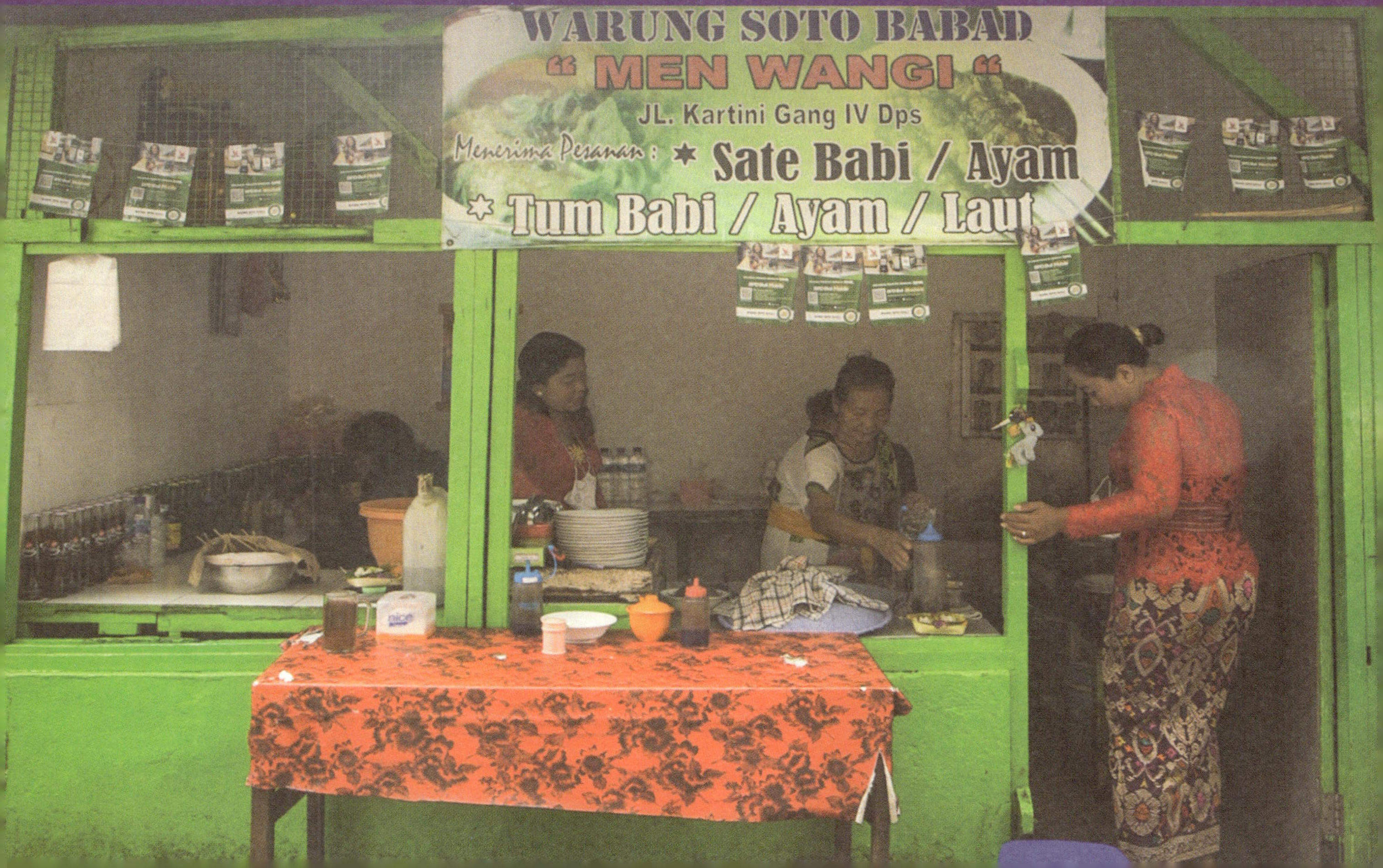

WARUNG SOTO BABAD
" MEN WANGI "
JL. Kartini Gang IV Dps
Menerima Pesanan : * Sate Babi / Ayam
* Tum Babi / Ayam / Laut

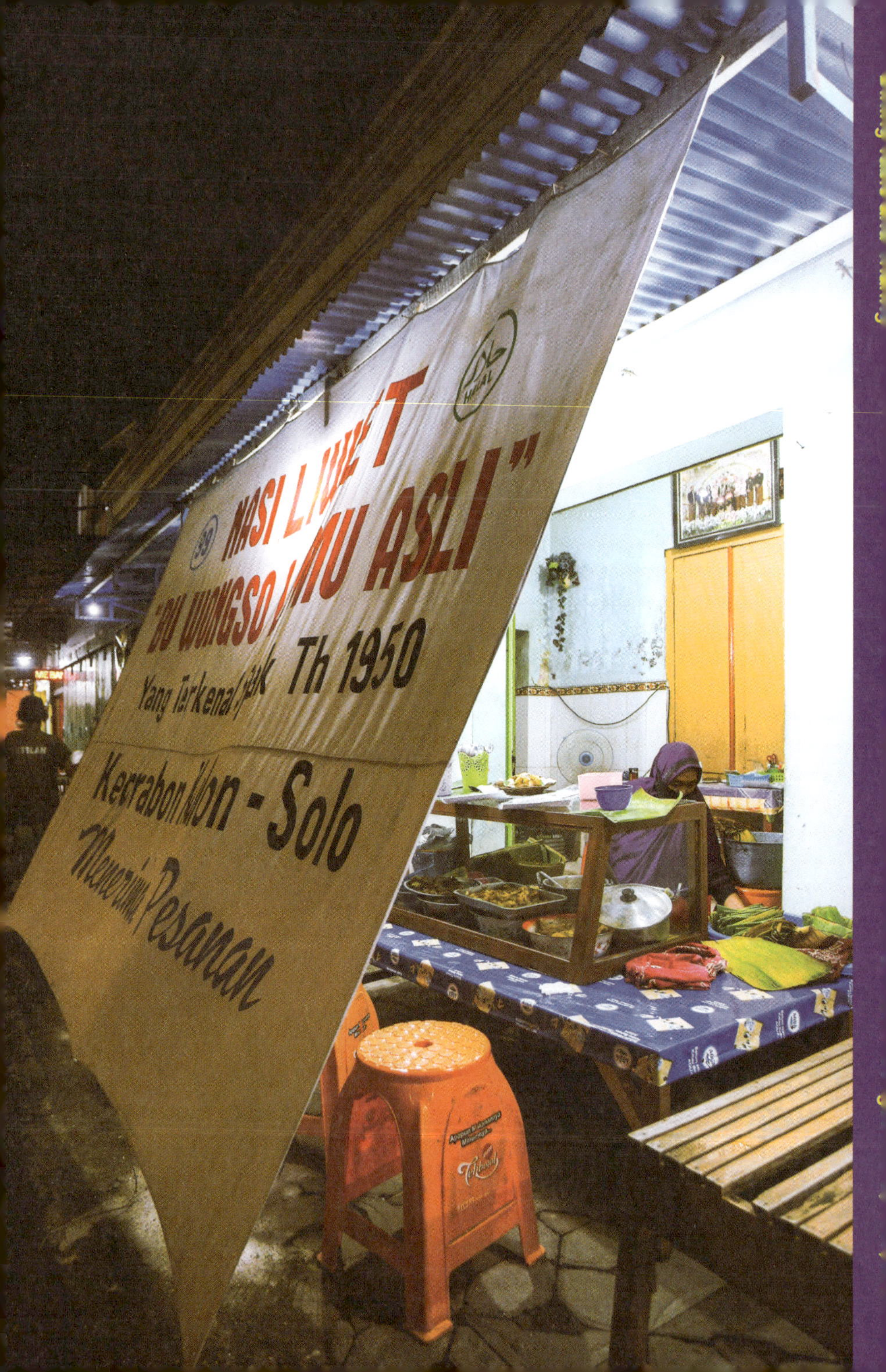
HALAL
39
"BU WONGSO
Th 1950
Yang Terkenal
- Solo
Menerima Pesanan

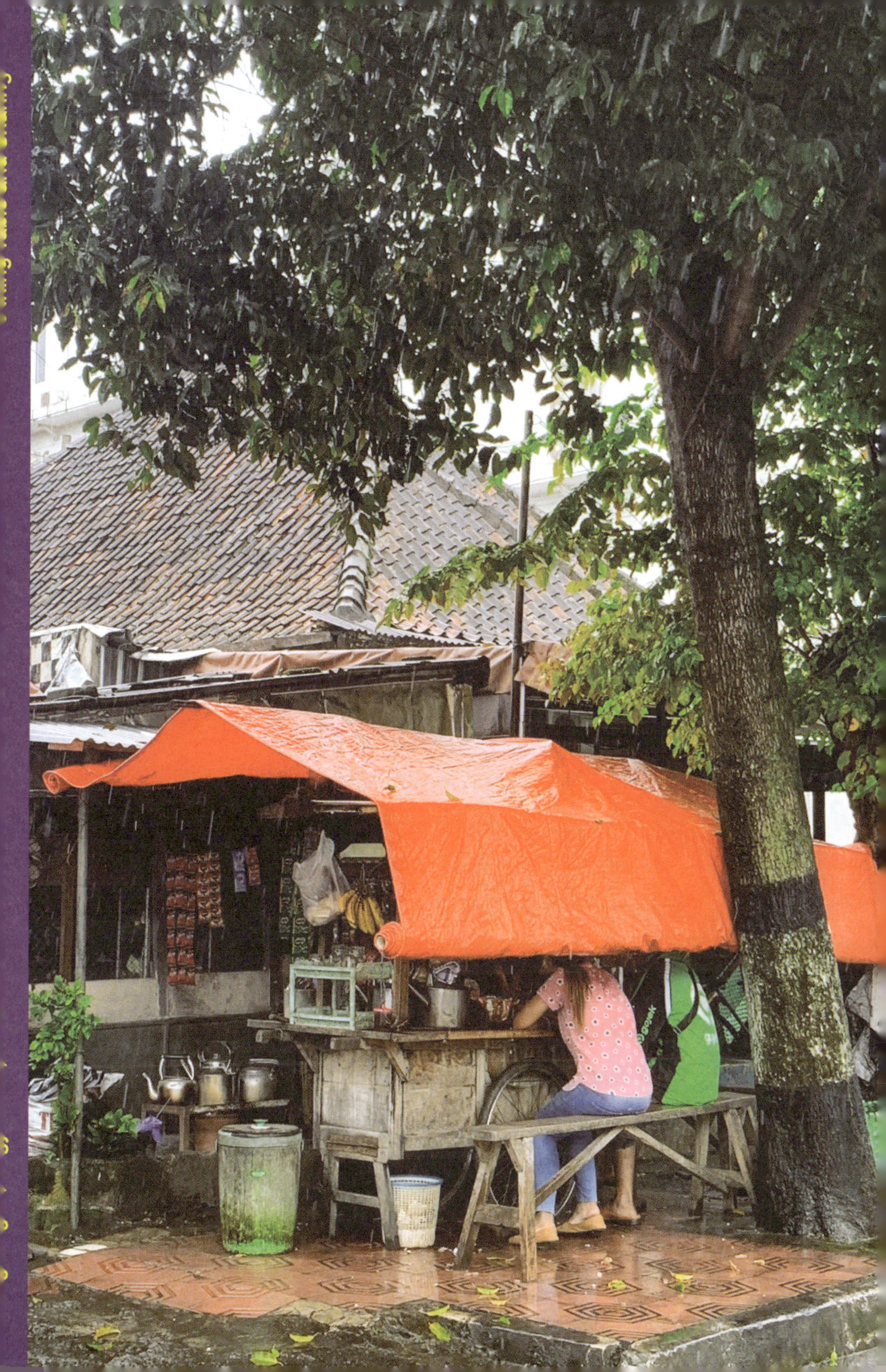

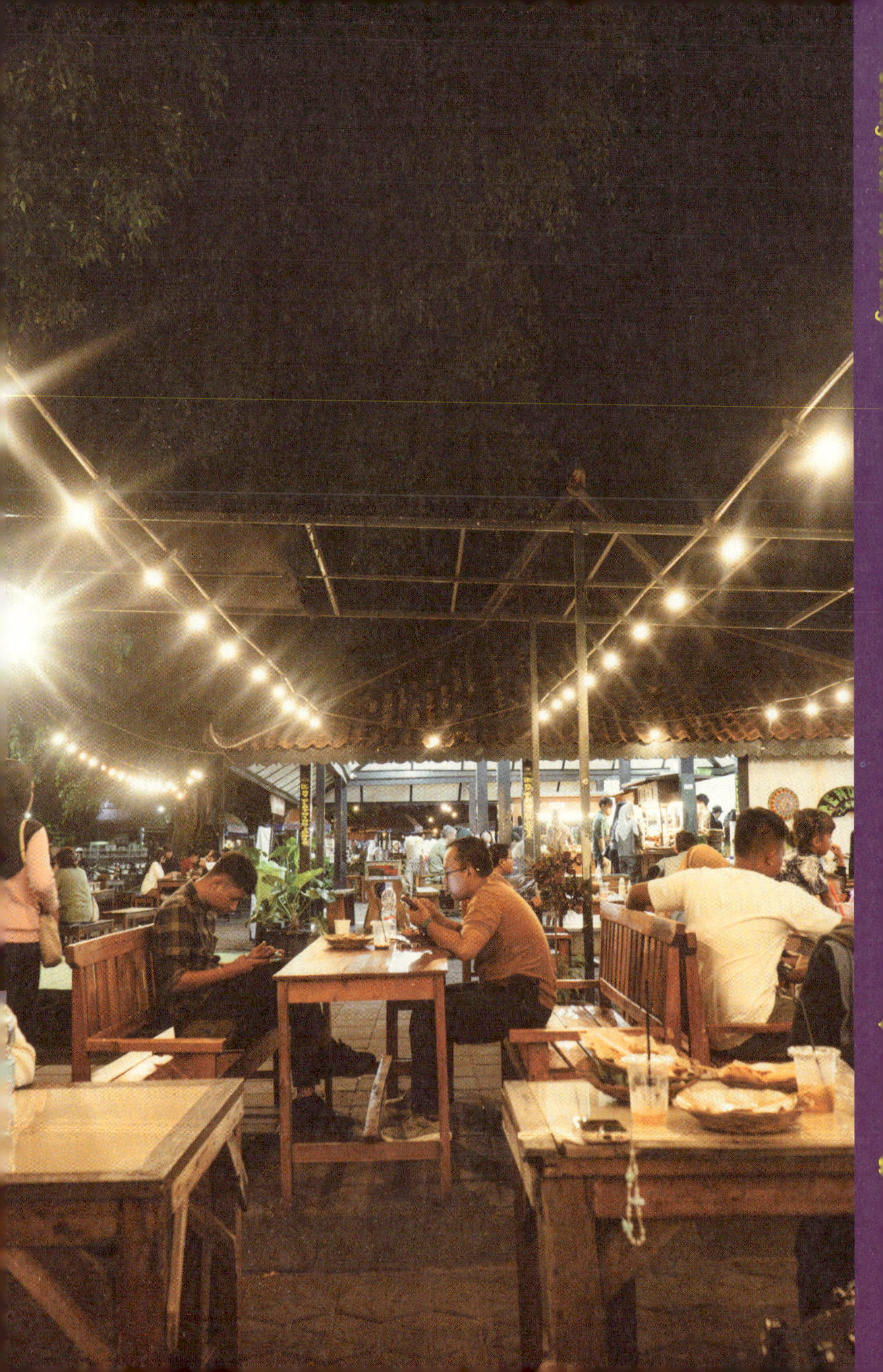

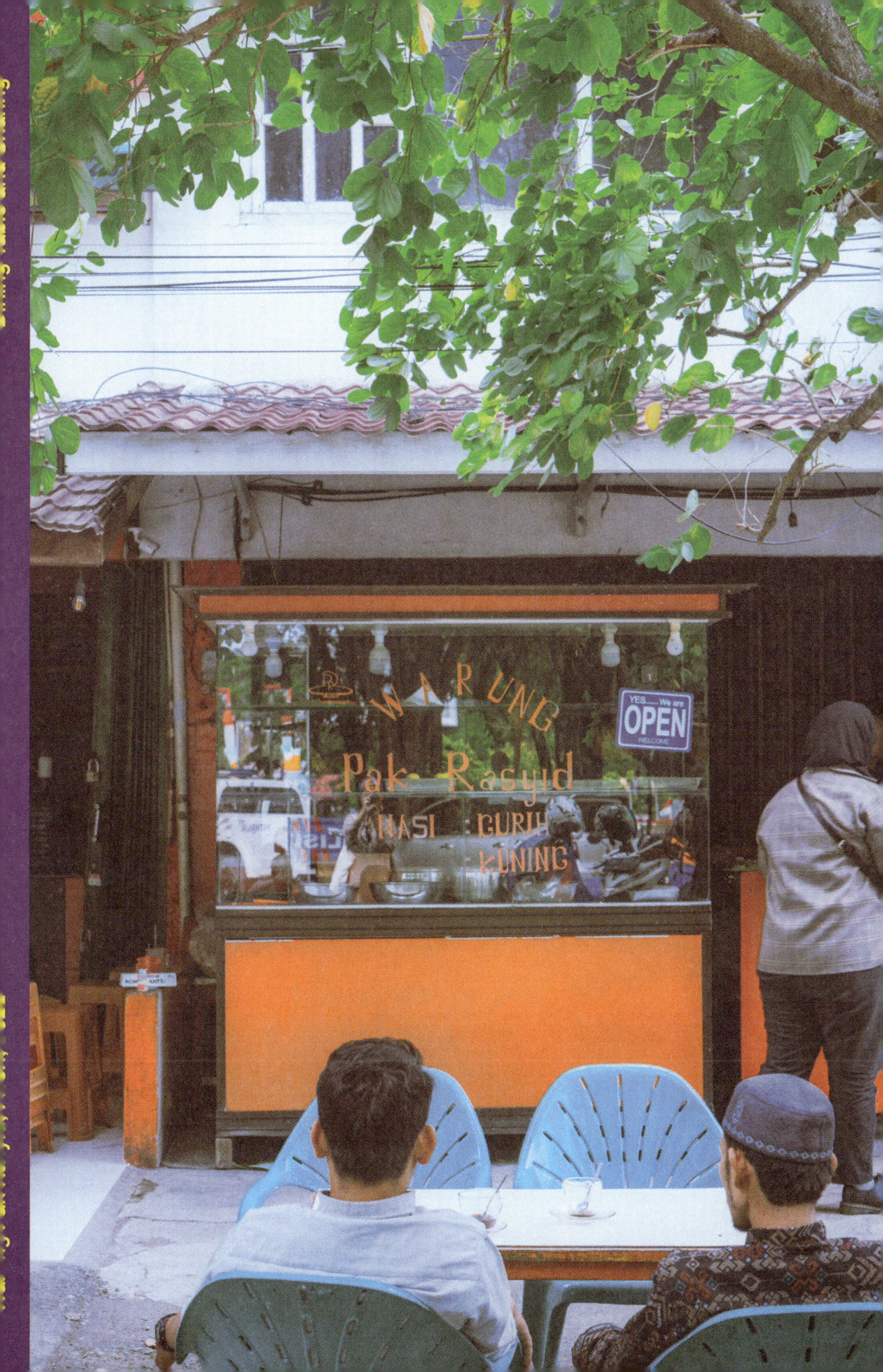
WARUNG
Pak Rasyid
NASI GURIH
KUNING
YES..... We are
OPEN

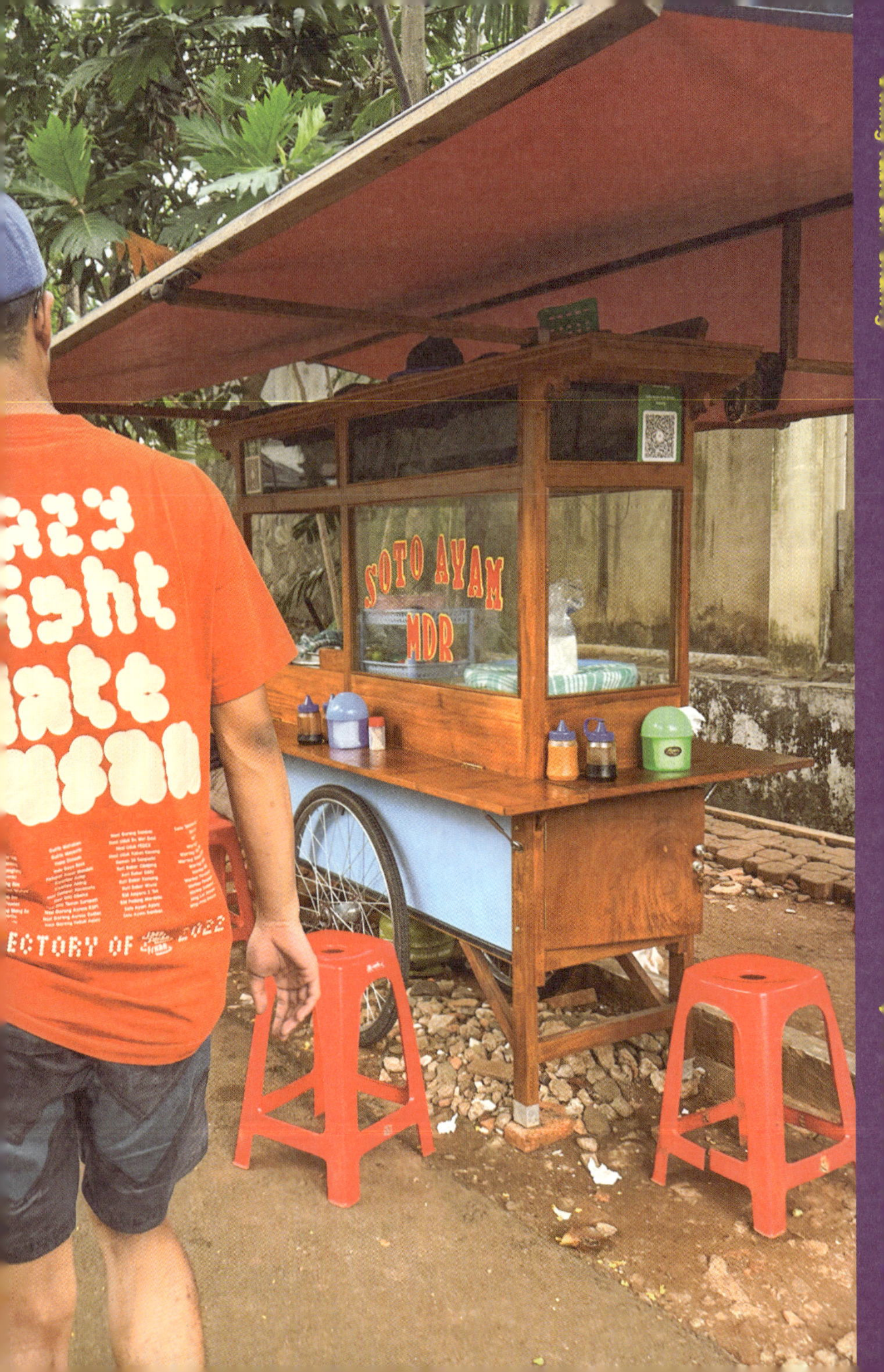
SOTO AYAM
MDR

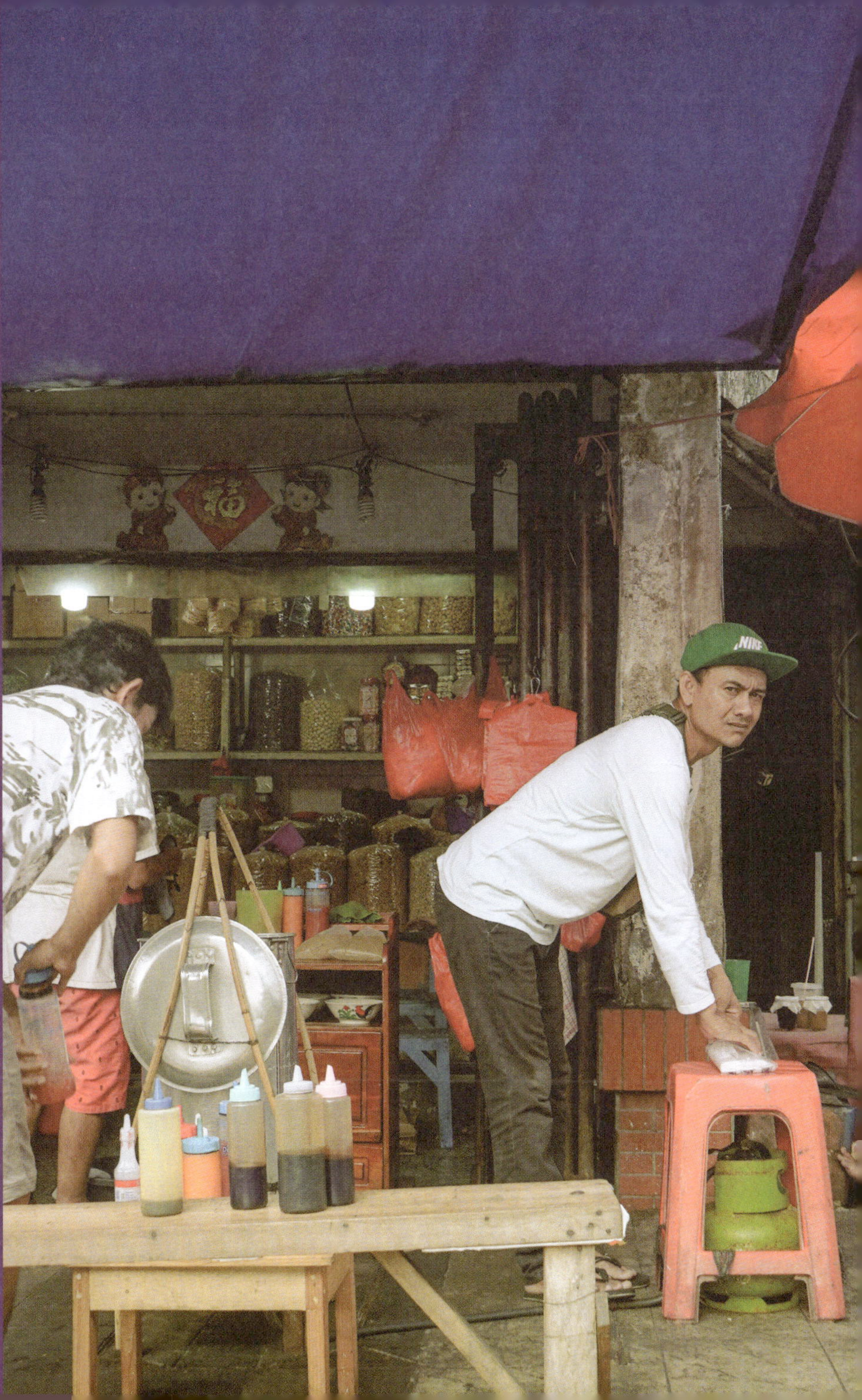

Bakso Pikul Pancoran, Jakarta, 2024

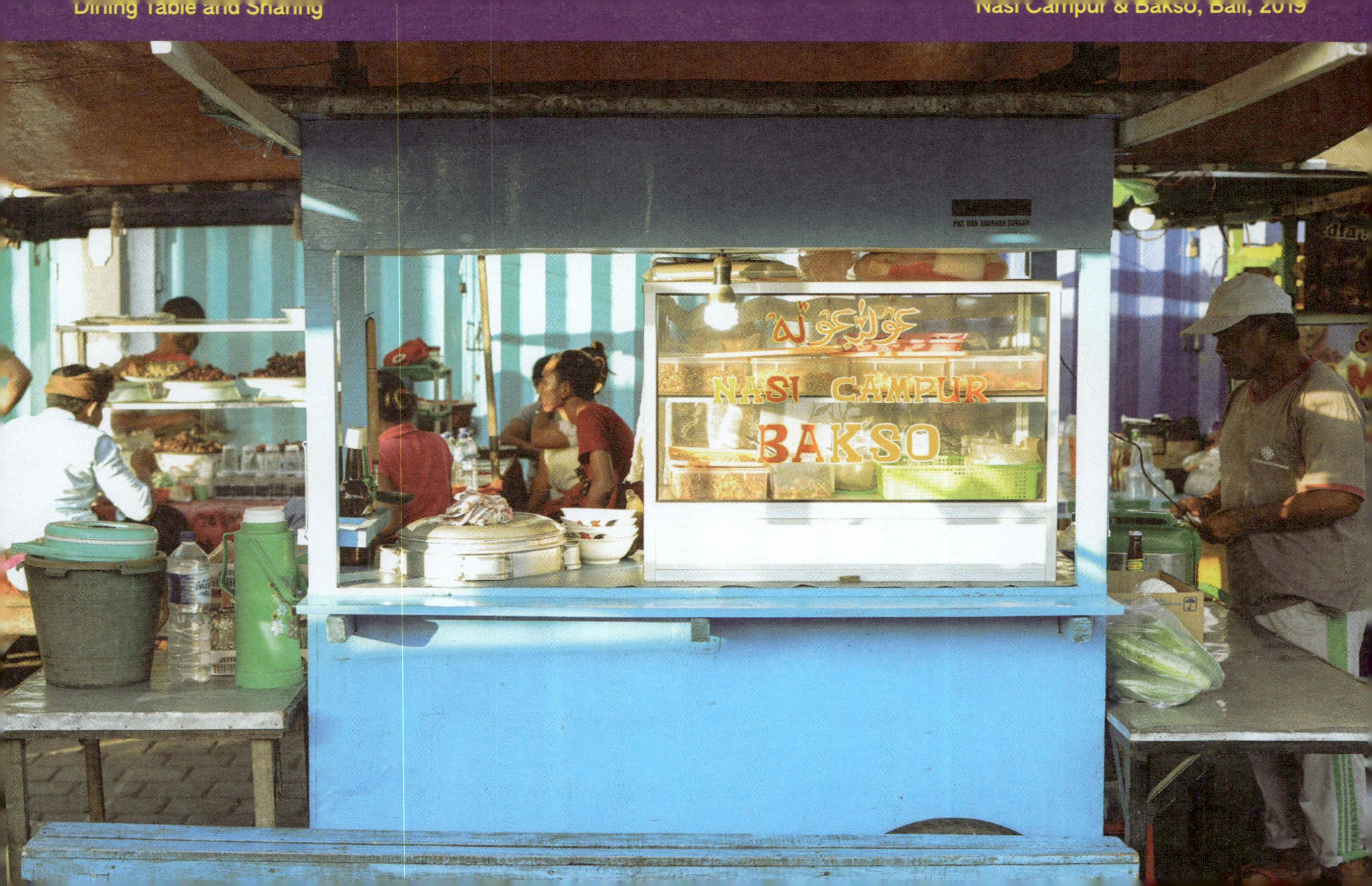

Nasi Campur & Bakso, Bali, 2019

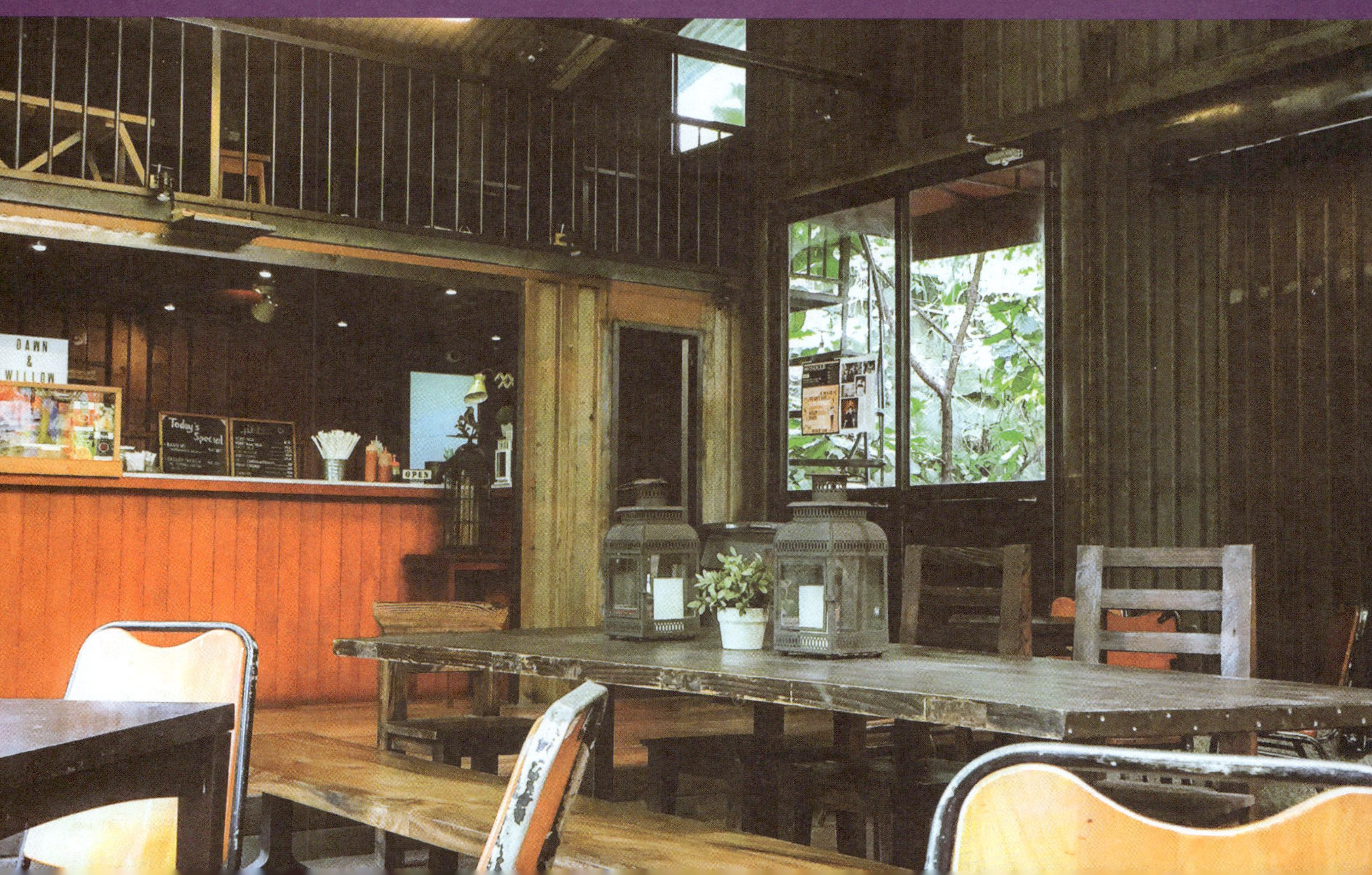

Dawn & Willow, Jakarta, 2018

lesehan

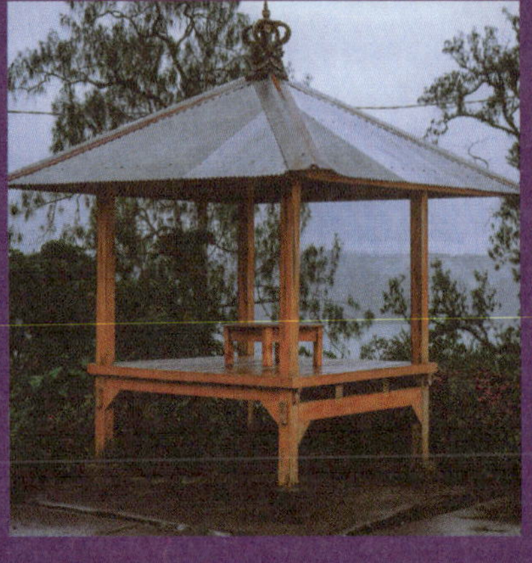

Traditional dining style where people sit on the floor or on low benches around a low table or mat, sometimes on the ground.

nongkrong

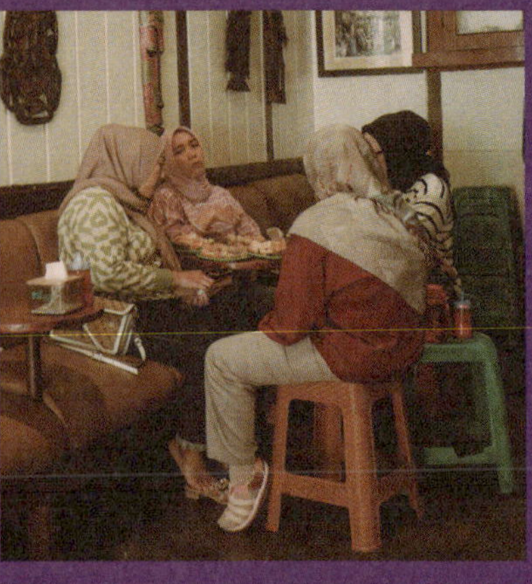

Dining Tables also function as a 'nongkrong' spot. Nongkrong is an Indonesian term coined as a spending time activity by doing nothing to fill the time.

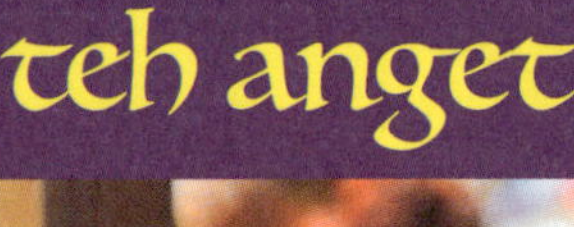

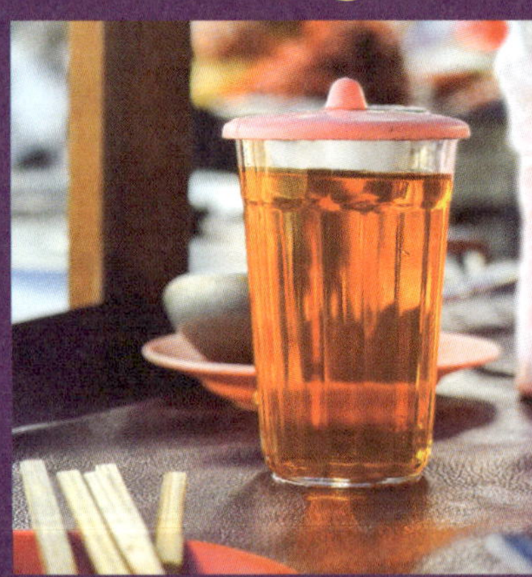

Usually free, always warm, sometimes sweet. A gesture of hospitality at its finest.

spanduk

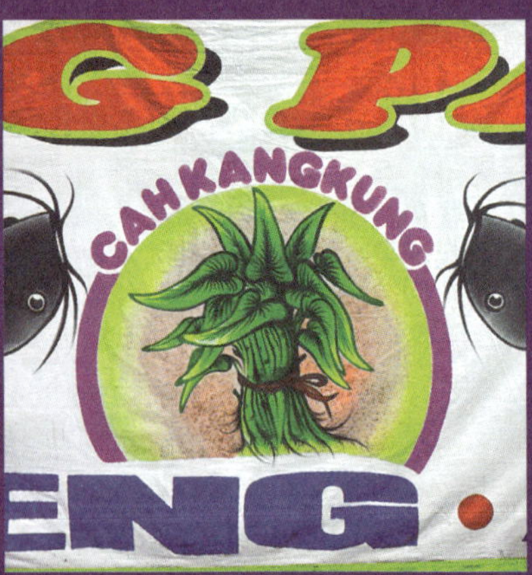

Banner turned signage. Faded by sun, flapping in the wind, but still shouting the menu louder than anything else.

food display

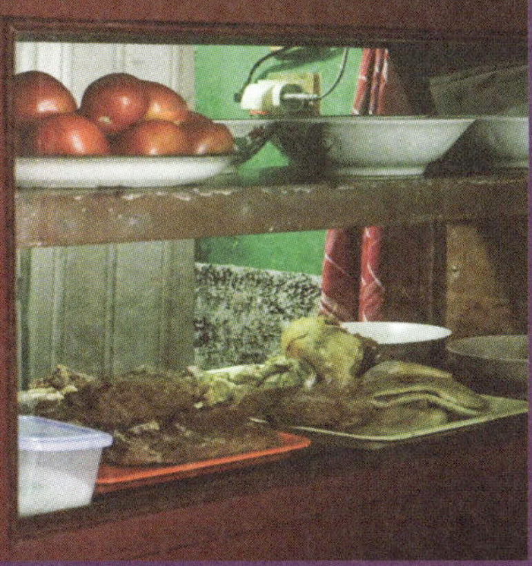

Eating in front of a food display is common in Indonesia. At street stalls, you pick your plate directly: carbs, proteins, veggies, sides. Locals jokingly call it a "touch screen."

plastic chair

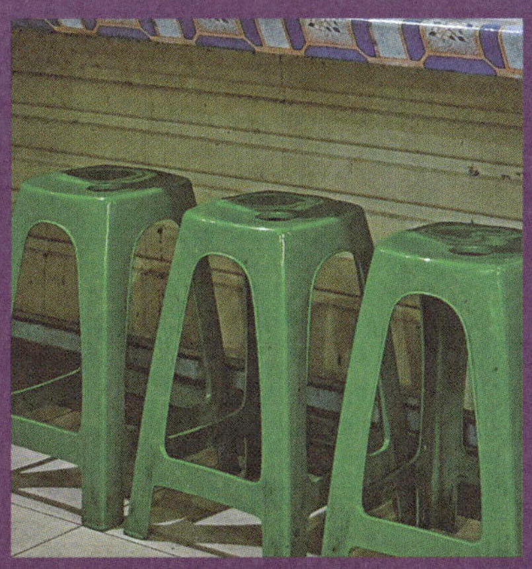

The chair some sees as 'the world's most perfectly designed object' and some others 'an evil of globalization' that is everywhere in the world are also here in Indonesia.

payung

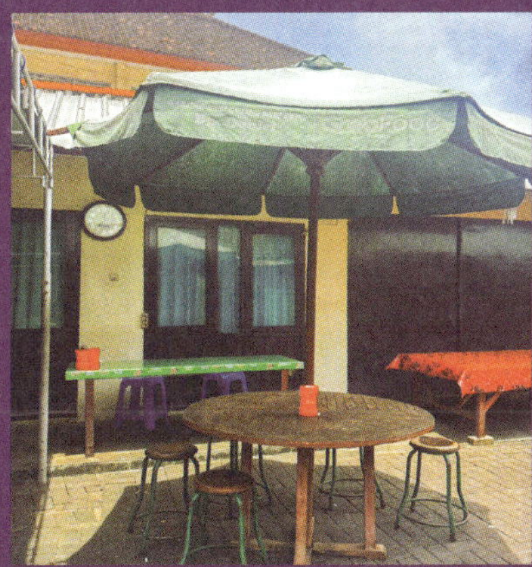

Big, worn, and branded — shields diners from sun and light rain, unofficially marks the territory of trusted warungs.

alat makan

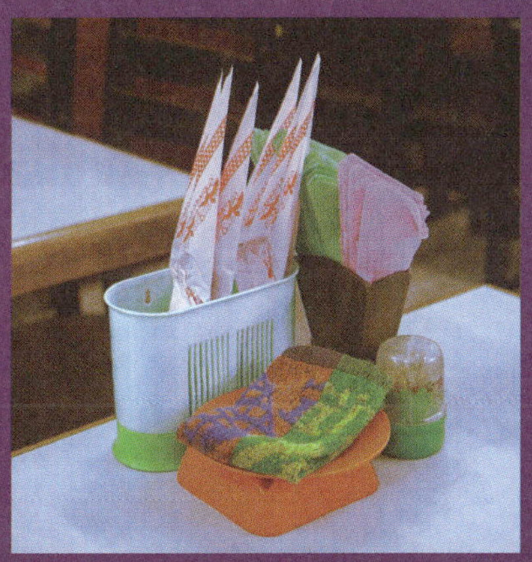

Wrapped spoon and fork, napkins, chili shaker, colorful mesh cloth, and a toothpick holder. Sometimes they get used, sometimes they're just decoration — but without them, the table just feels incomplete.

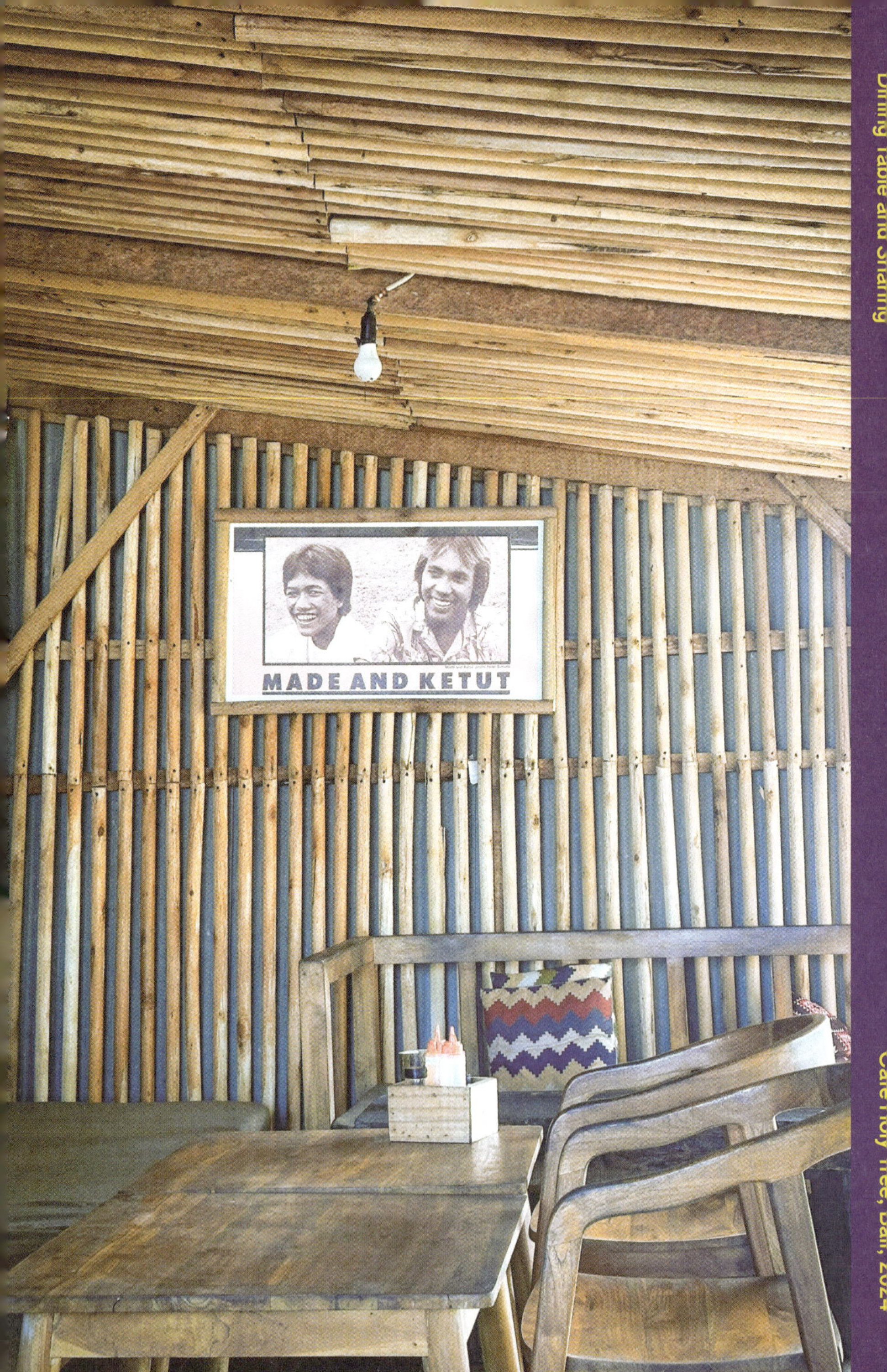
MADE AND KETUT

dining table and celebration

Dining tables in Indonesia are central to celebrations, bringing families and communities together through food. These tables are the heart of many life events — from weddings and religious ceremonies to harvest festivals and even funerals. In Minangkabau culture, for example, it's common to host communal gatherings with over 200 people, where guests are served in shifts, and food is shared in generous platters.

Indonesians have a deep-rooted penchant for marking every occasion, no matter how big or small. From pre-birth rituals to coming-of-age milestones, from marriages to memorials, the act of gathering, sitting, and eating together becomes a way to honor and witness life's transitions.

More than just meals, these moments reflect unity, joy, and shared meaning. Chairs are borrowed from neighbors, tables are dressed in lace or newspaper, and dishes are prepared not for show, but for love. Even the most modest celebration feels full when people are present — bringing with them stories, laughter, and a sense of togetherness that turns food into memory.

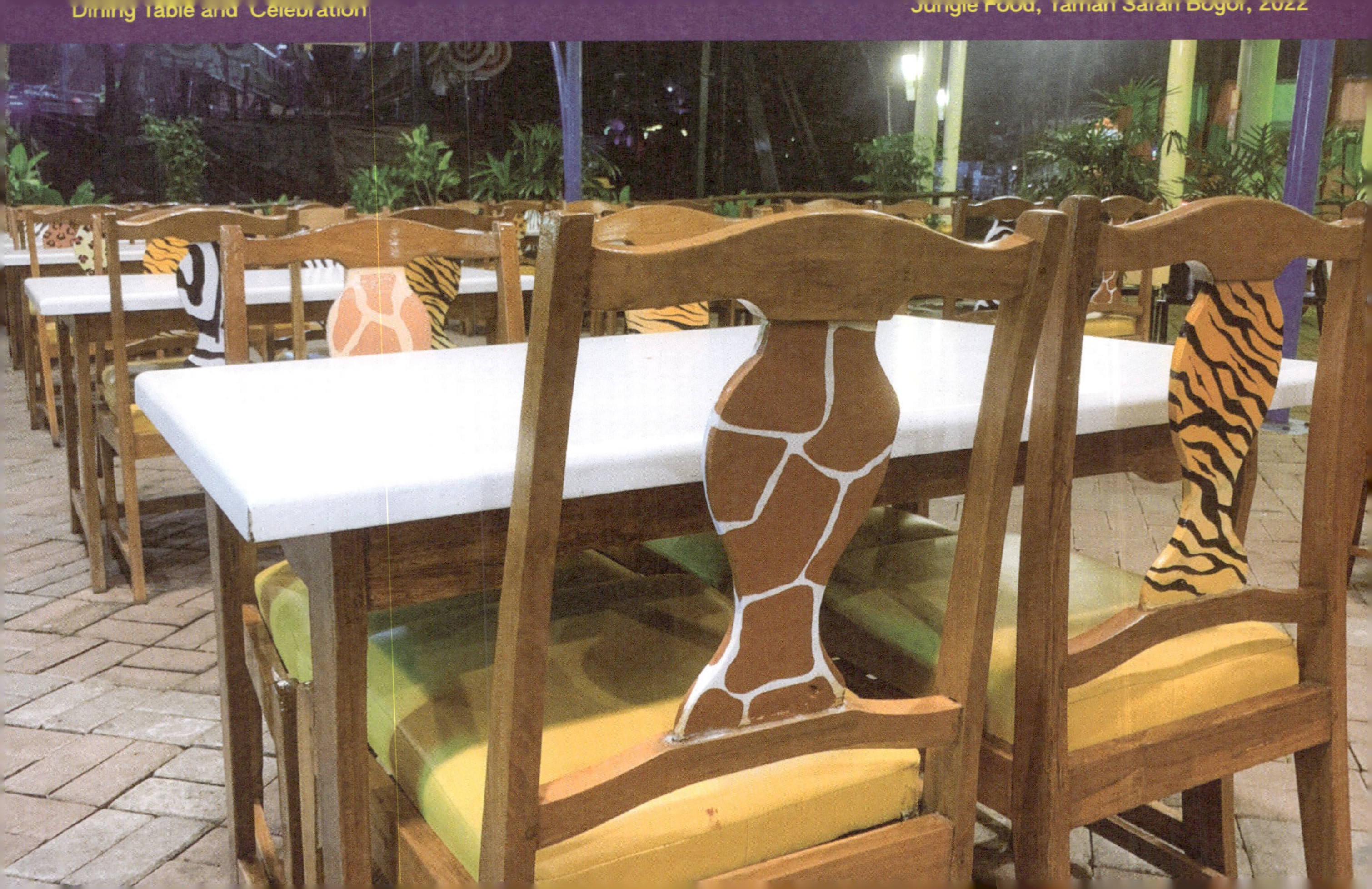

Dining Table and Celebration

Jungle Food, Taman Safari Bogor, 2022

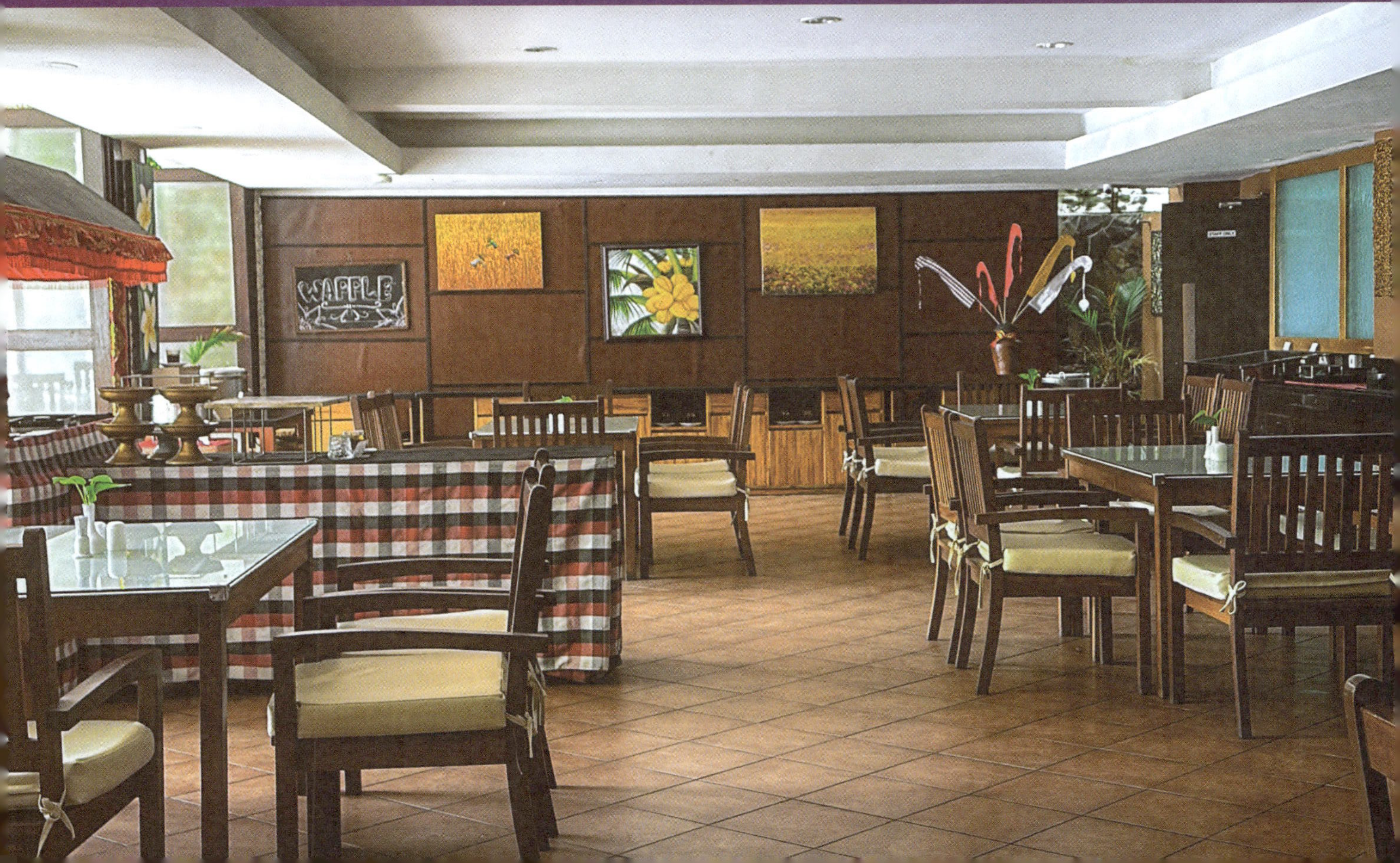

Ambrosia Restaurant, Bali, 2024

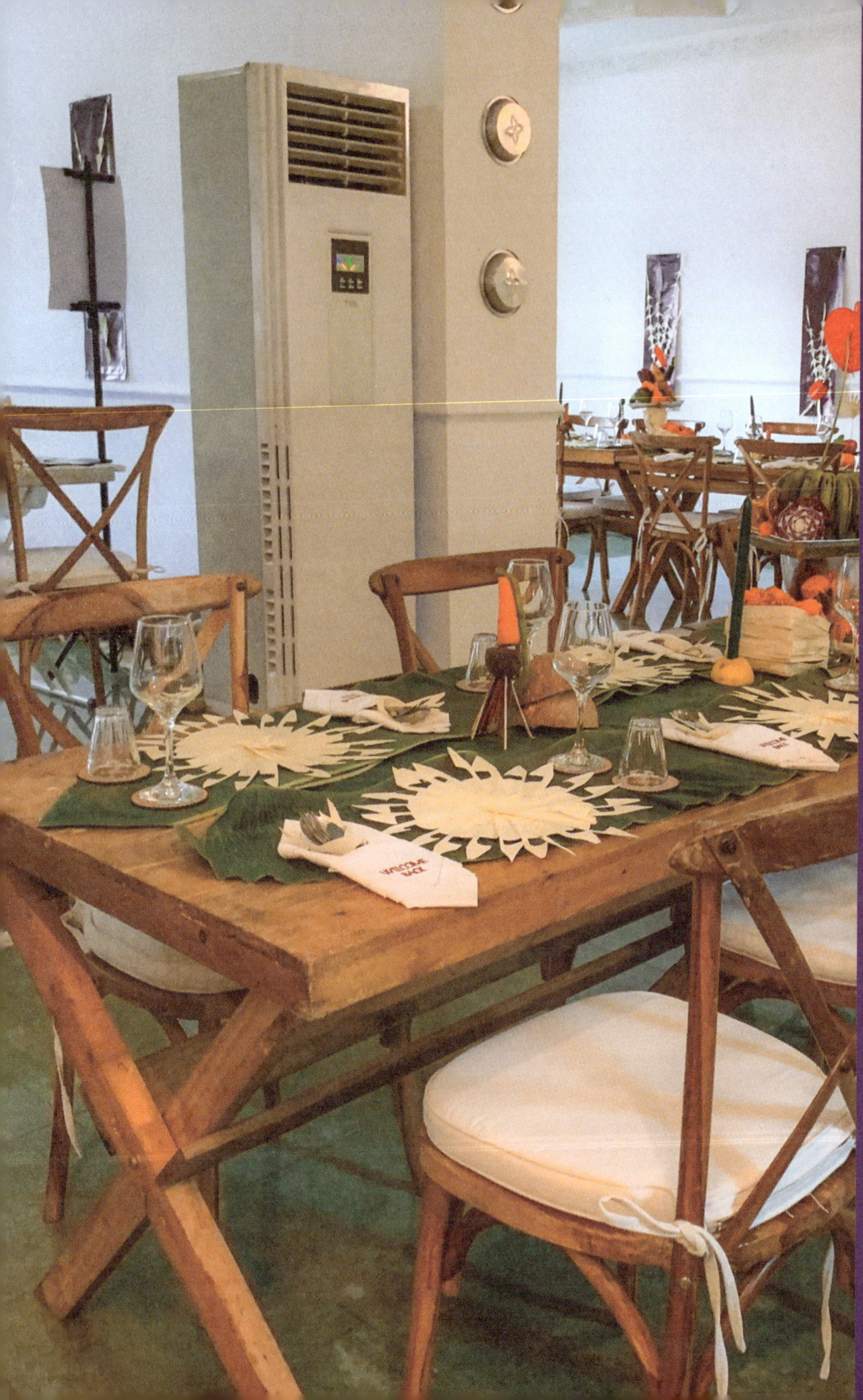

Mewali at Cipete, Jakarta, 2022

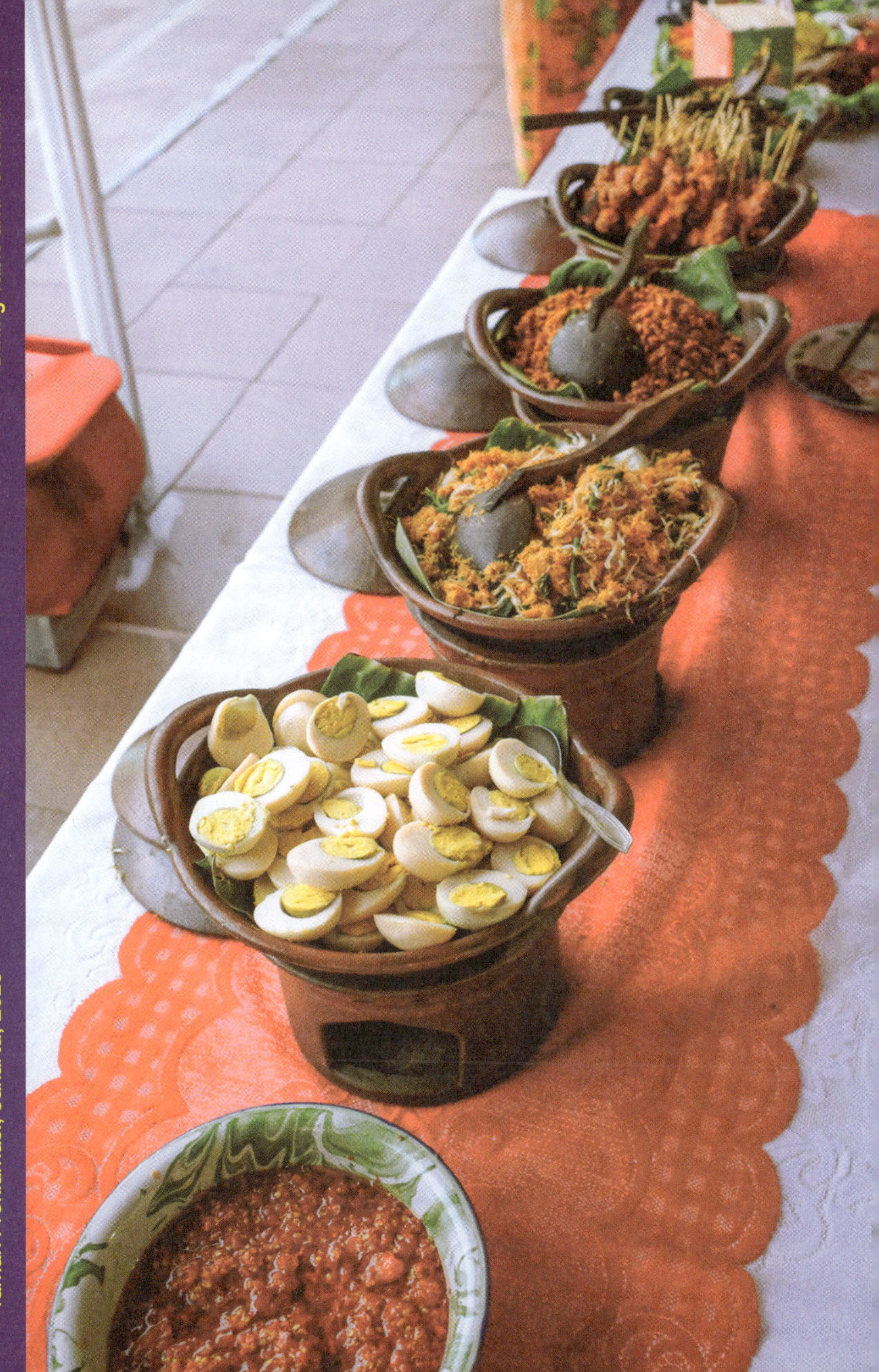

Taman Proklamasi, Jakarta, 2023

Dining Table and Celebration

Aceh Food Festival, Aceh, 2022

dining table and diversity

Indonesia, with its 1,300+ ethnic groups and over 270 million people, is a melting pot of cultures. Each culture has its own unique take on dining tables, eating habits, and chair designs. Whether it's a low table in a Javanese home or a communal table in a Batak house, these pieces reflect the rich traditions of their people — passed down through generations, shaped by landscape, values, and daily life.

While Indonesia became independent in 1945, its culture has been shaped by outside influences for centuries. Chinese and Dutch traditions, for example, have left their mark on how Indonesians dine. The Chinese introduced round tables and communal eating, while the Dutch brought Western-style dining tables and chairs, shaping the way many urban households still eat today. Indian and Arab influences are also present: seen in the use of shared platters, floor seating, and richly spiced dishes eaten by hand, especially in Aceh, West Sumatra, and coastal communities.

Today, this cultural layering continues. Restaurants serving food from all over the world — from Japanese izakayas to Middle Eastern diners — are thriving across Indonesian cities. This didn't happen overnight, nor is it a sign of abandoning local identity, but a reflection of how expansive and adaptable the Indonesian palate has always been. Perhaps our collective palate is still evolving — not yet fully formed, but full of curiosity, openness, and experimentation. We are not a "third world" country with limited taste — we are a dynamic, expressive nation that embraces flavor, form, and influence, and makes them our own.

This blend of local and global traditions creates a vibrant, diverse dining culture that varies from one region to another.

You'll see this reflected in the chapter — not just across regions, but across generations. The types of chairs, table heights, materials, and even the decorations around them all differ. From wood to plastic to cement, from patterned tiles to hanging calendars, from a warung's green plastic stools to a grandma's lace tablecloth — every detail speaks to a different time, place, and way of gathering.

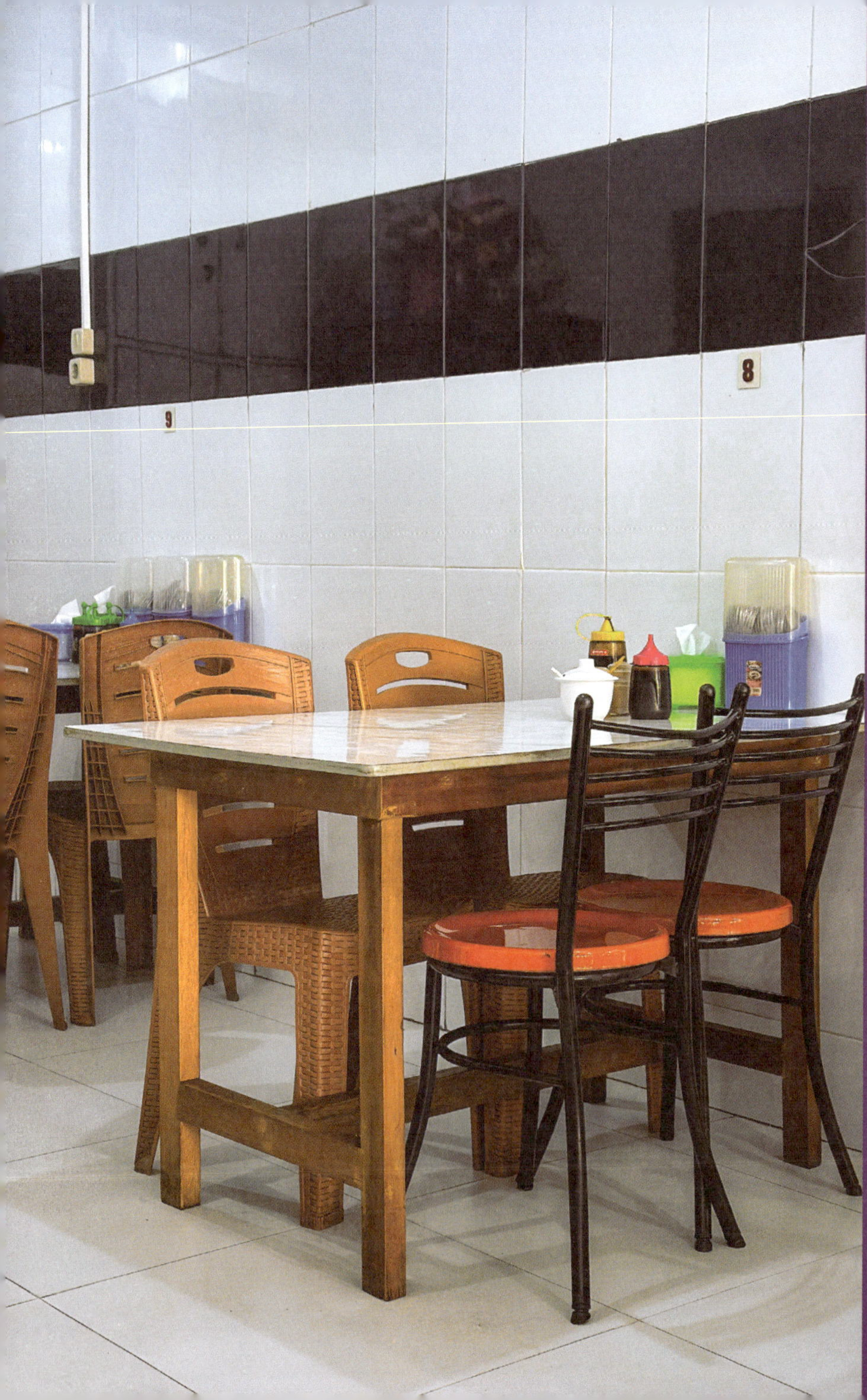

Nasi Ayam Afu, Pontianak, 2024

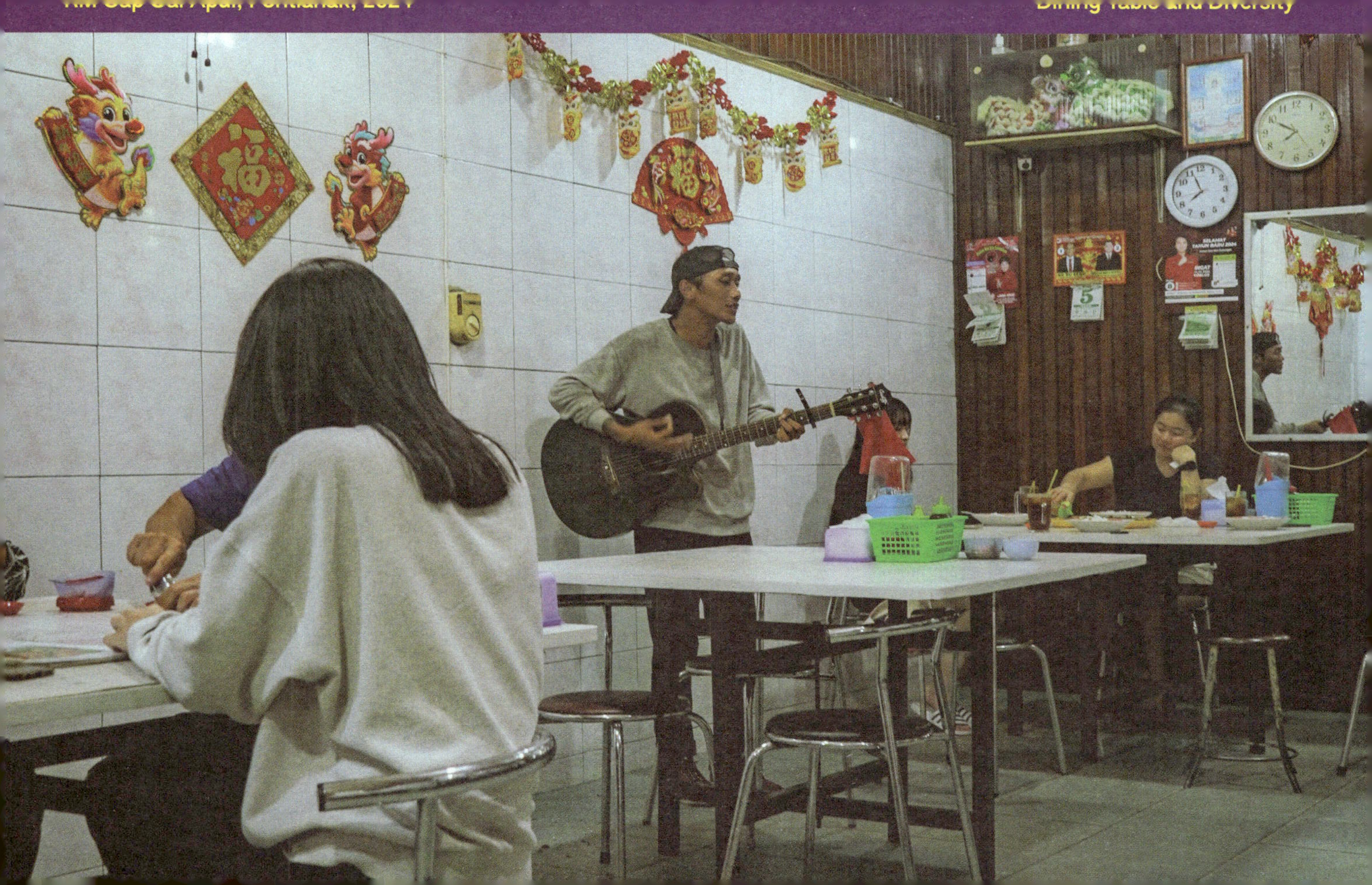

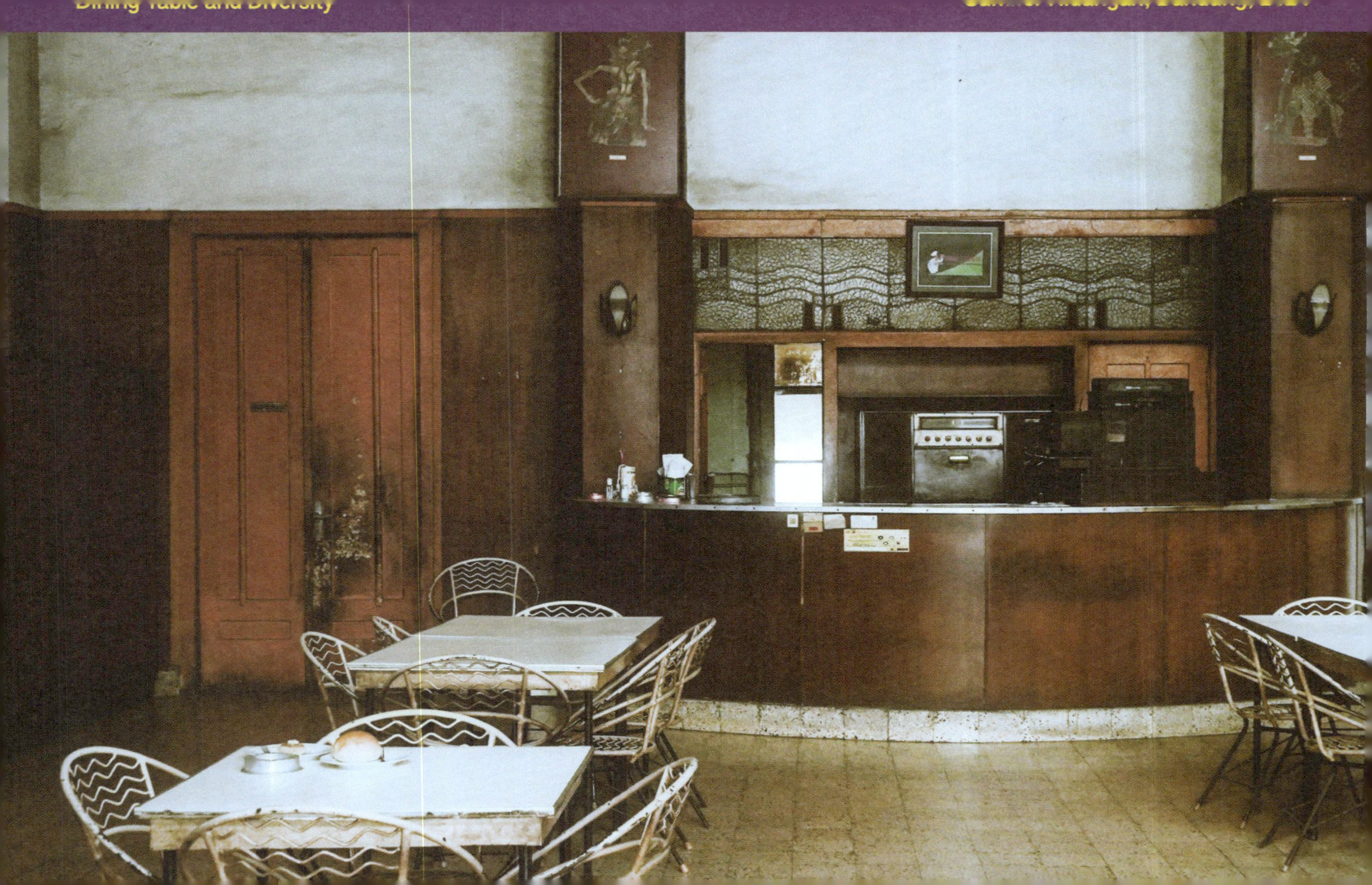

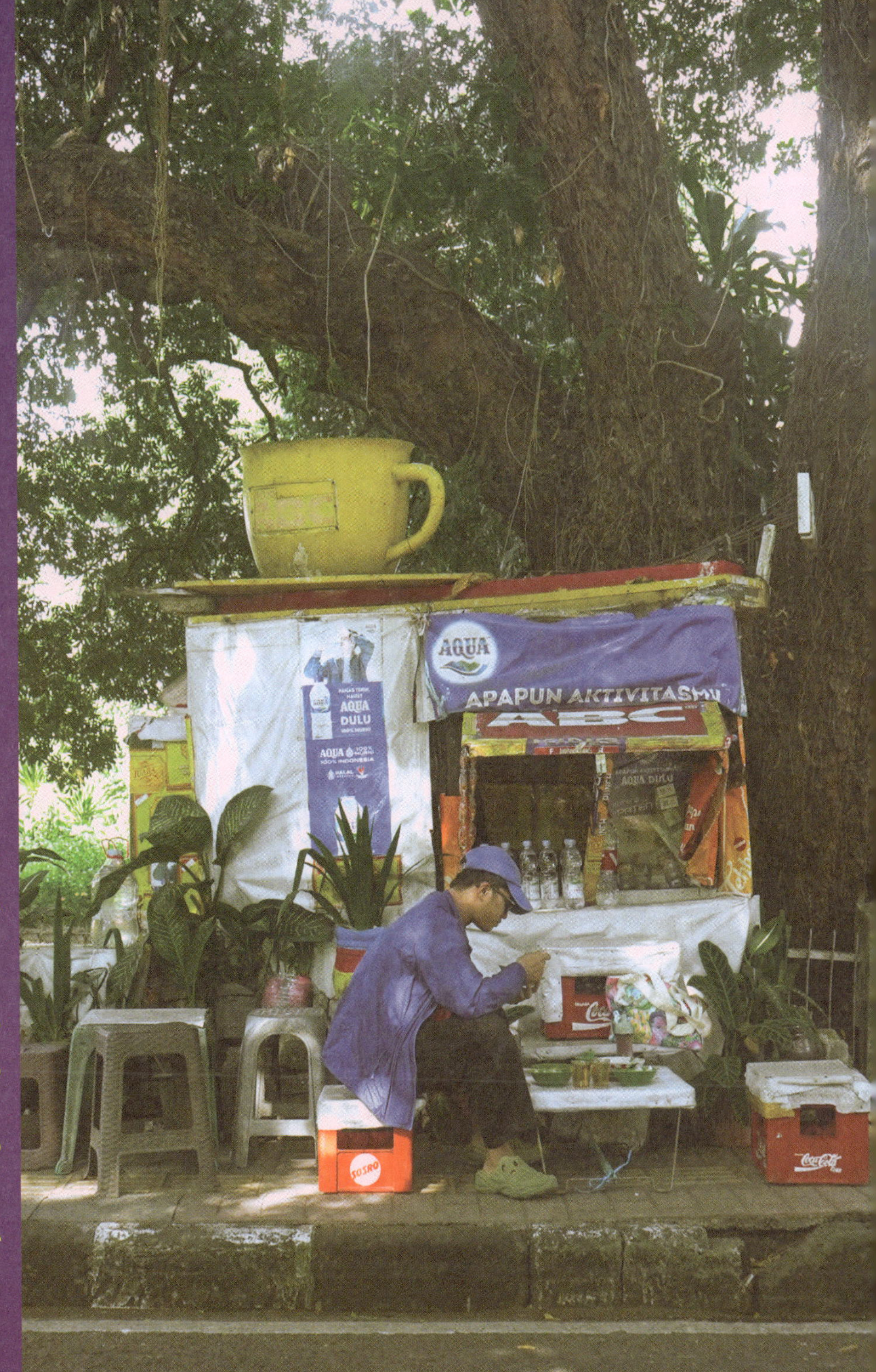

Bubur Ayam Sangkuriang Dago, Bandung, 2024

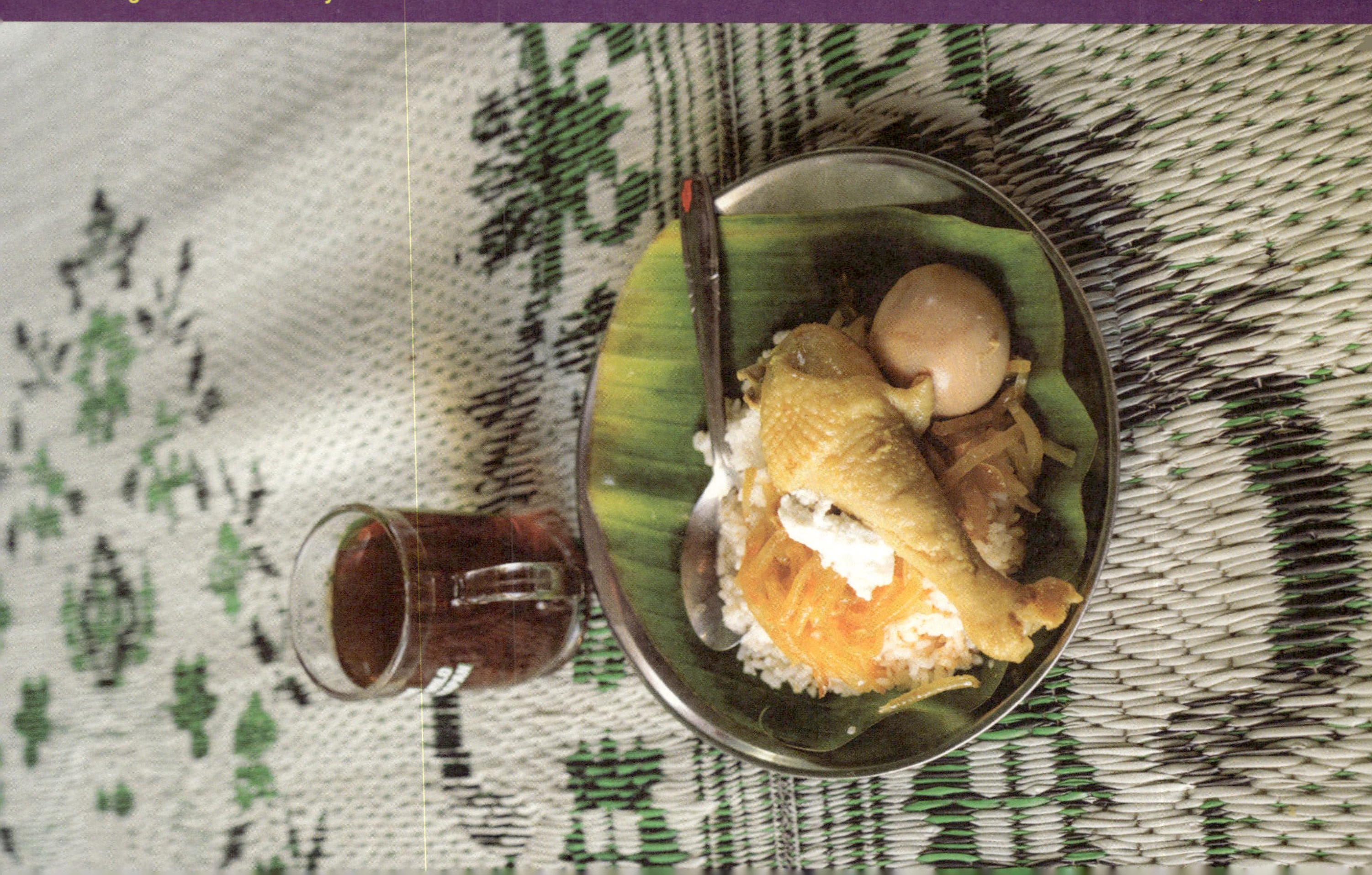

Nasi Liwet Bu Waris, Solo, 2023

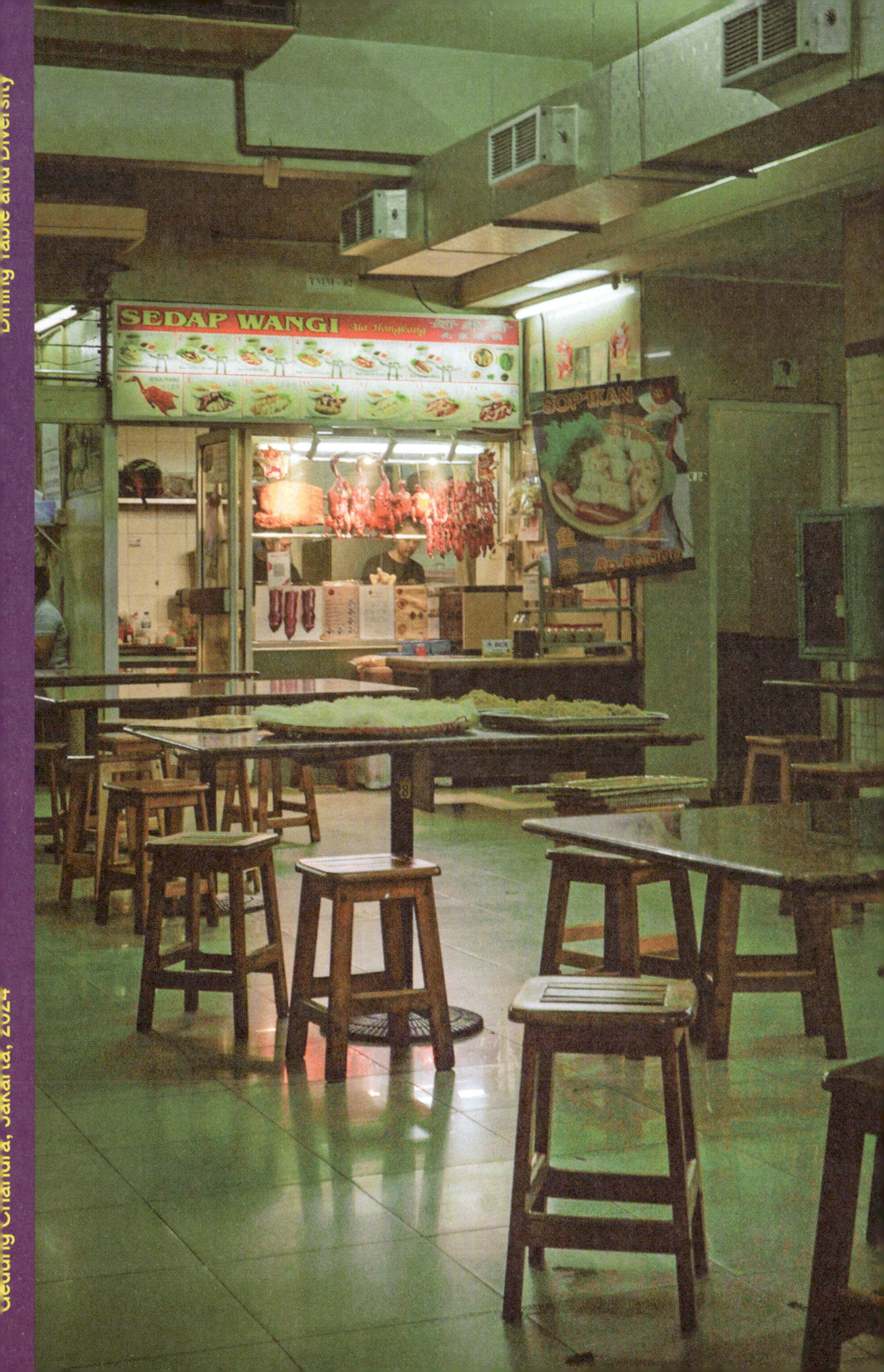

Gedung Chandra, Jakarta, 2024

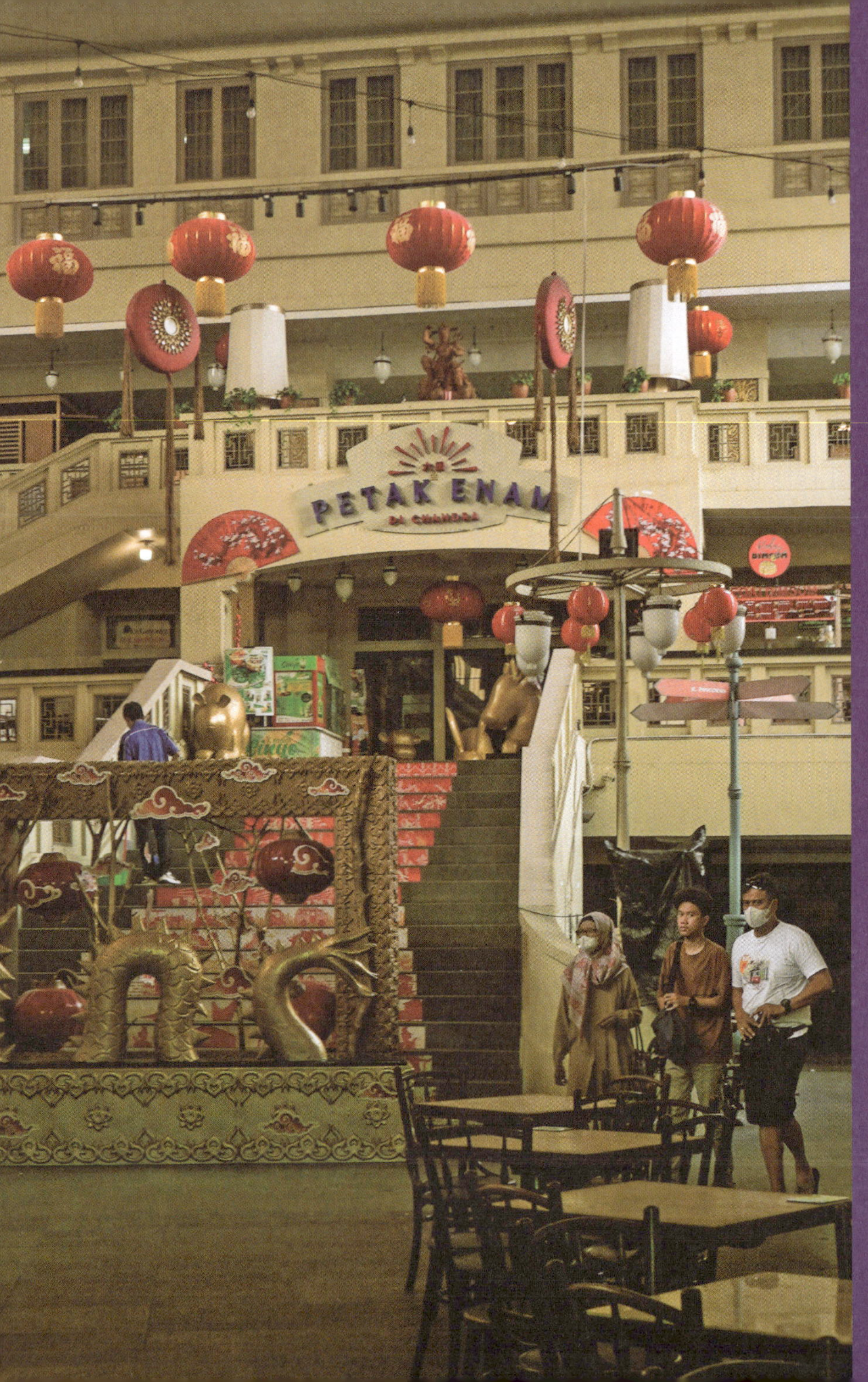

Petak Enam, Jakarta, 2024

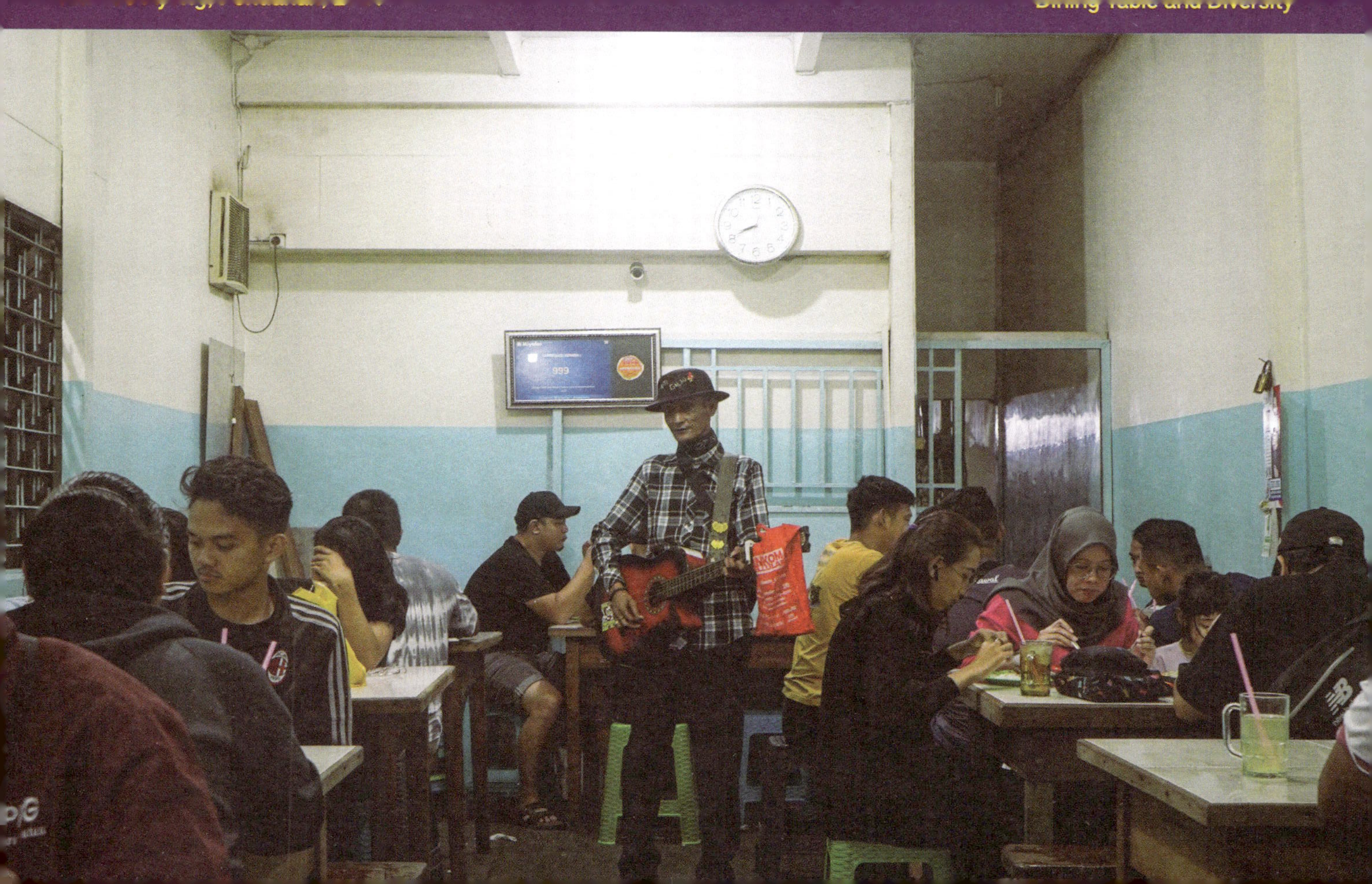

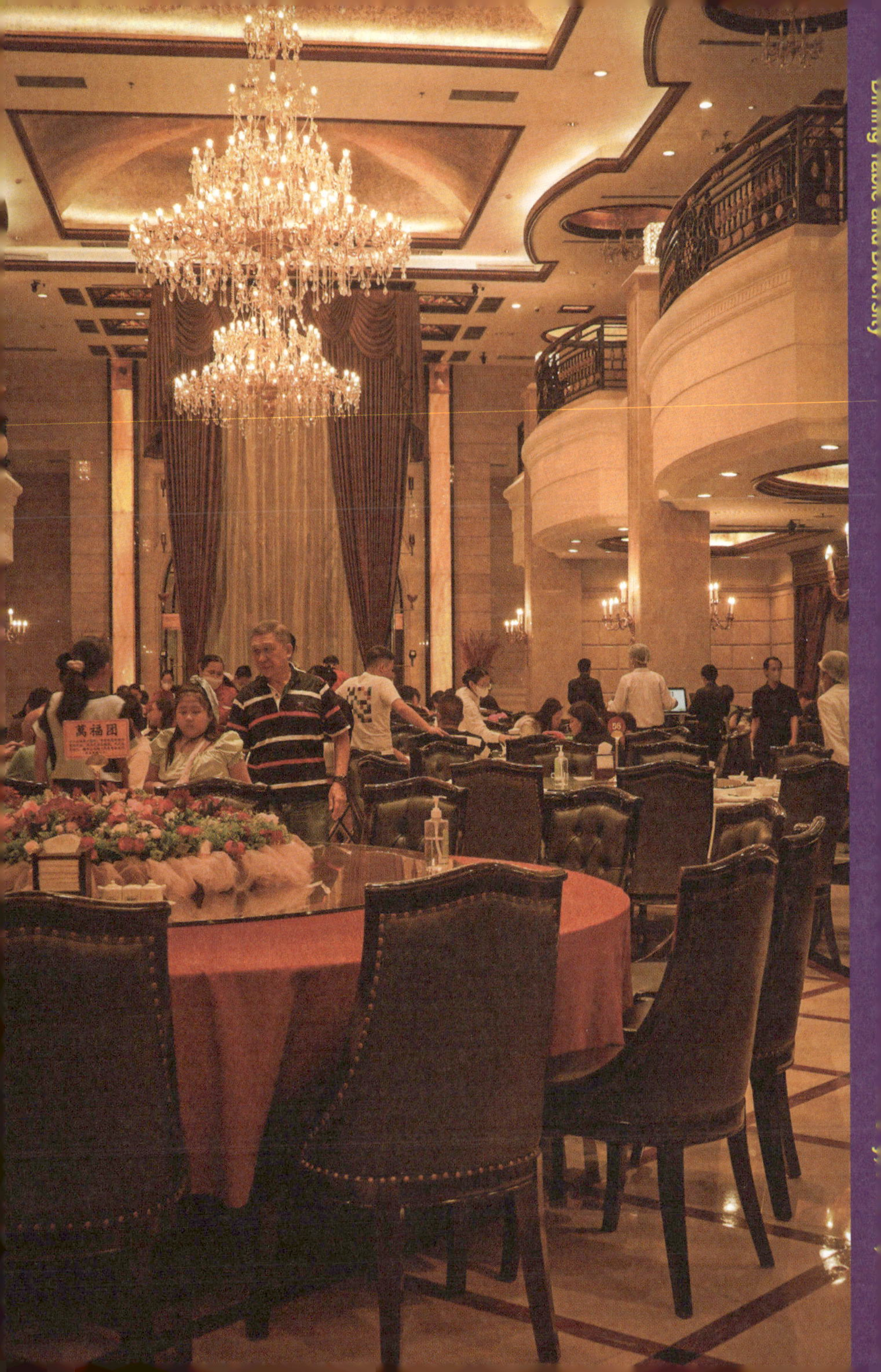
萬福園

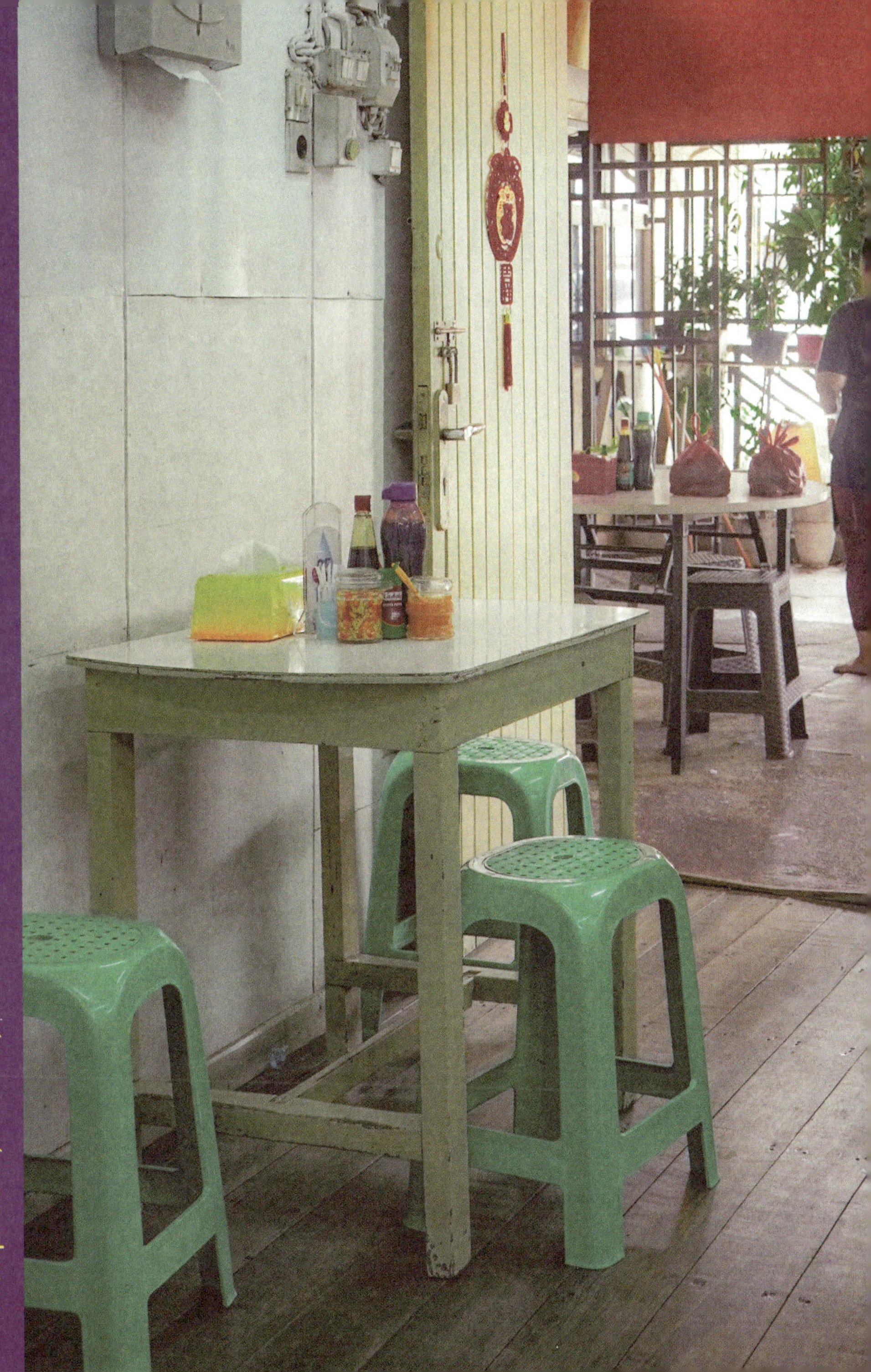

Kwecap Veteran, Pontianak, 2024

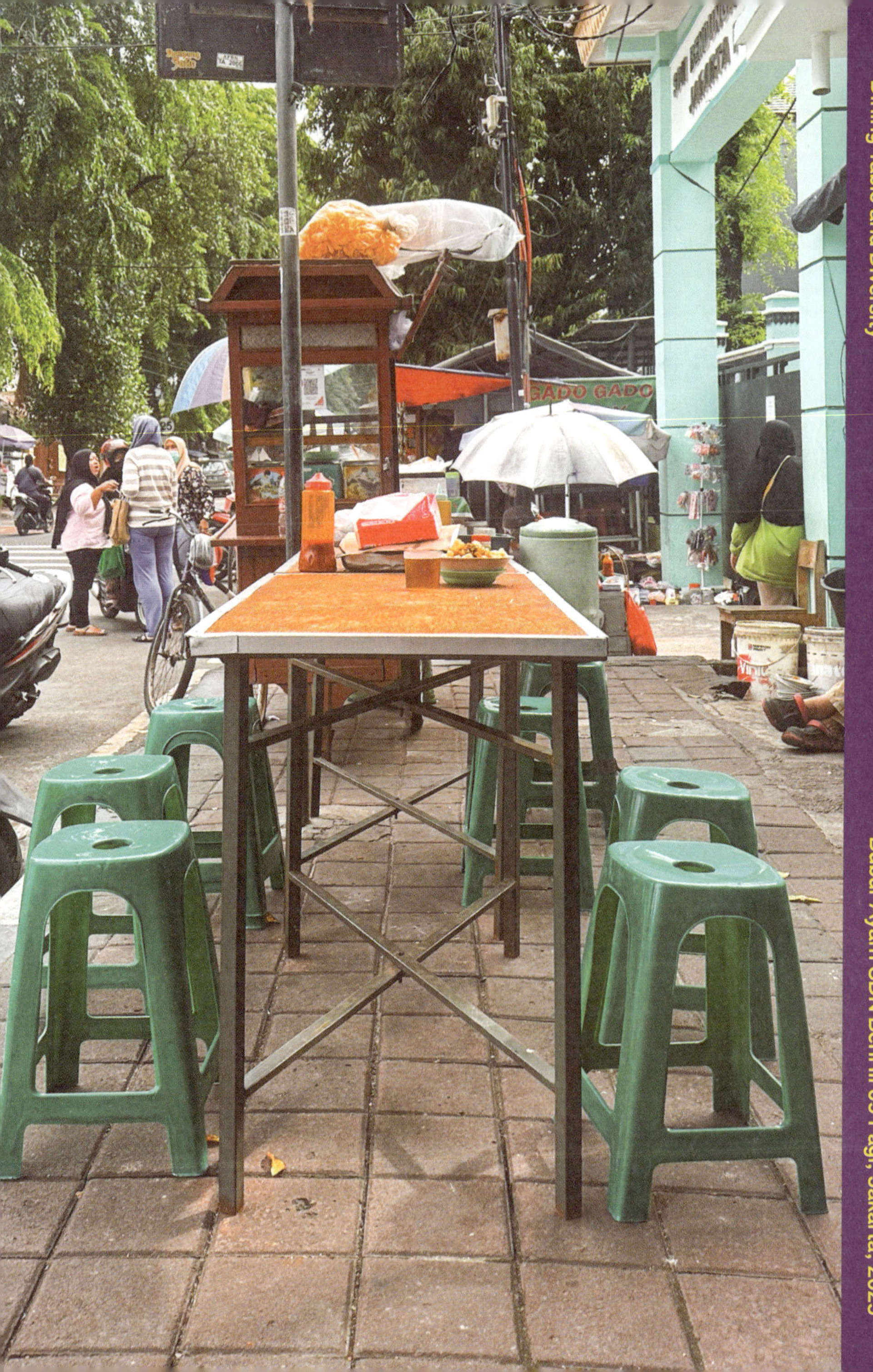

Bubur Ayam SDN Benhil 09 Pagi, Jakarta, 2023

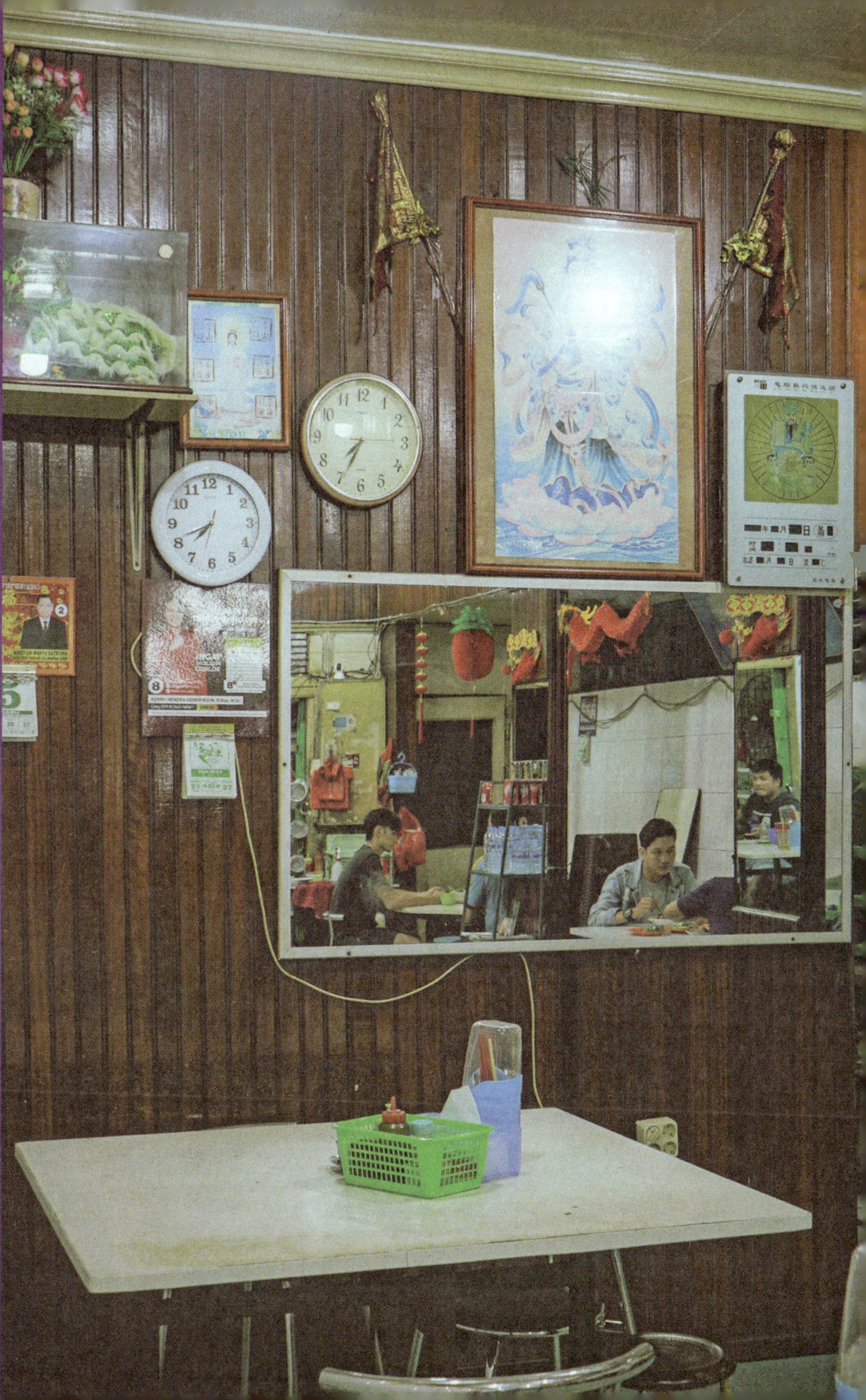

Kwi Cap Cai Apui, Pontianak, 2024

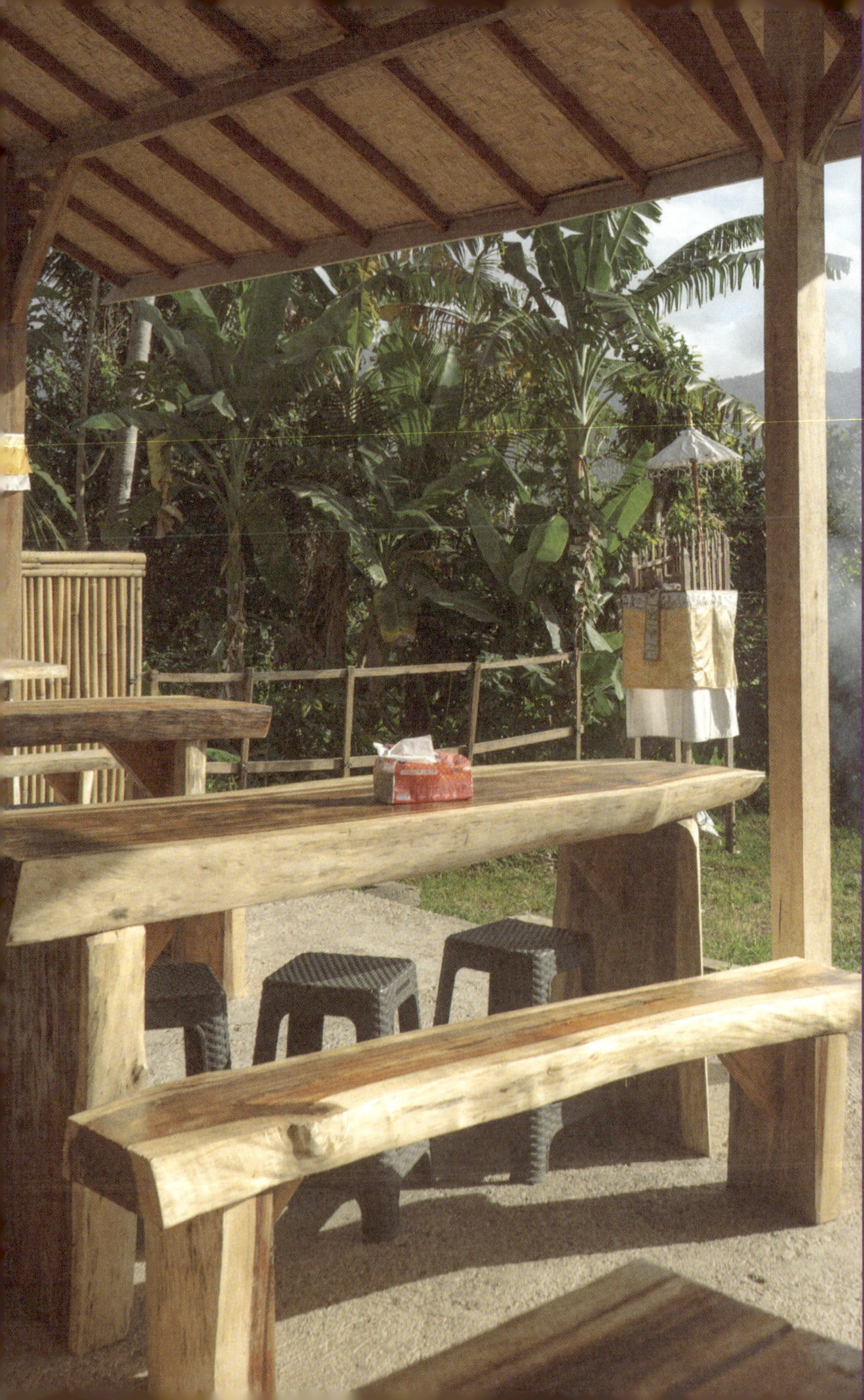

Babi Guling Pan Beryek, Bali, 2023

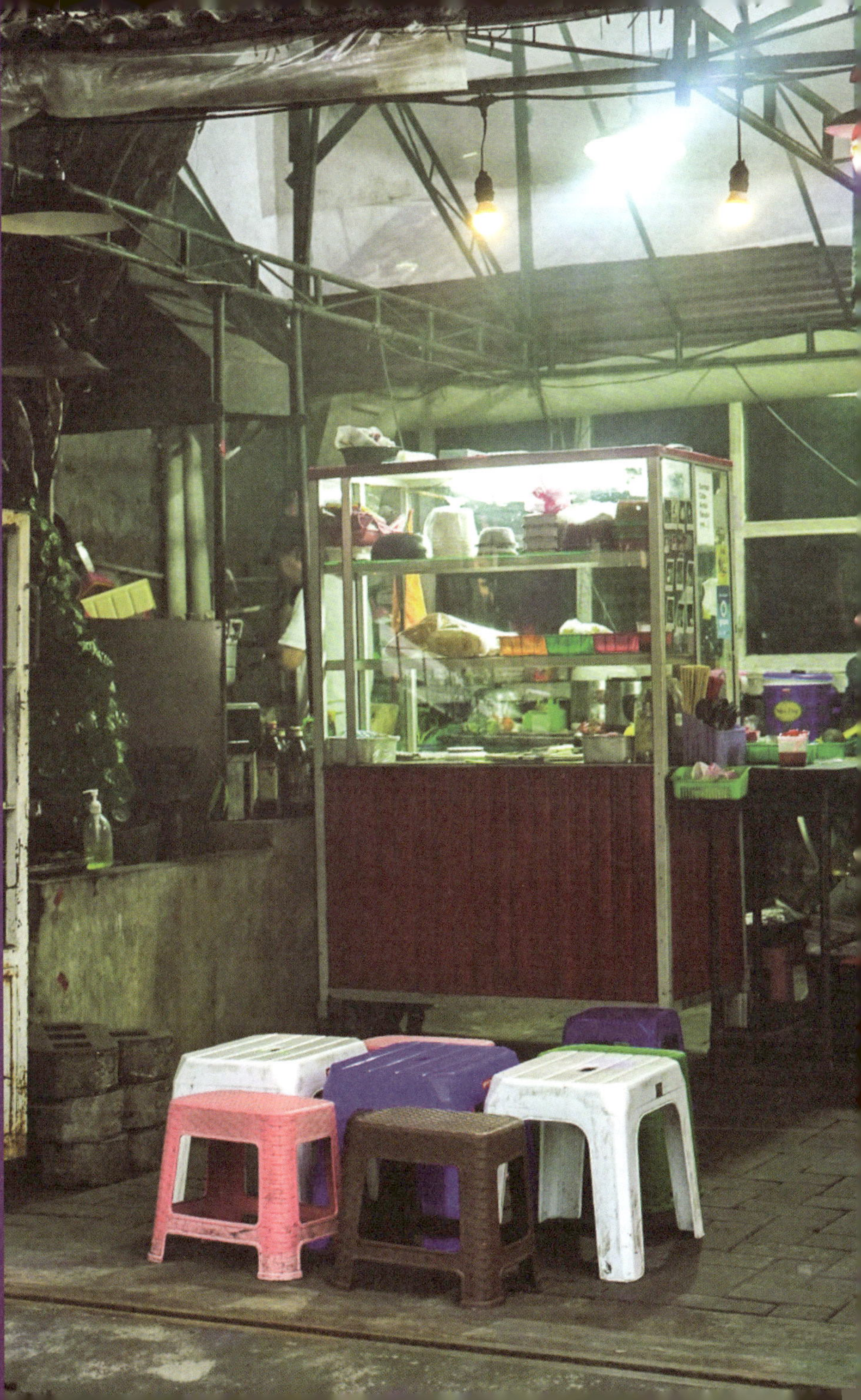

Mimbar Si Baud, Yogyakarta, 2022

Rumah Makan Sepakat Blok M, Jakarta, 2023

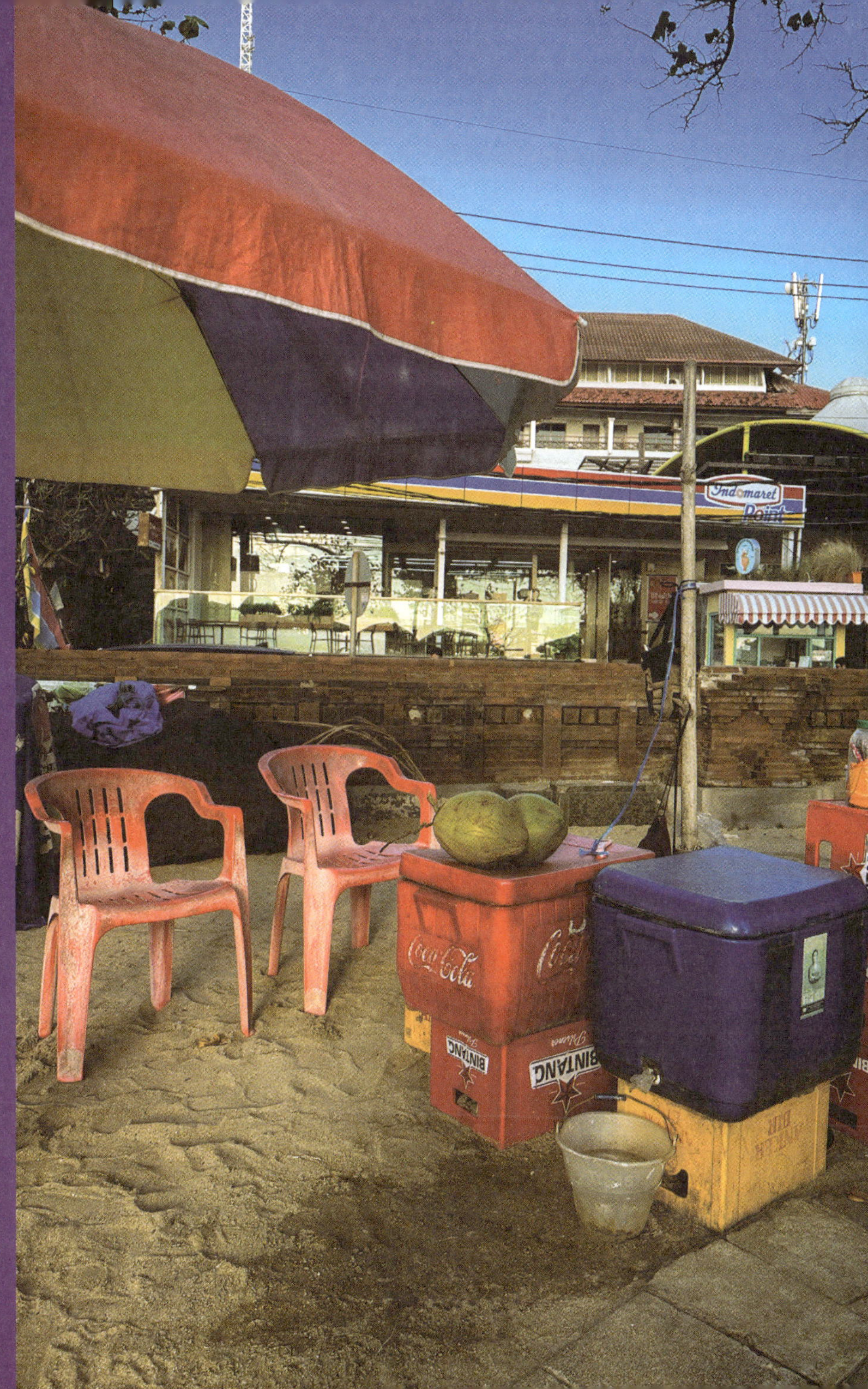

Warung in Kuta Beach, Bali, 2024

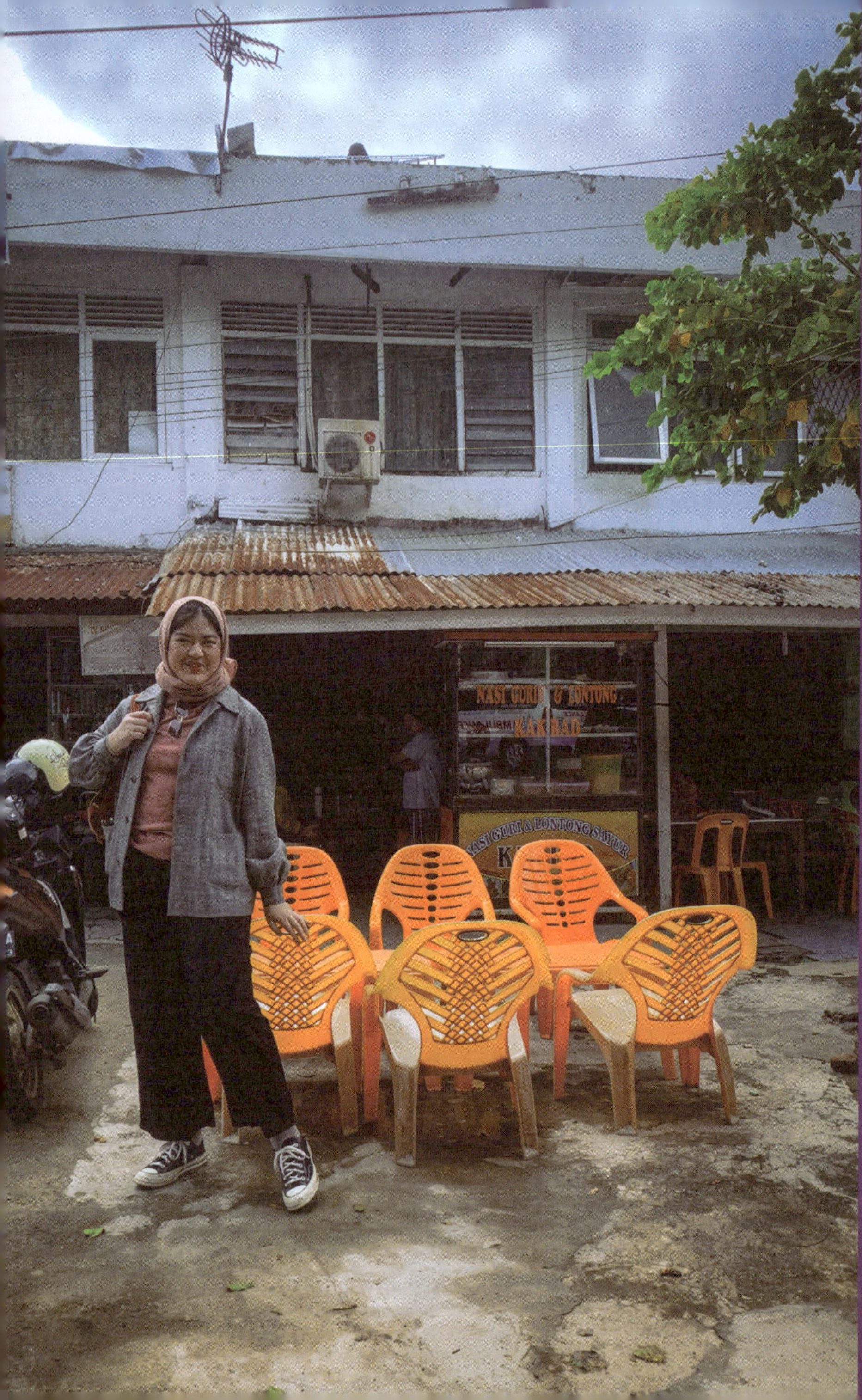

Nasi Gurih, Aceh, 2024

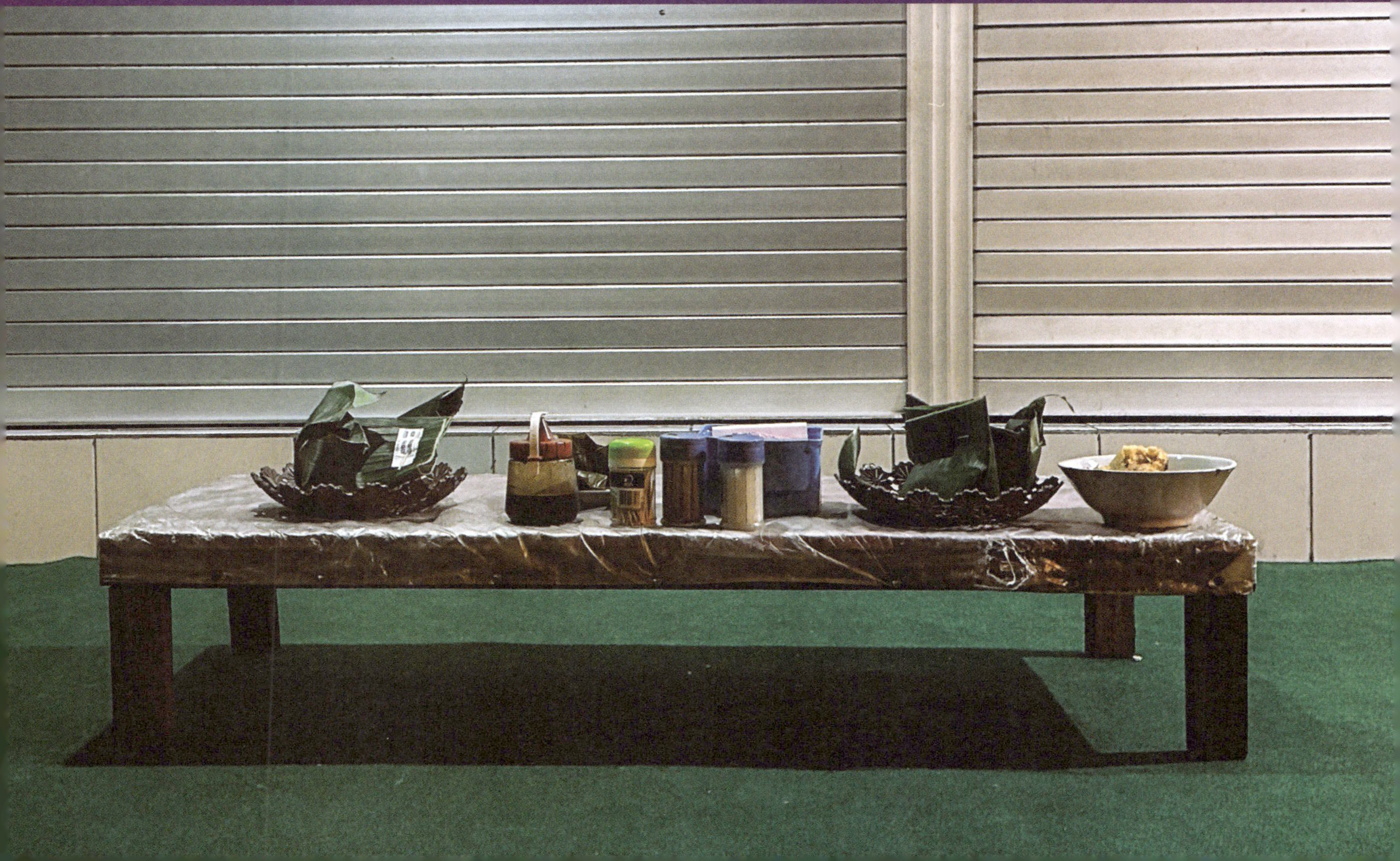

Jinggo Pinggiran, Bali, 2024

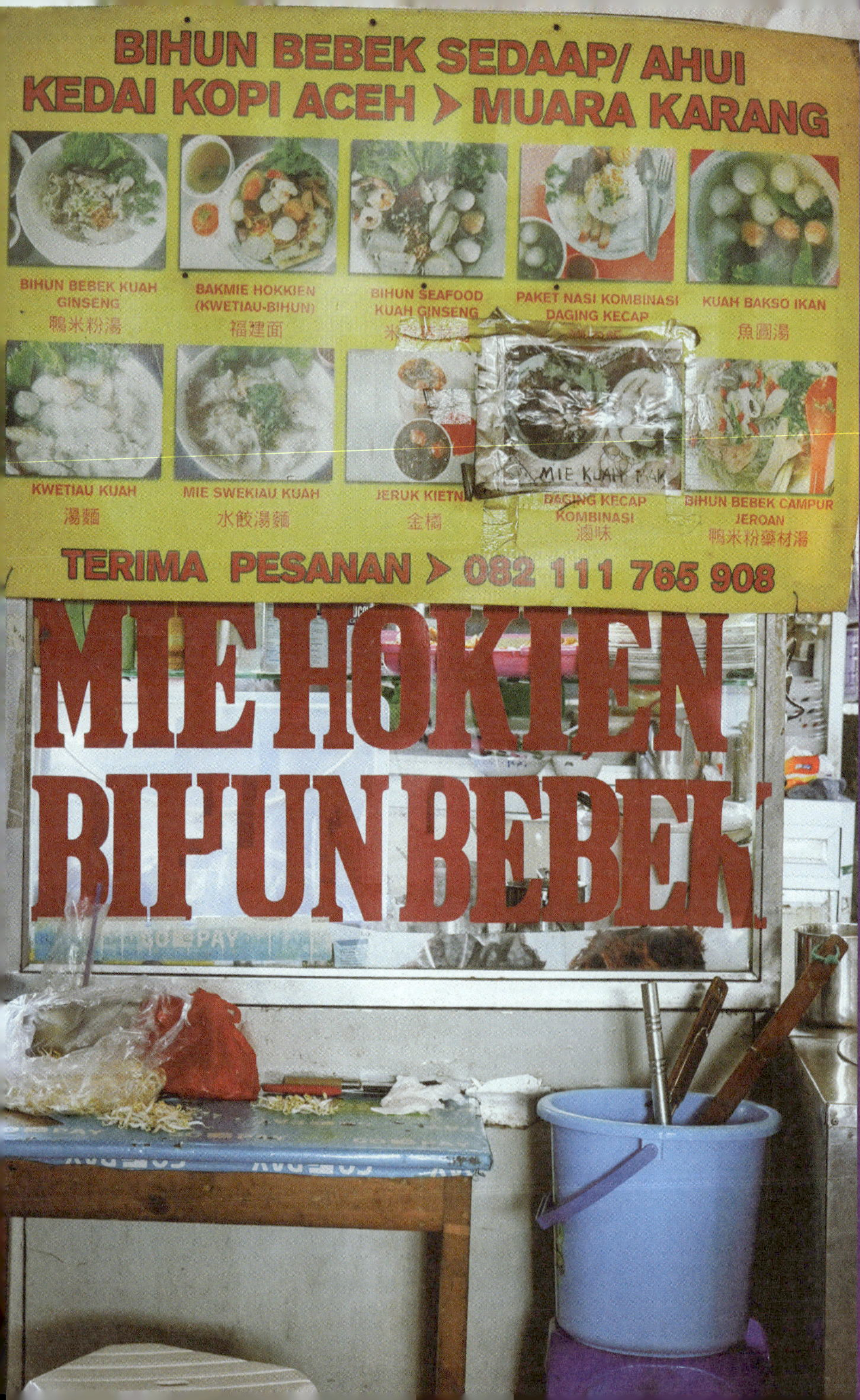

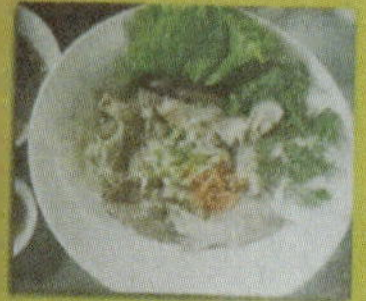

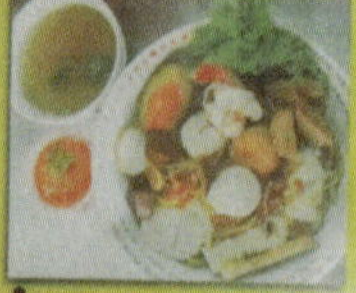

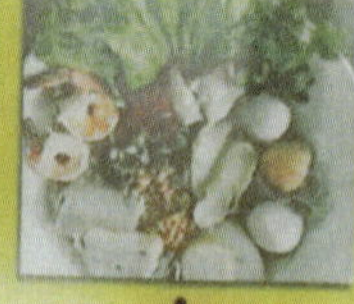

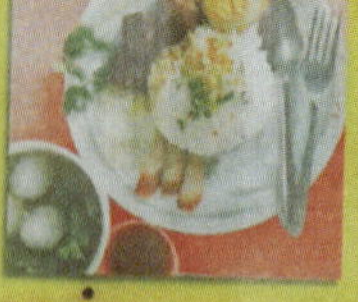

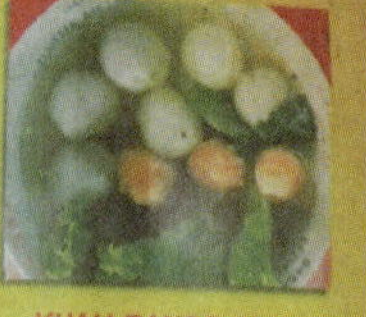

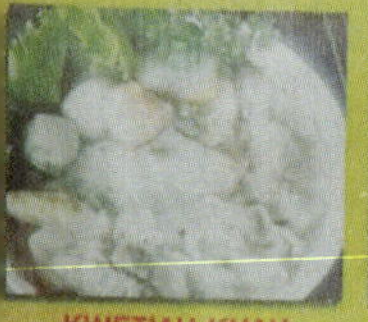

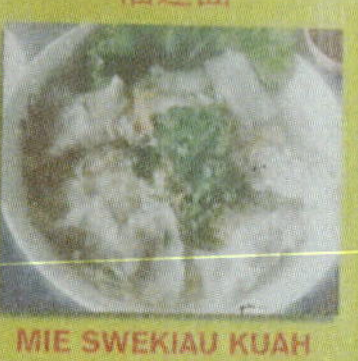

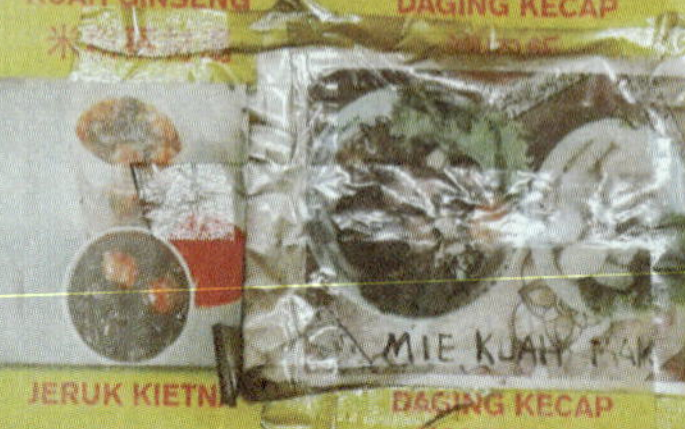

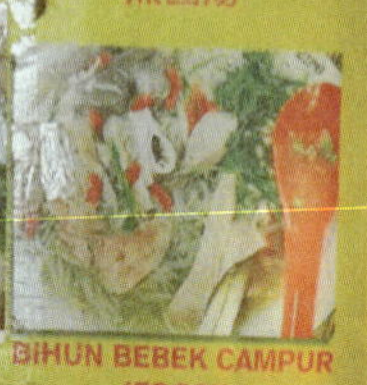

Bihun Bebek Ahui, Muara Karang, 2021

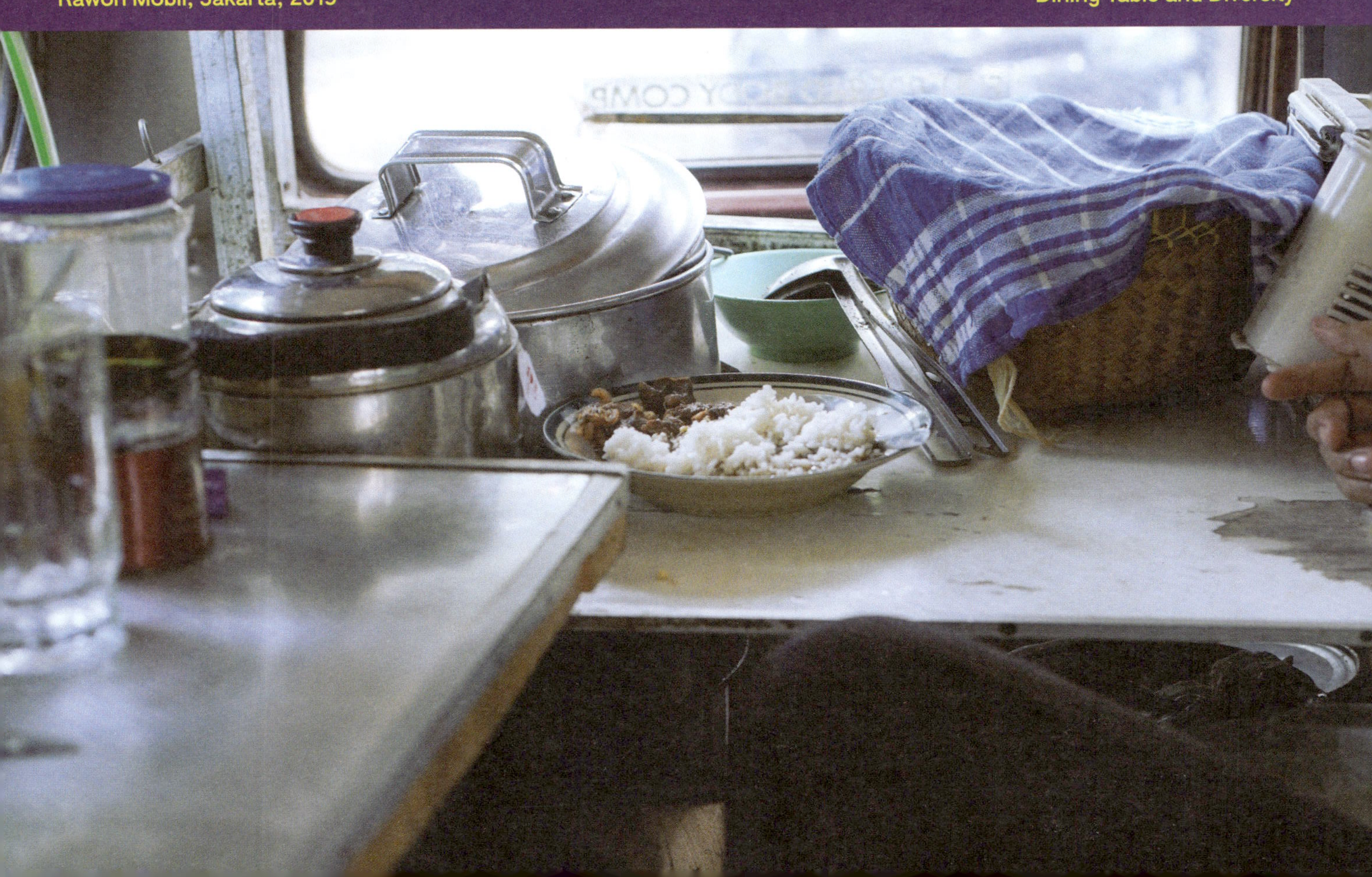

Rawon Mobil, Jakarta, 2019

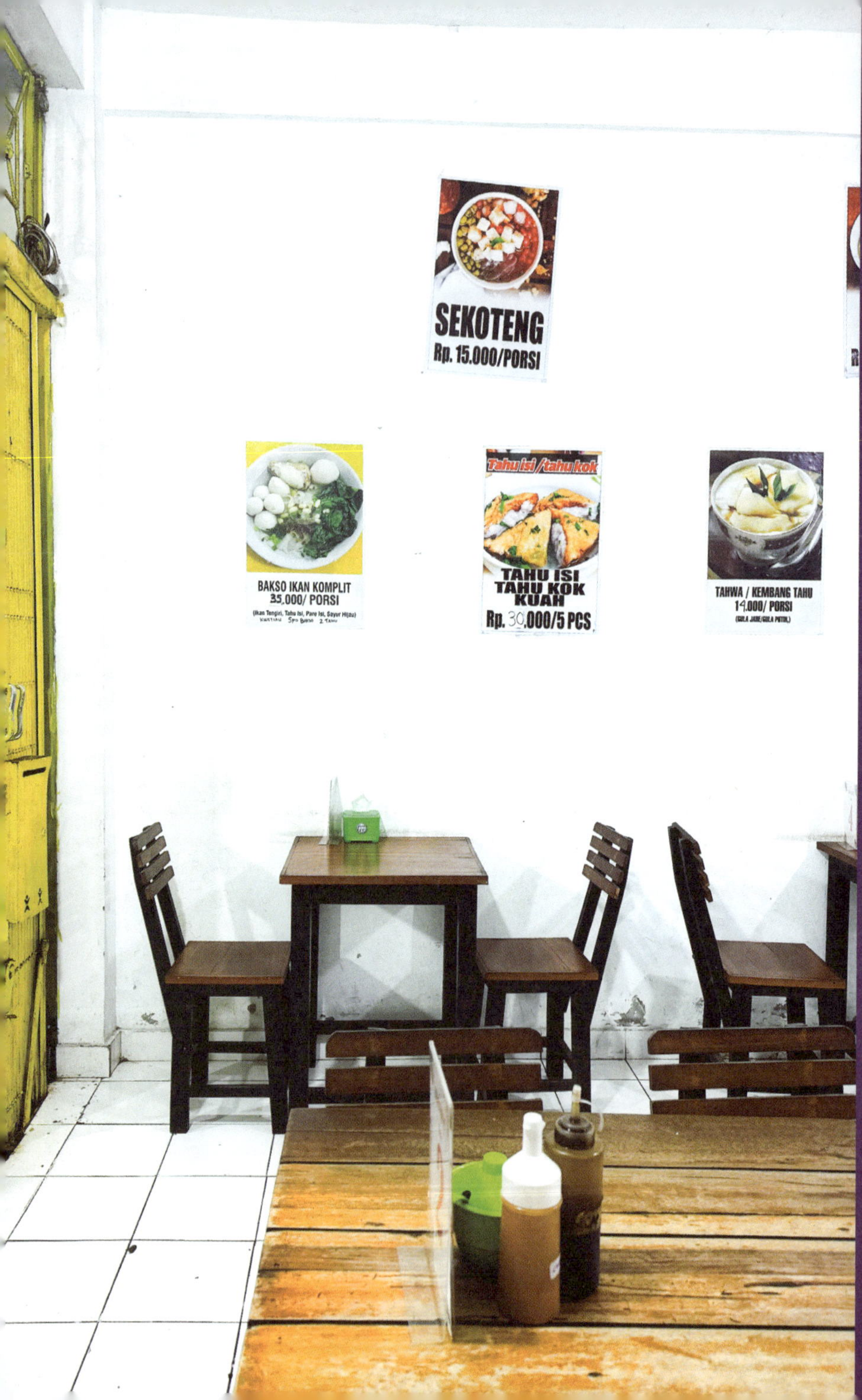

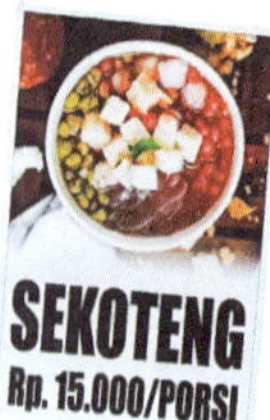

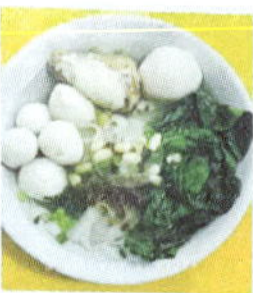

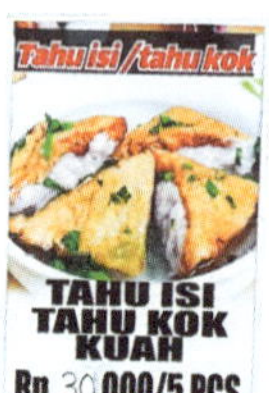

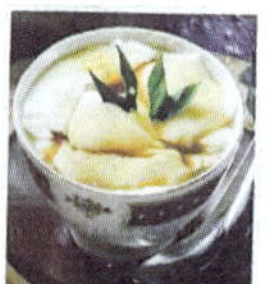

Tahwa Ahim58, Bali, 2024

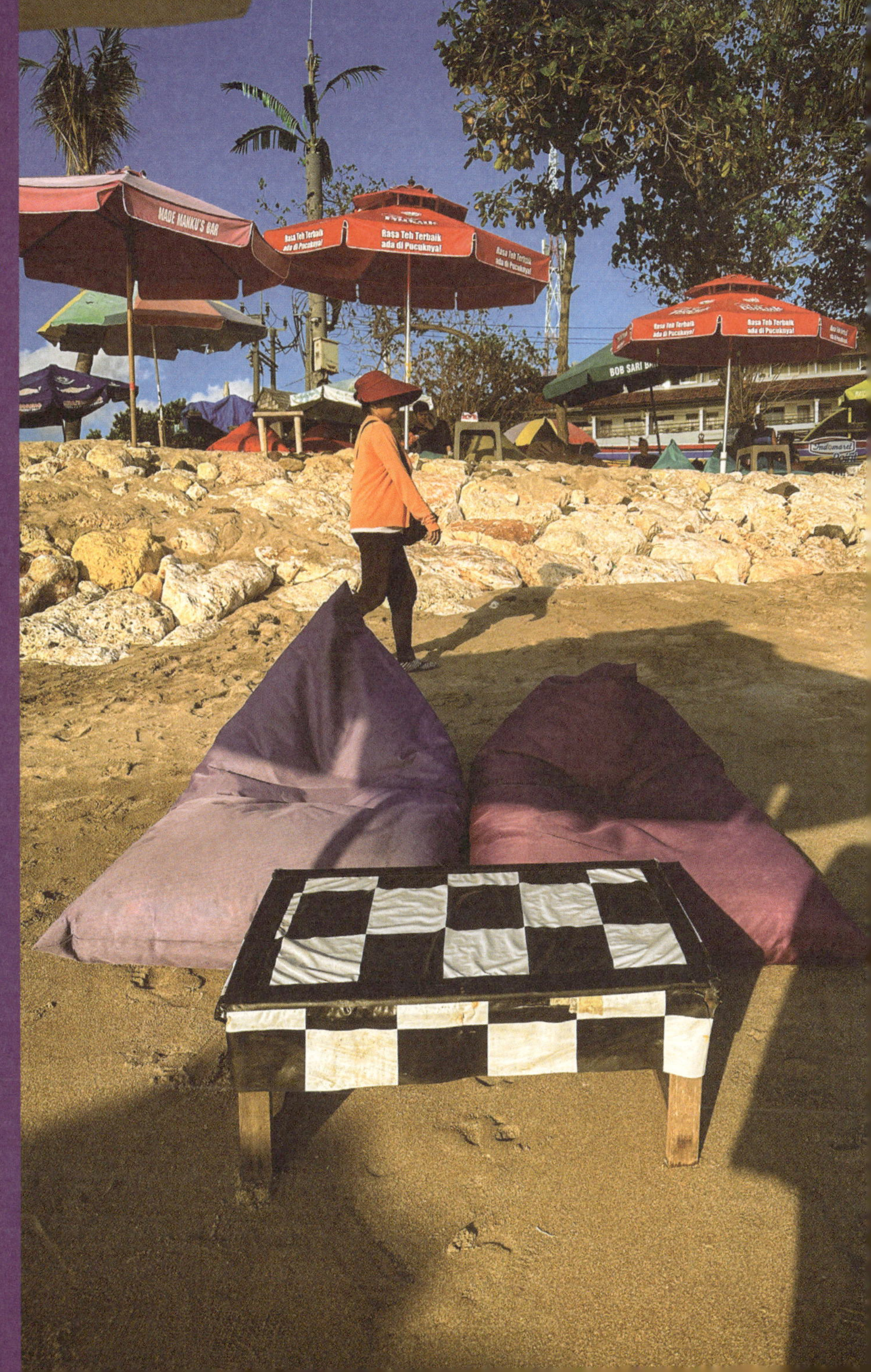

Kuta Beach, Bali, 2024

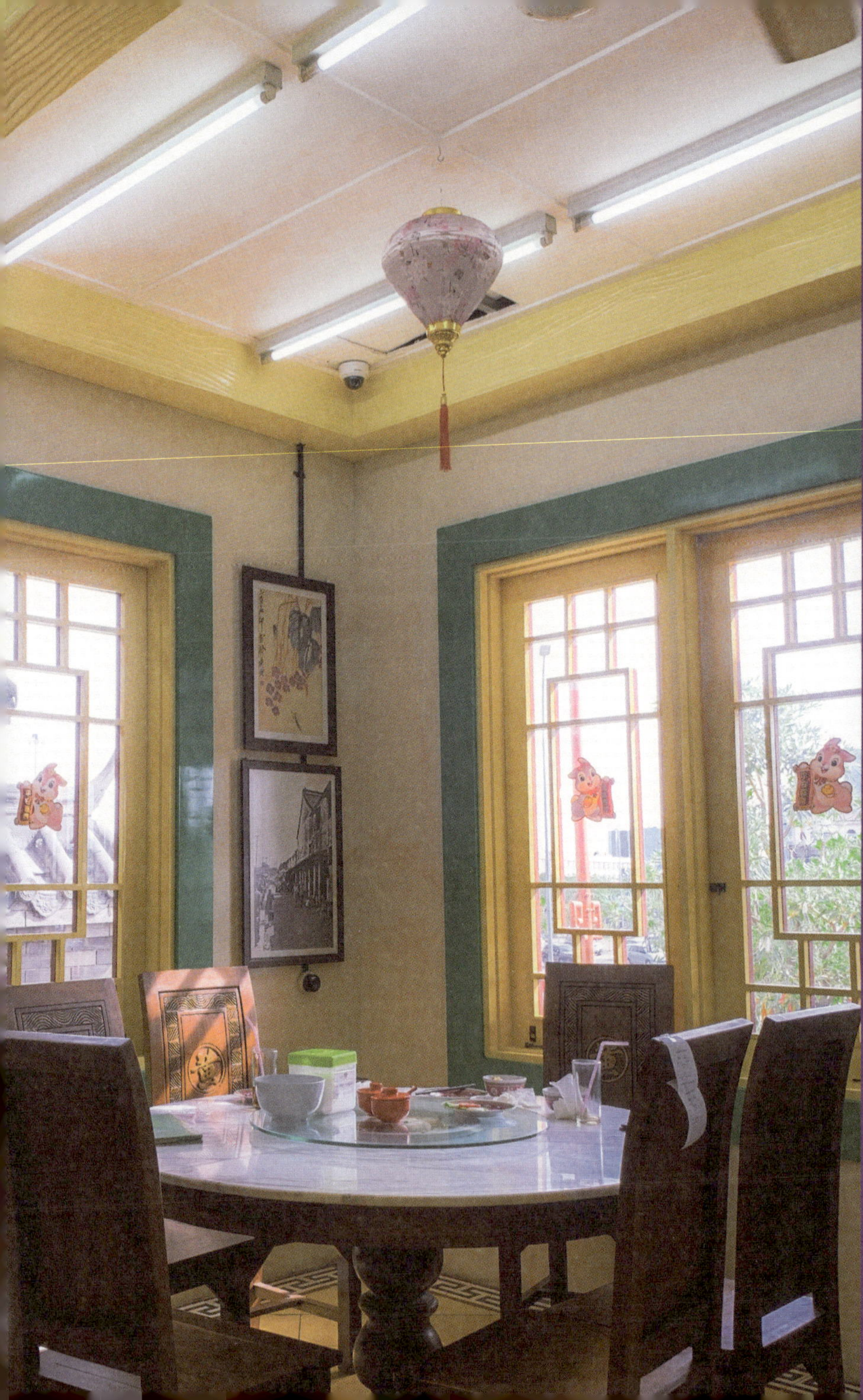

Wong Fu Kie, Jakarta, 2023

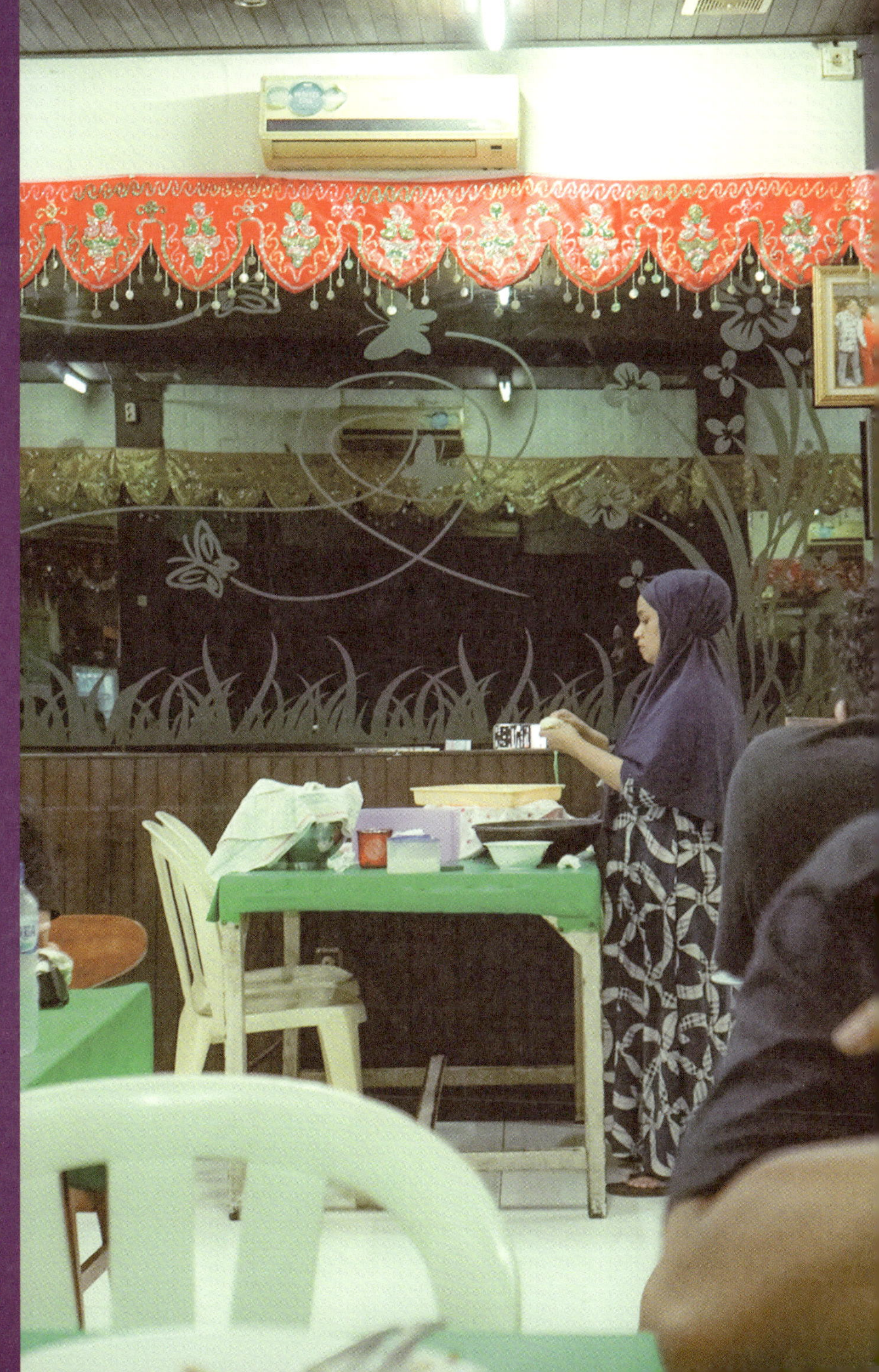

Coto Makassar Kuta, Bali, 2024

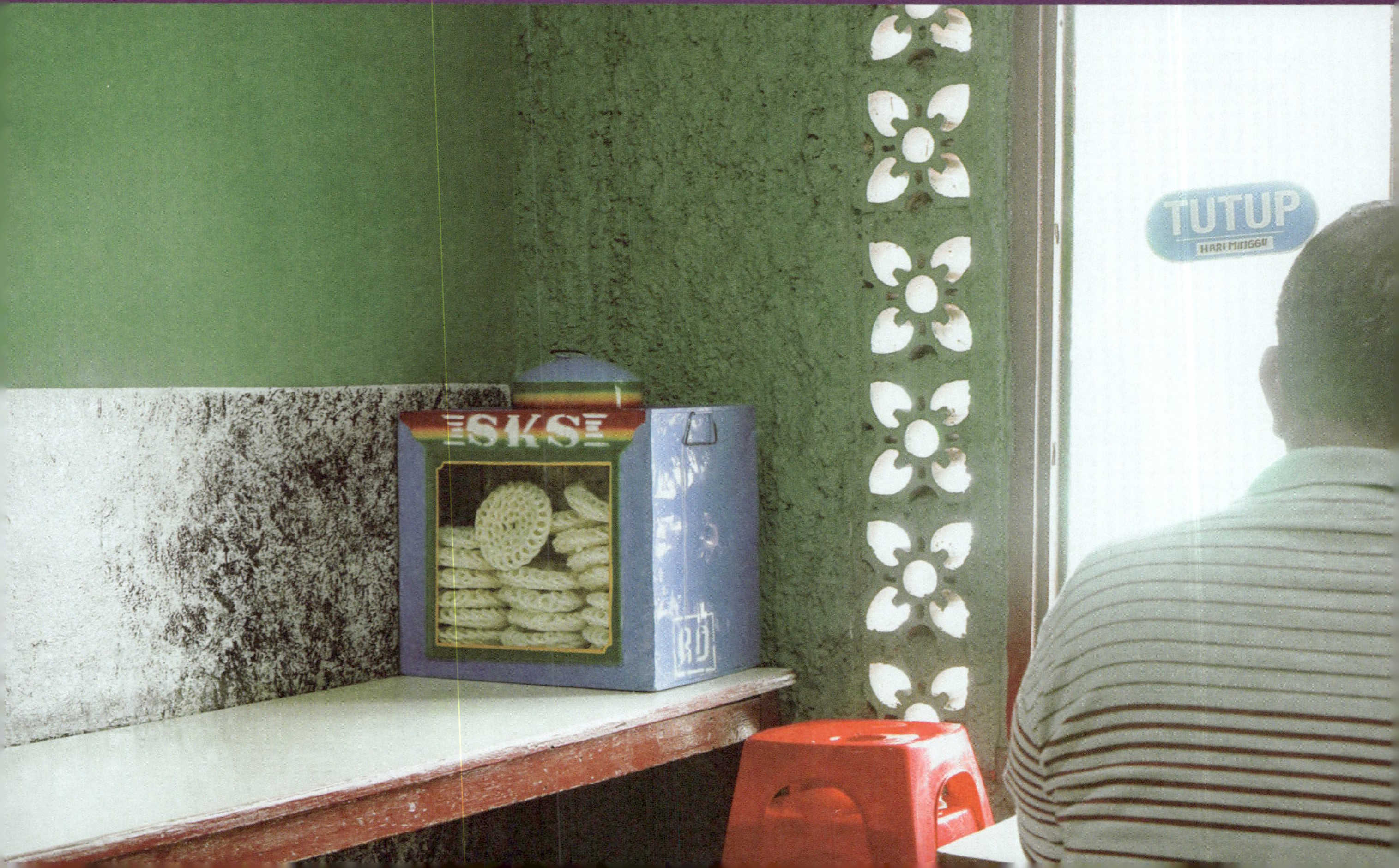

Soto Moroseneng, Jakarta, 2023

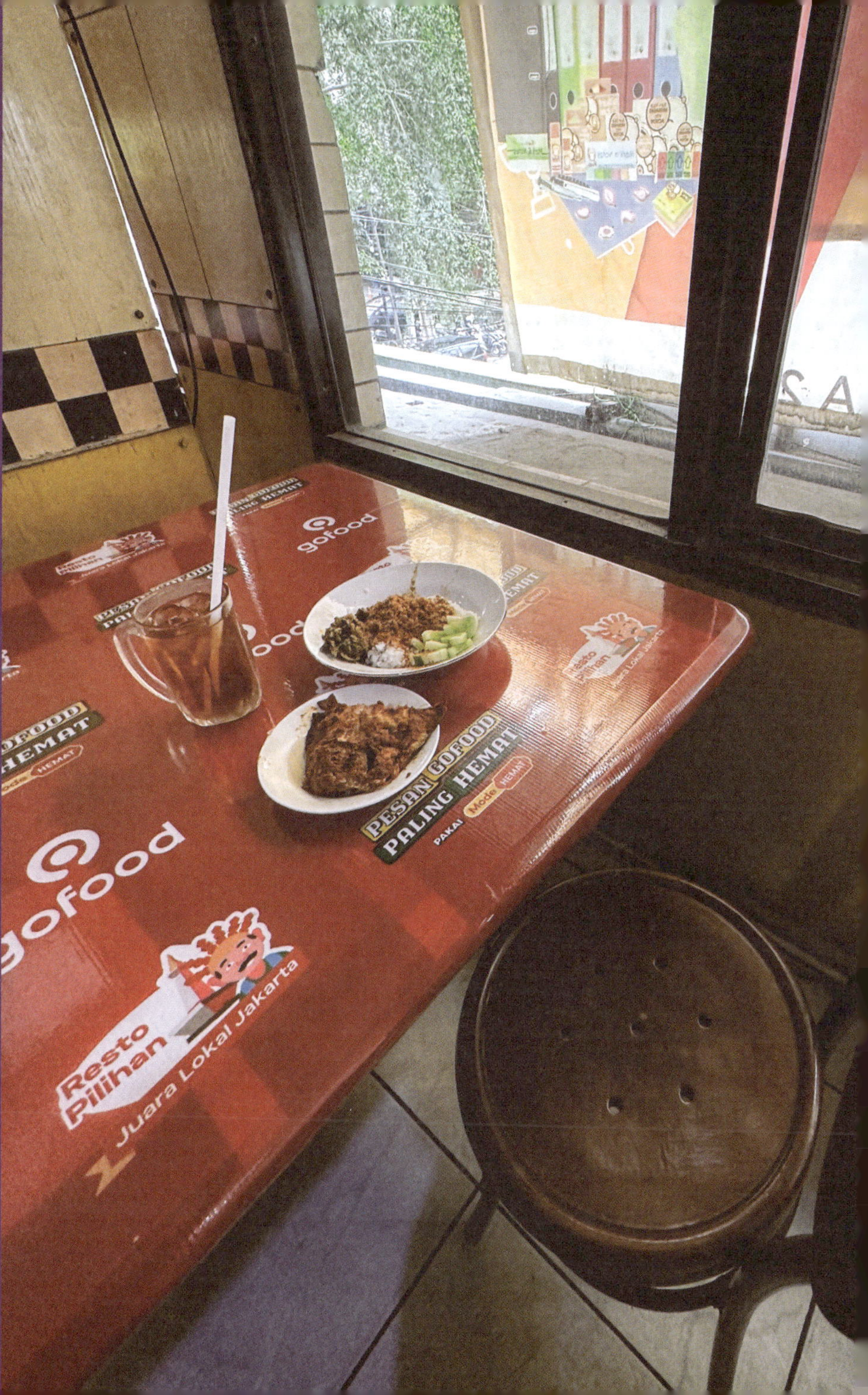

Rumah Makan Sepakat, Jakarta, 2023

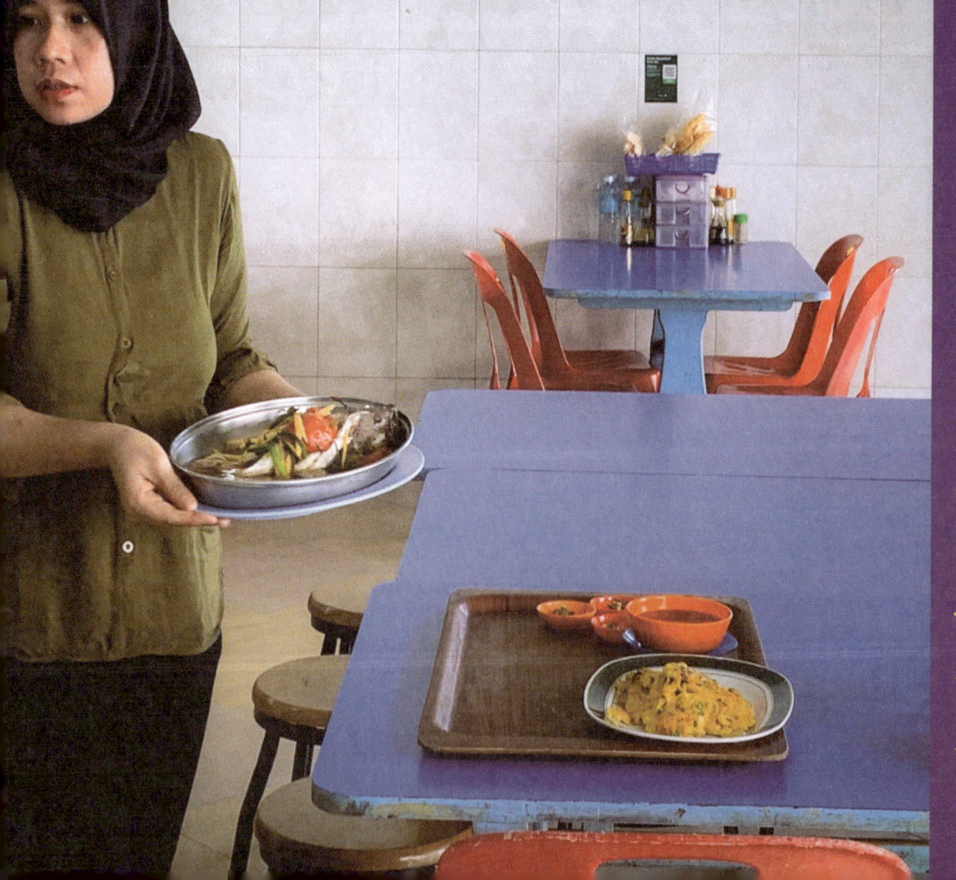

Rumah Makan Sedap Sari, Aceh, 2022

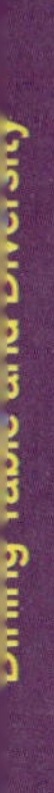

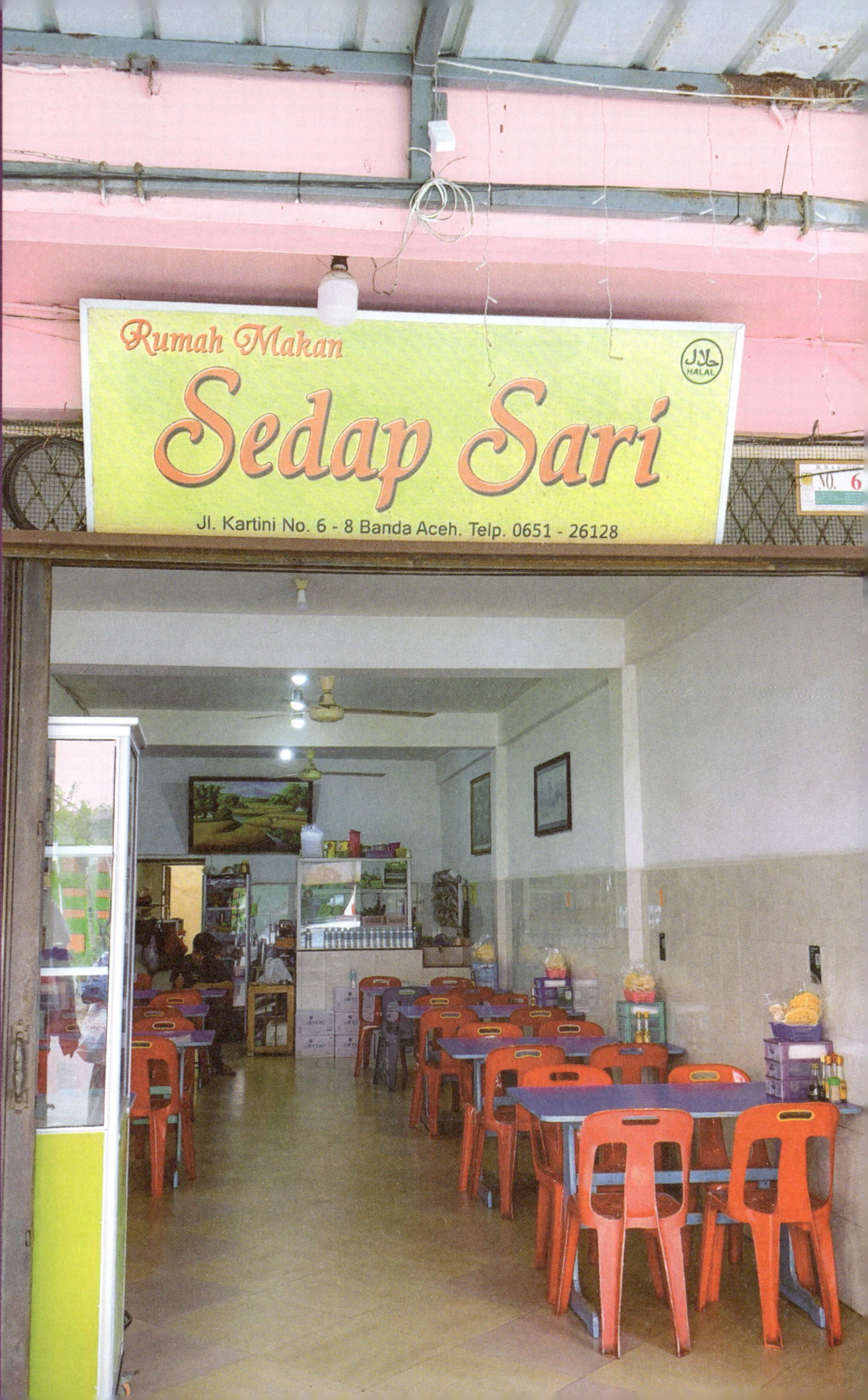

Rumah Makan Sedap Sari, Aceh, 2022

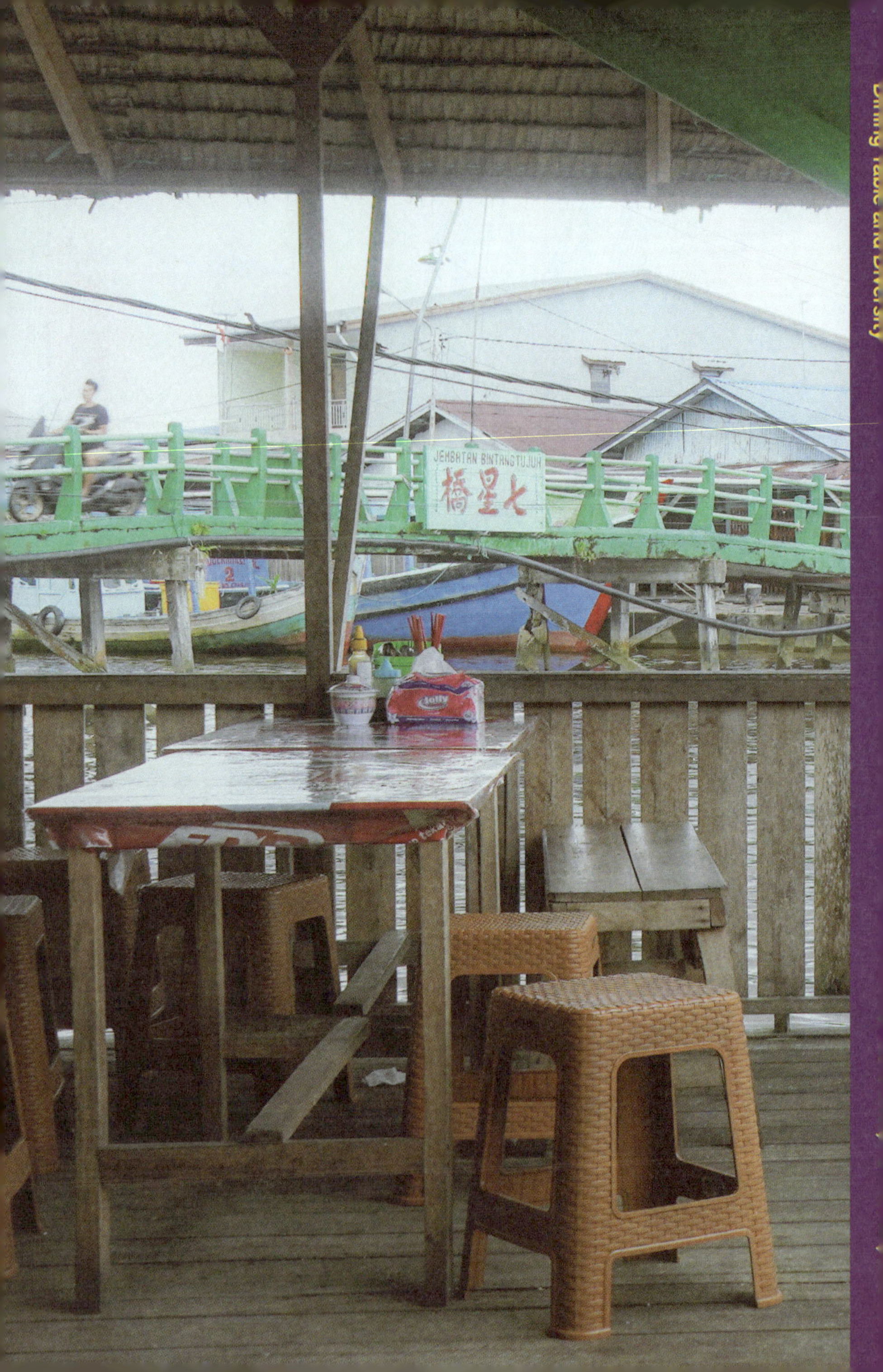
JEMBATAN BINTANG TUJUH
七星橋
Jolly

dining table and nature

With the rich blend of cultures in Indonesia, it can be hard to pinpoint what's truly native. But one thing that stands out is nature's abundance, blessing us with beautiful views and an incredible variety of produce that nourishes both the body and soul.

Our dining tables, often made from local woods, reflect this natural beauty. From the days of hunting and gathering to our more advanced civilization, dining culture has always been tied to mother nature.

Even as years we've modernized, meals in outdoor settings are still enjoyed, reminding us that dining and nature are inseparable around the world and especially in Indonesia.

As we continue to evolve, it's crucial to remember to care for and protect the world that sustains us.

Dining culture and nature will always be intertwined.

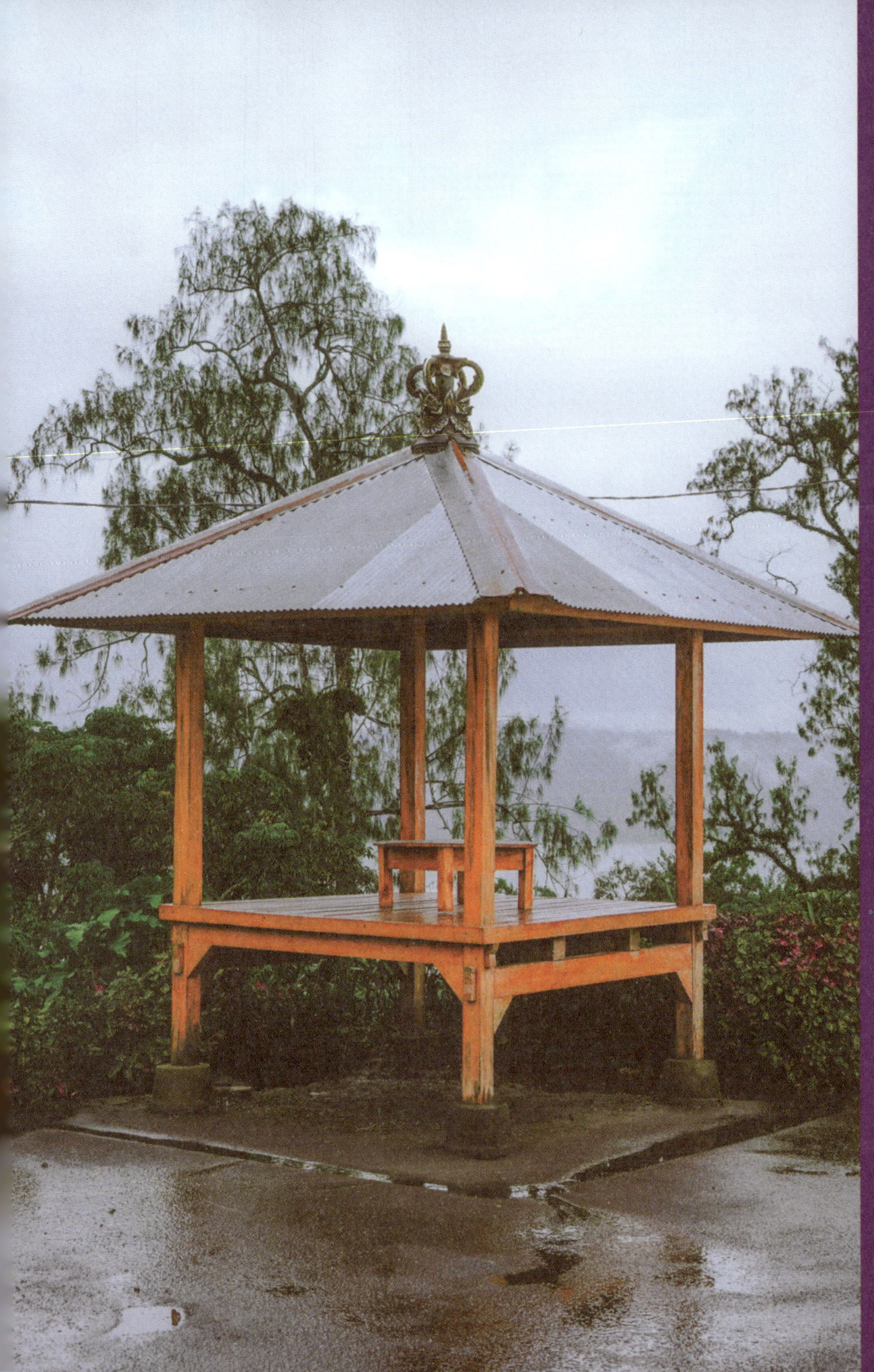

Lake Tamblingan, Bali, 2024

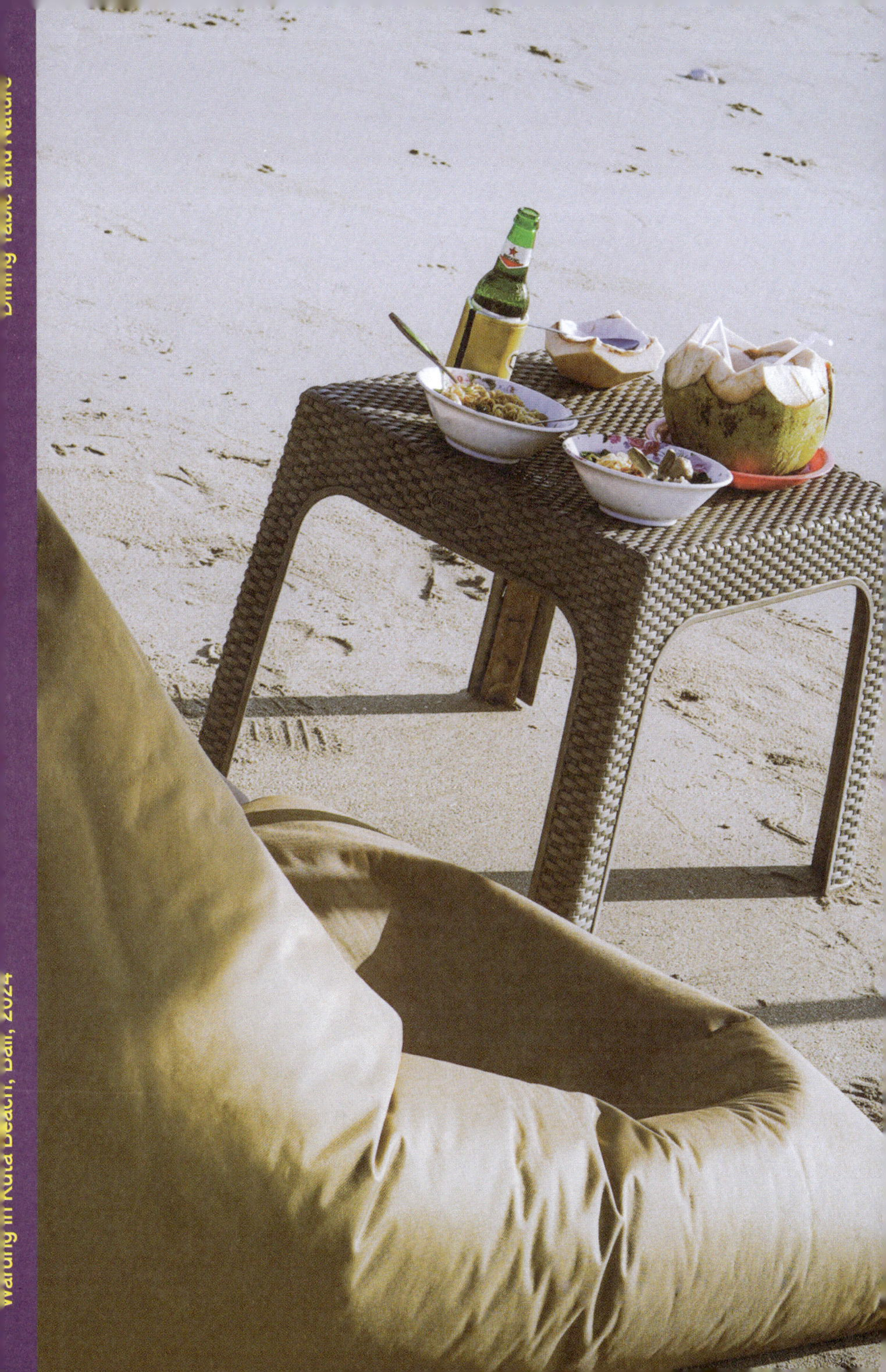

Warung in Kuta Beach, Bali, 2024

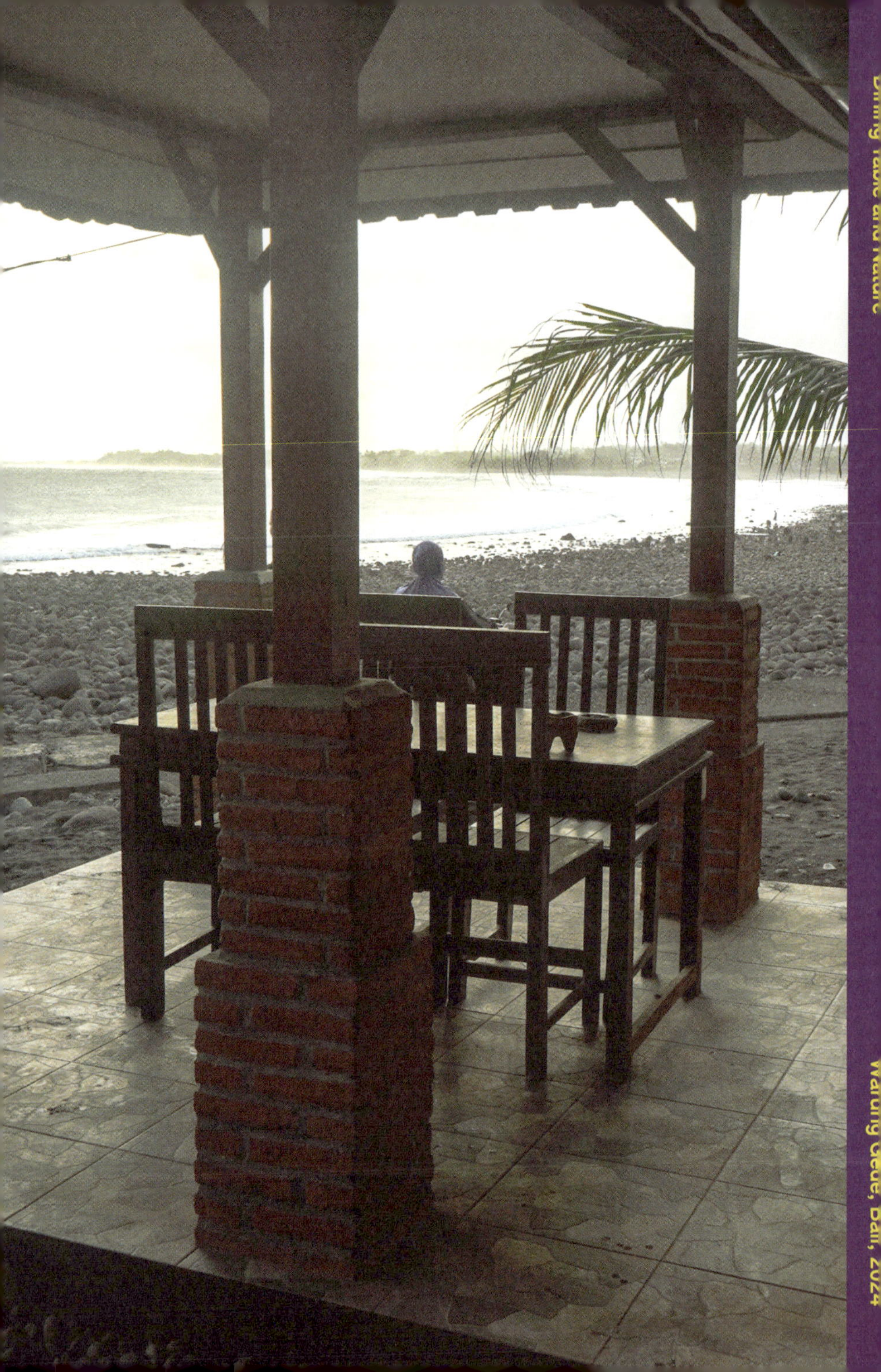

Dining Table and Nature

Warung Gede, Bali, 2024

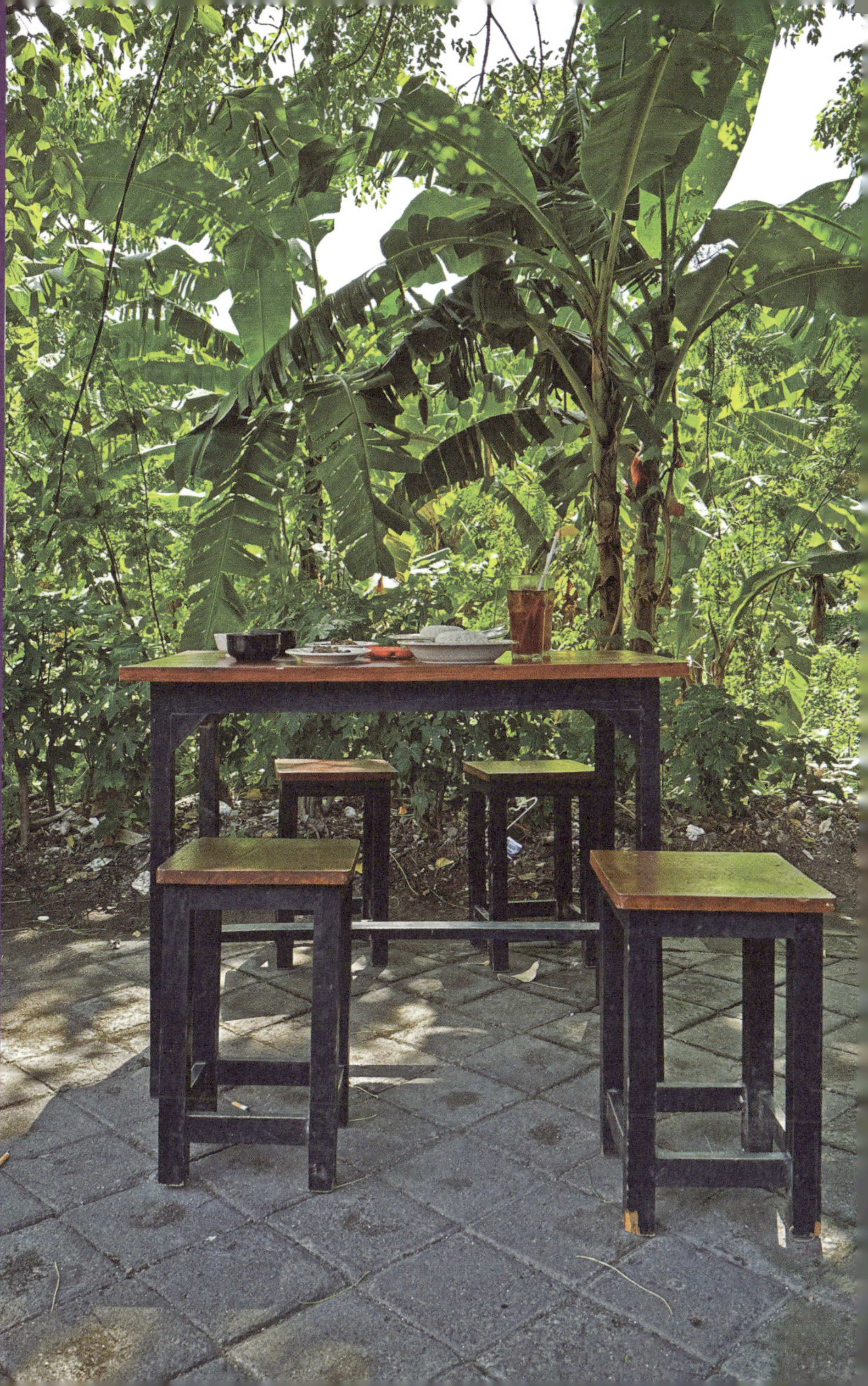

Lapo Tabo, Bali, 2024

Dining Table and Nature

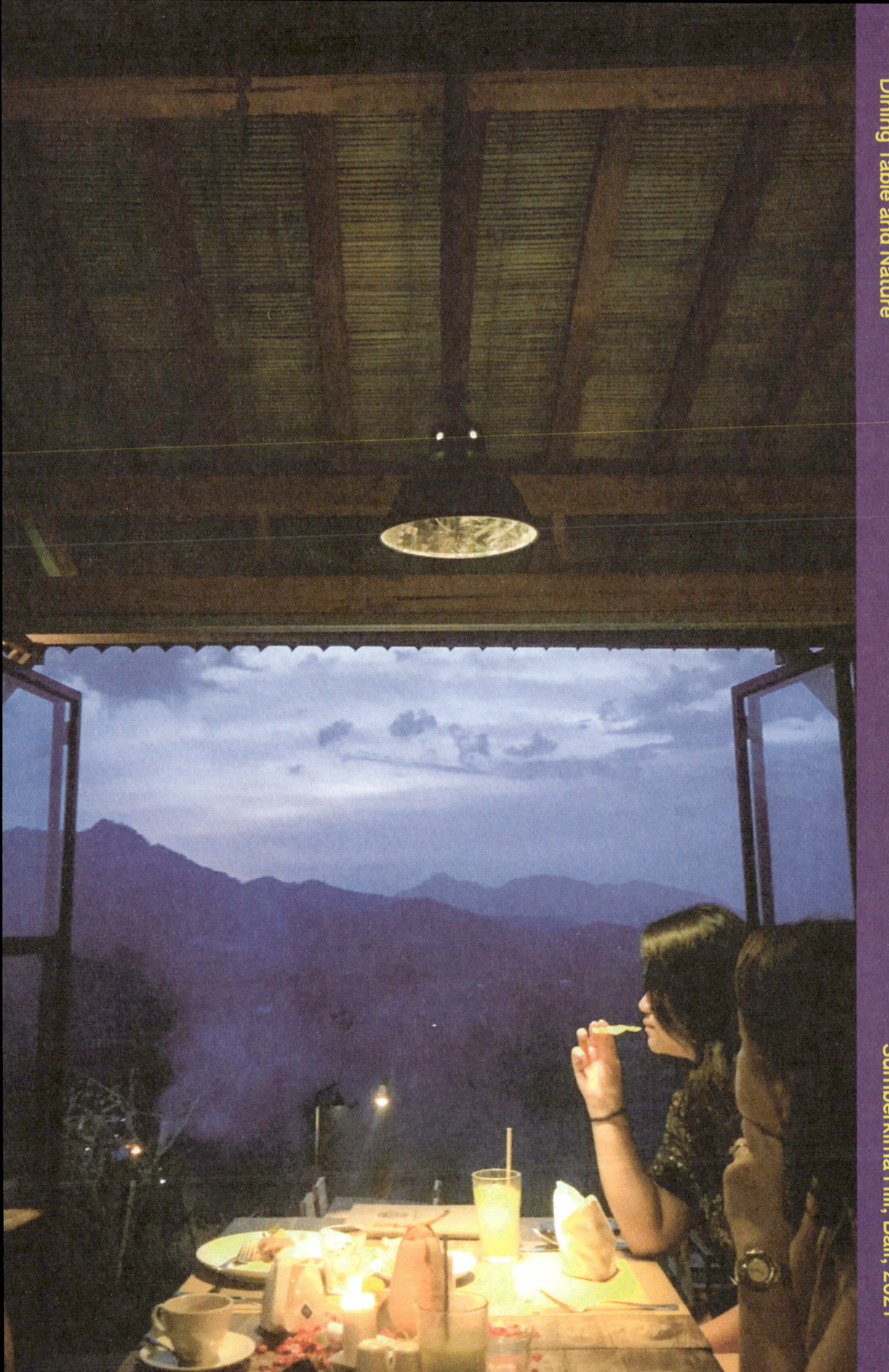

Dining Table and Nature

Sumberkima Hill, Bali, 2021

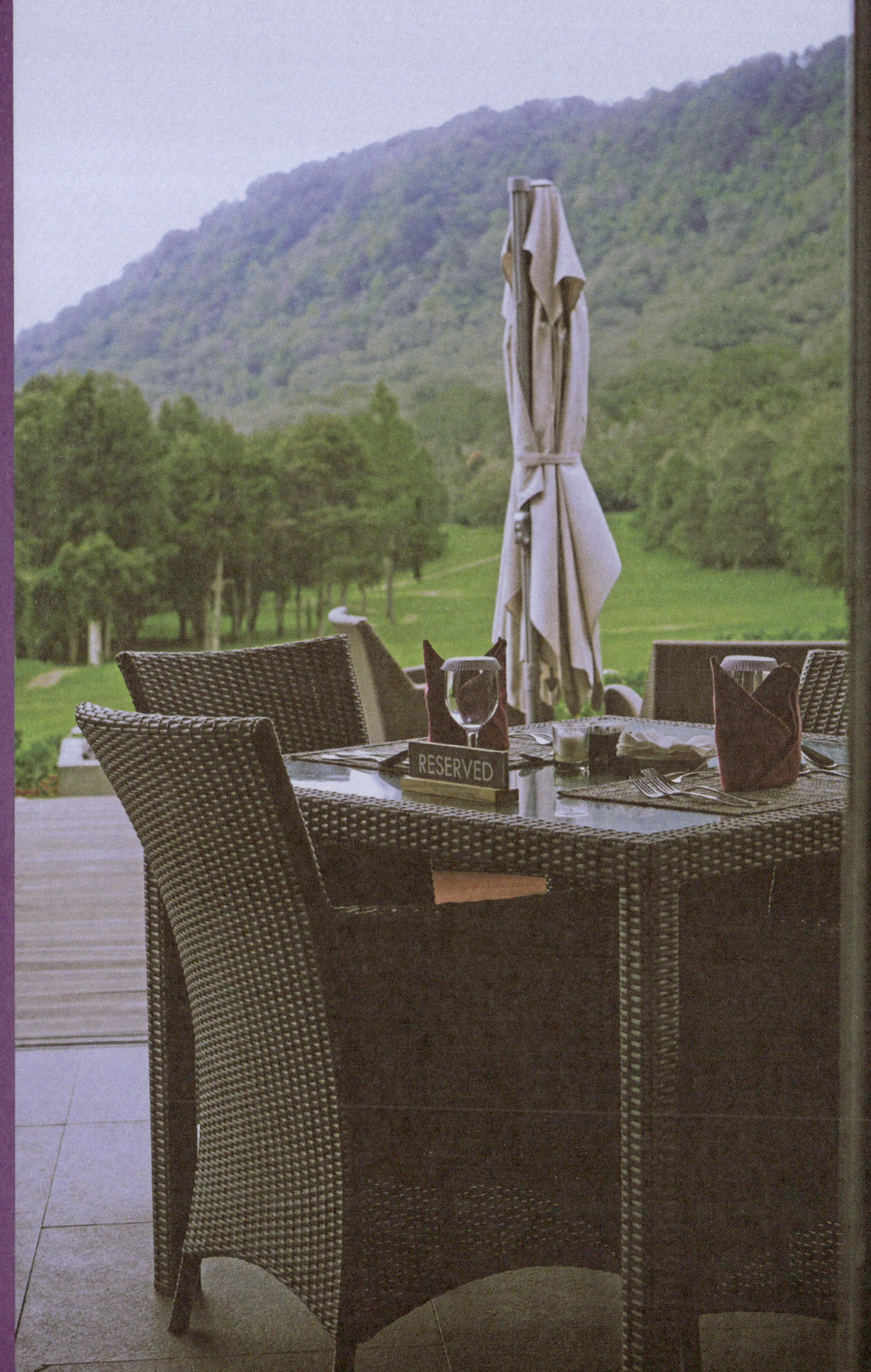

Dining Table and Nature

Handara, Bali, 2024

Dining Table and Nature

MMX Cafe, Sumba, 2019

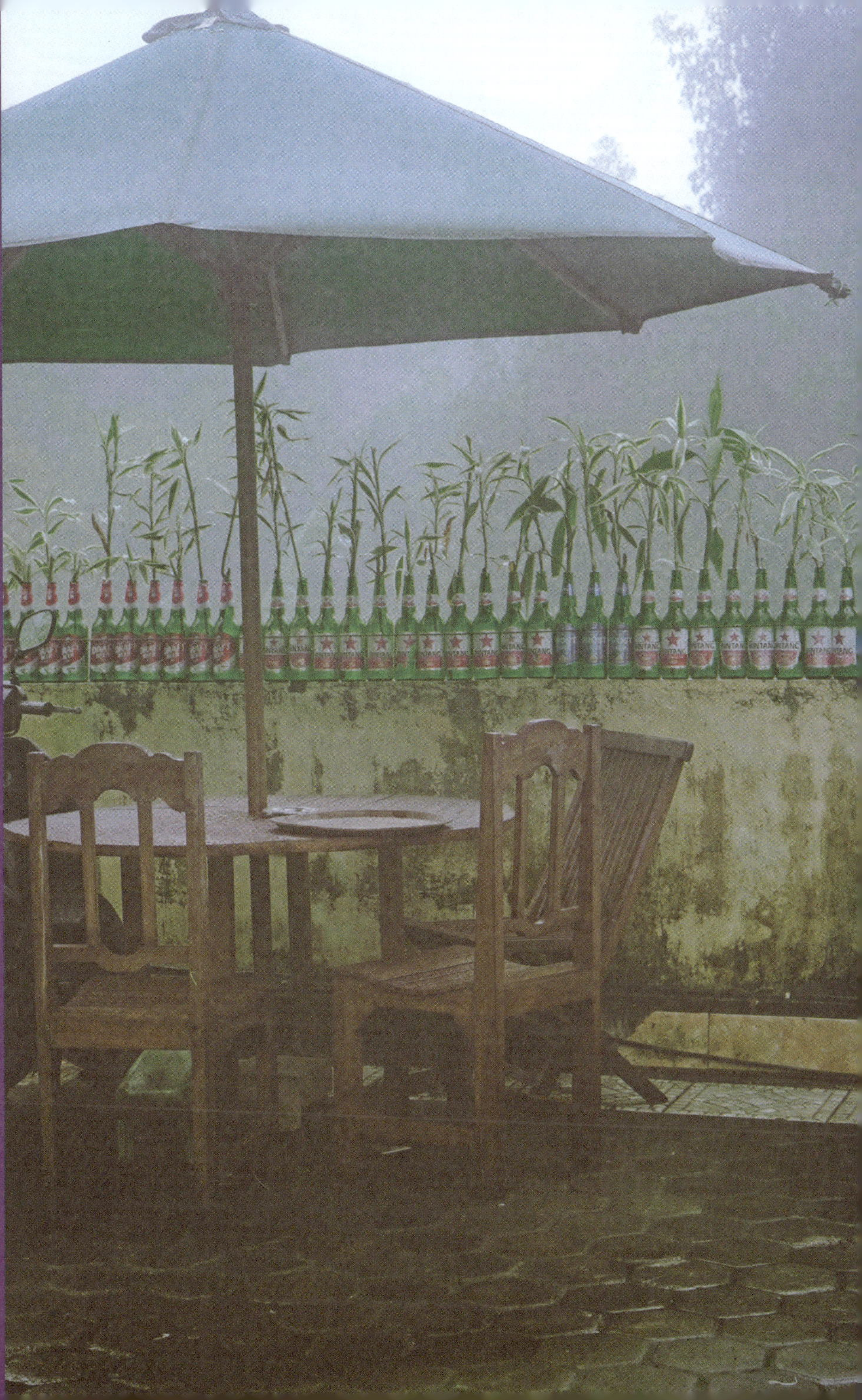

Dining Table and Nature

Munduk, Bali, 2024

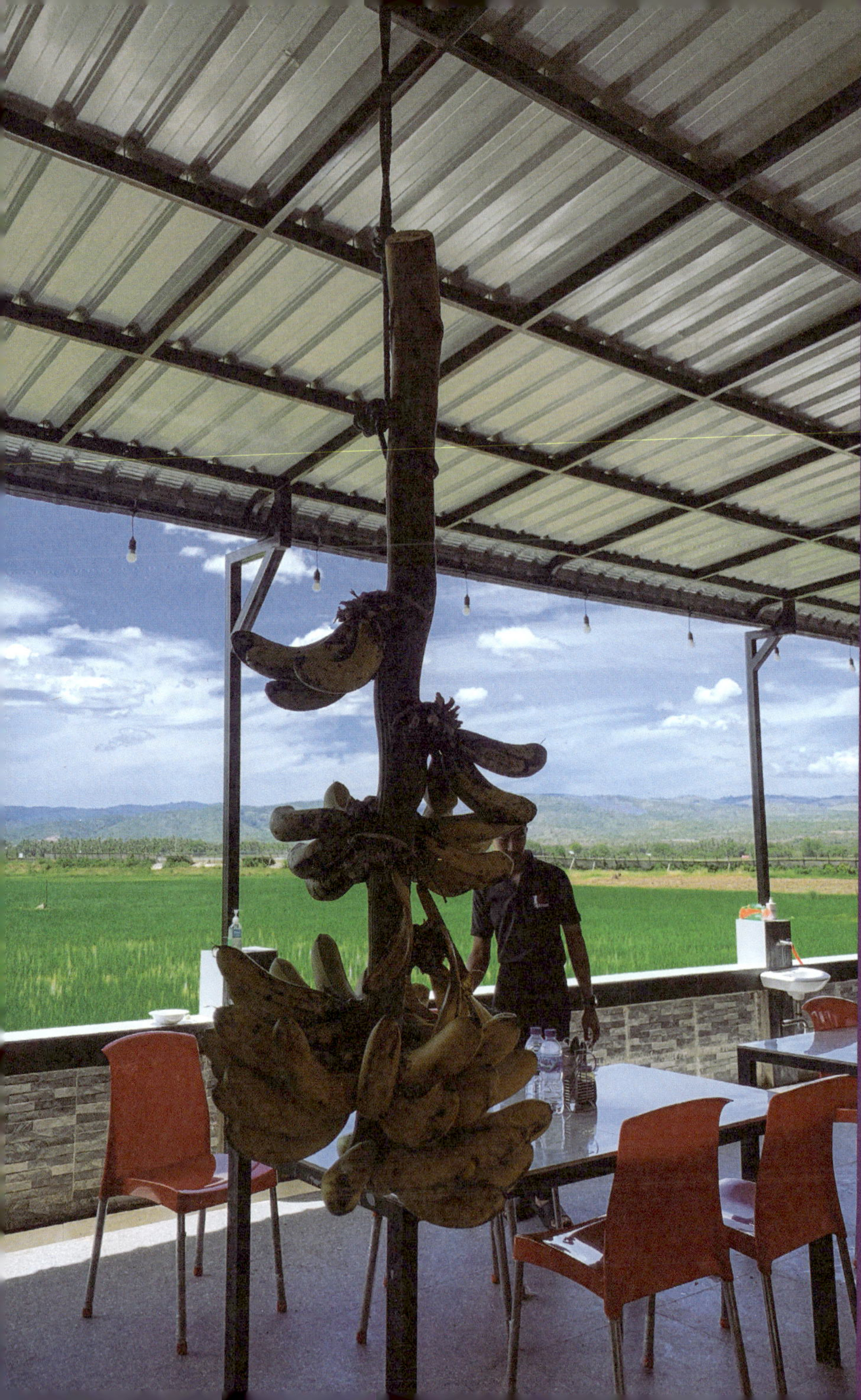

Ayam Pramugari, Aceh, 2022

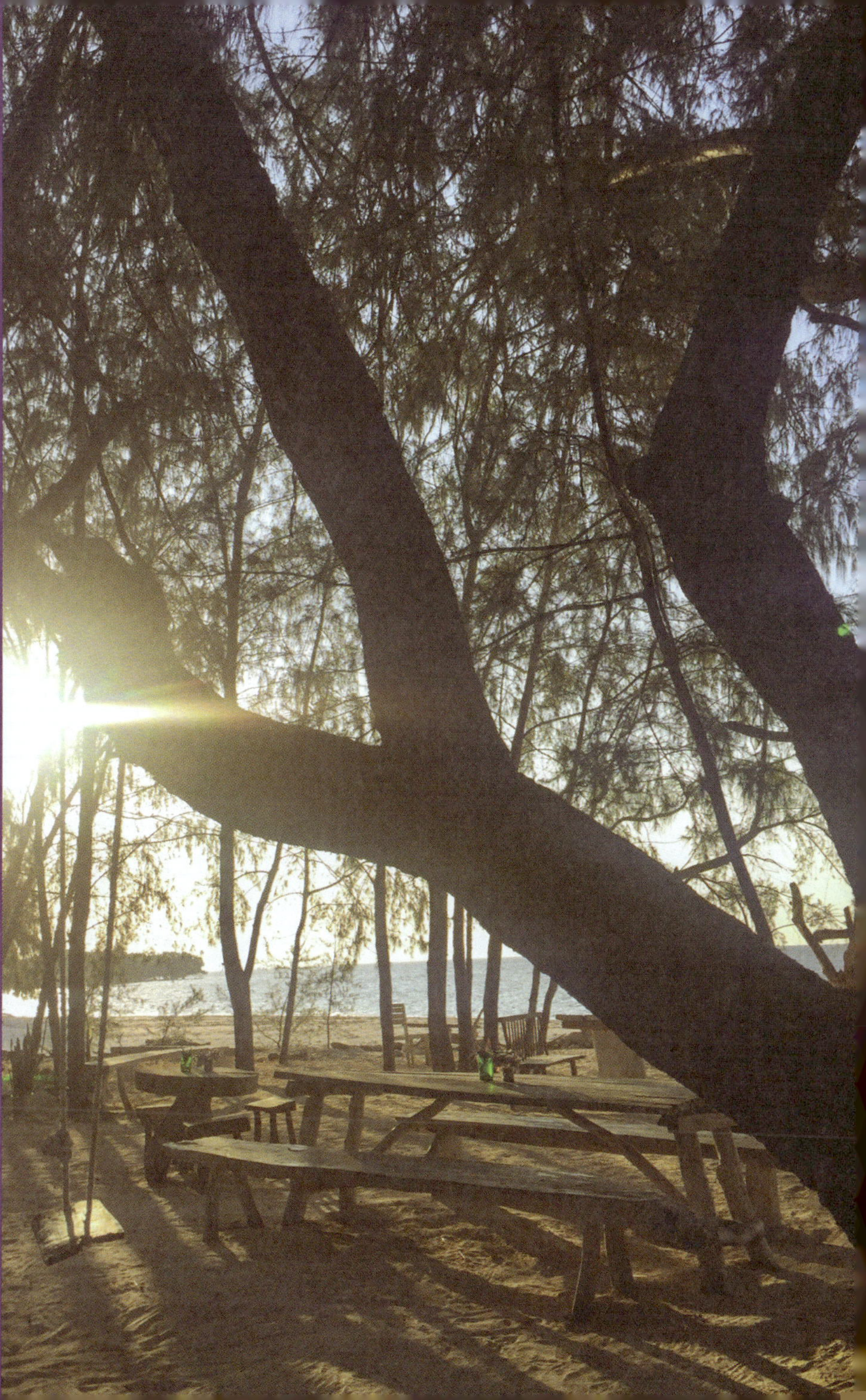

Dining Table and Nature

Pantai Cemara, Sumba, 2018

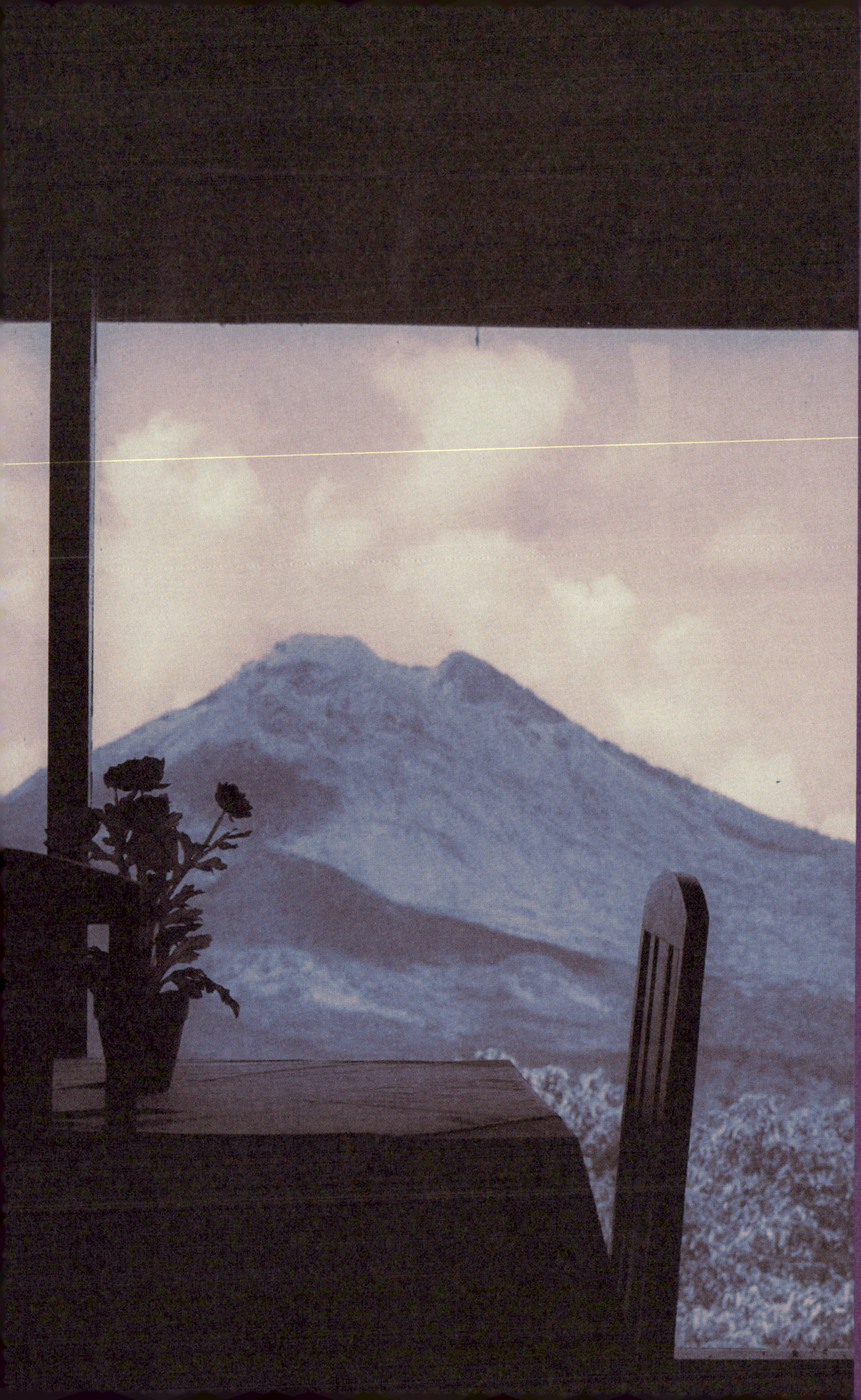

Dining Table and Nature

Restoran Gunung Sari, Bali, 2021

Inti Coffee 78, Aceh, 2022

Stalls at Tamblingan Lake, Bali, 2024

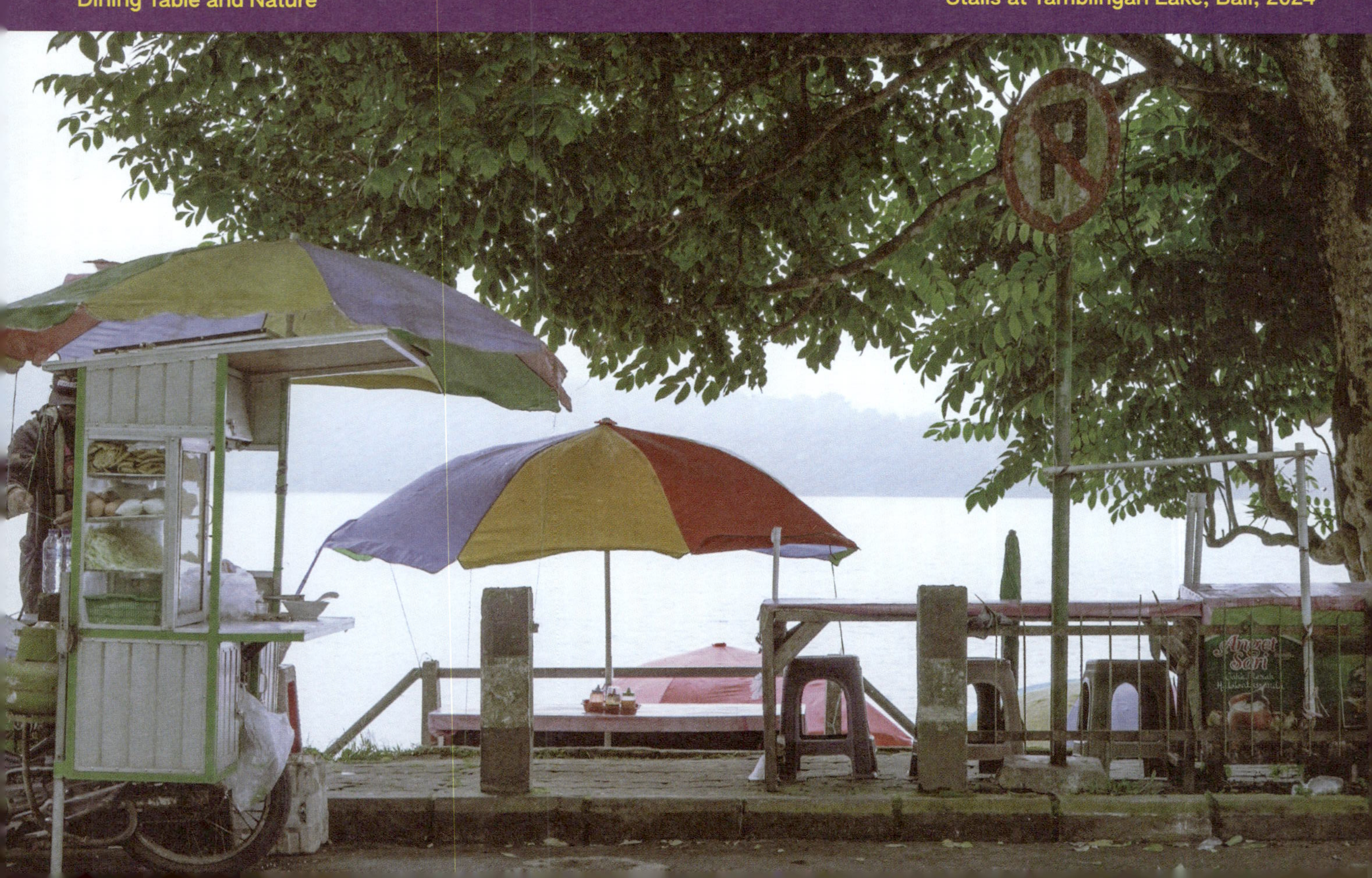

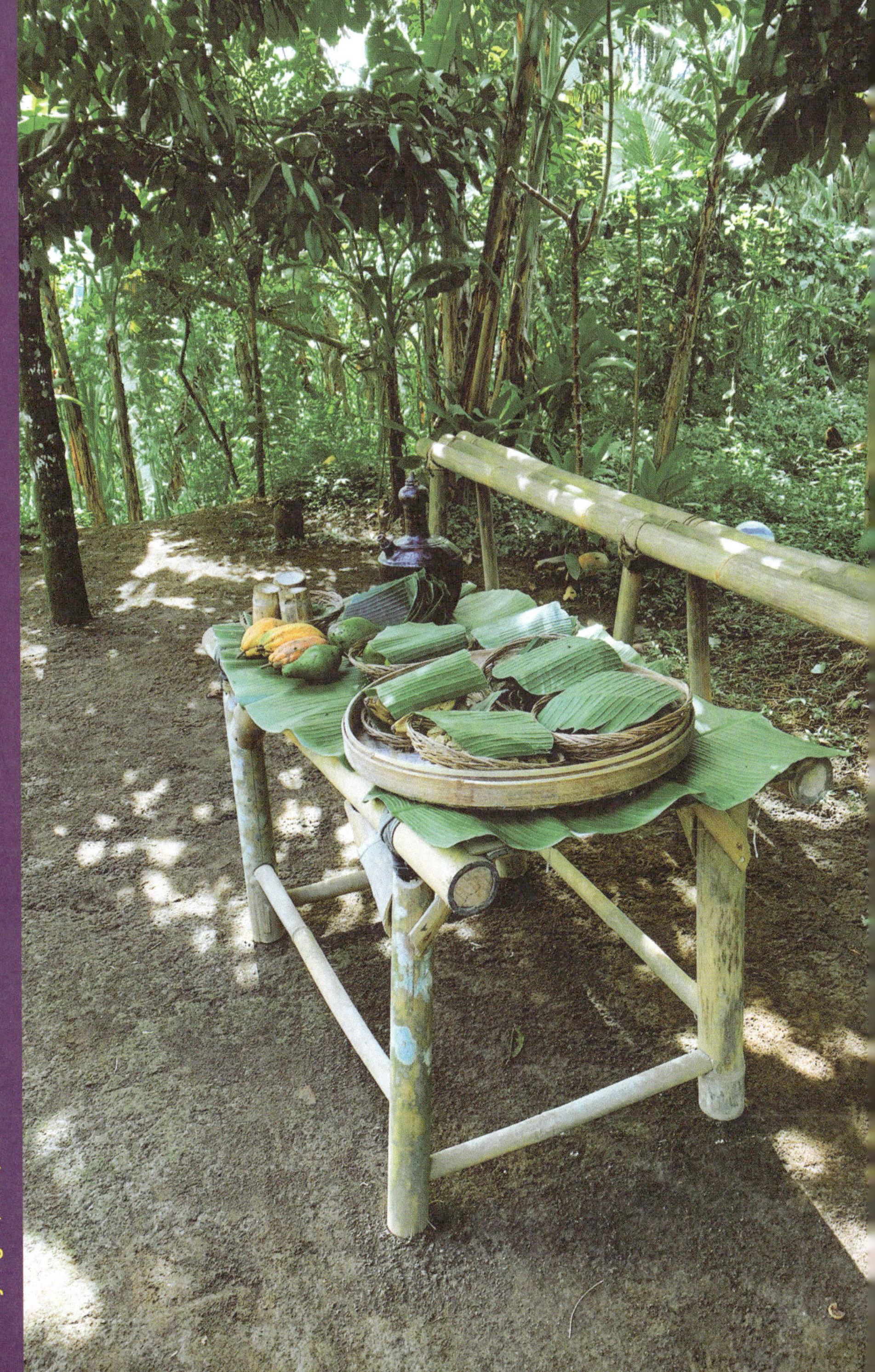

Payangan, Bali, 2024

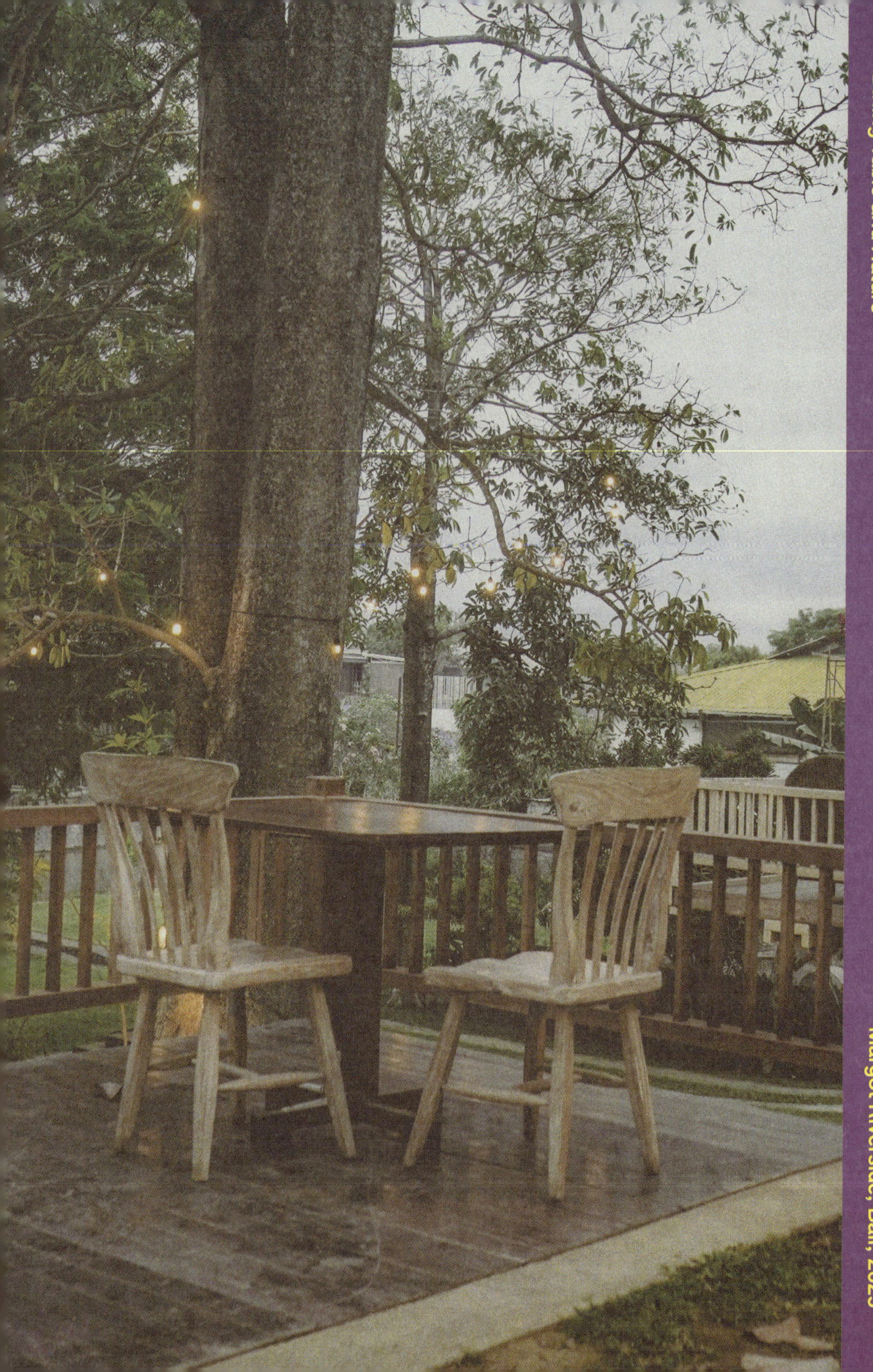

Dining Table and Nature

Margot Riverside, Bali, 2025

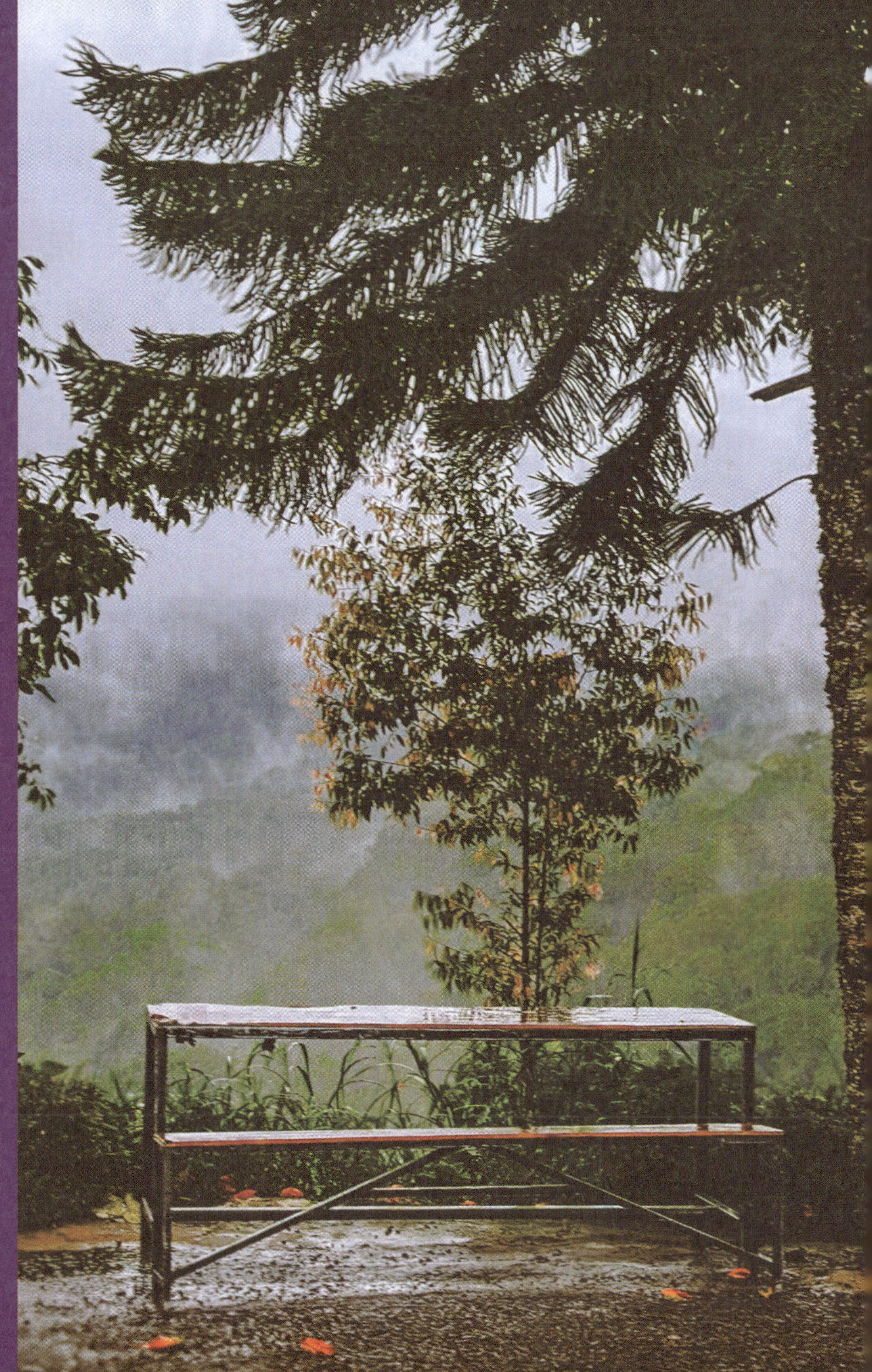

Wanagiri, Bali, 2024

Dining Table and Nature

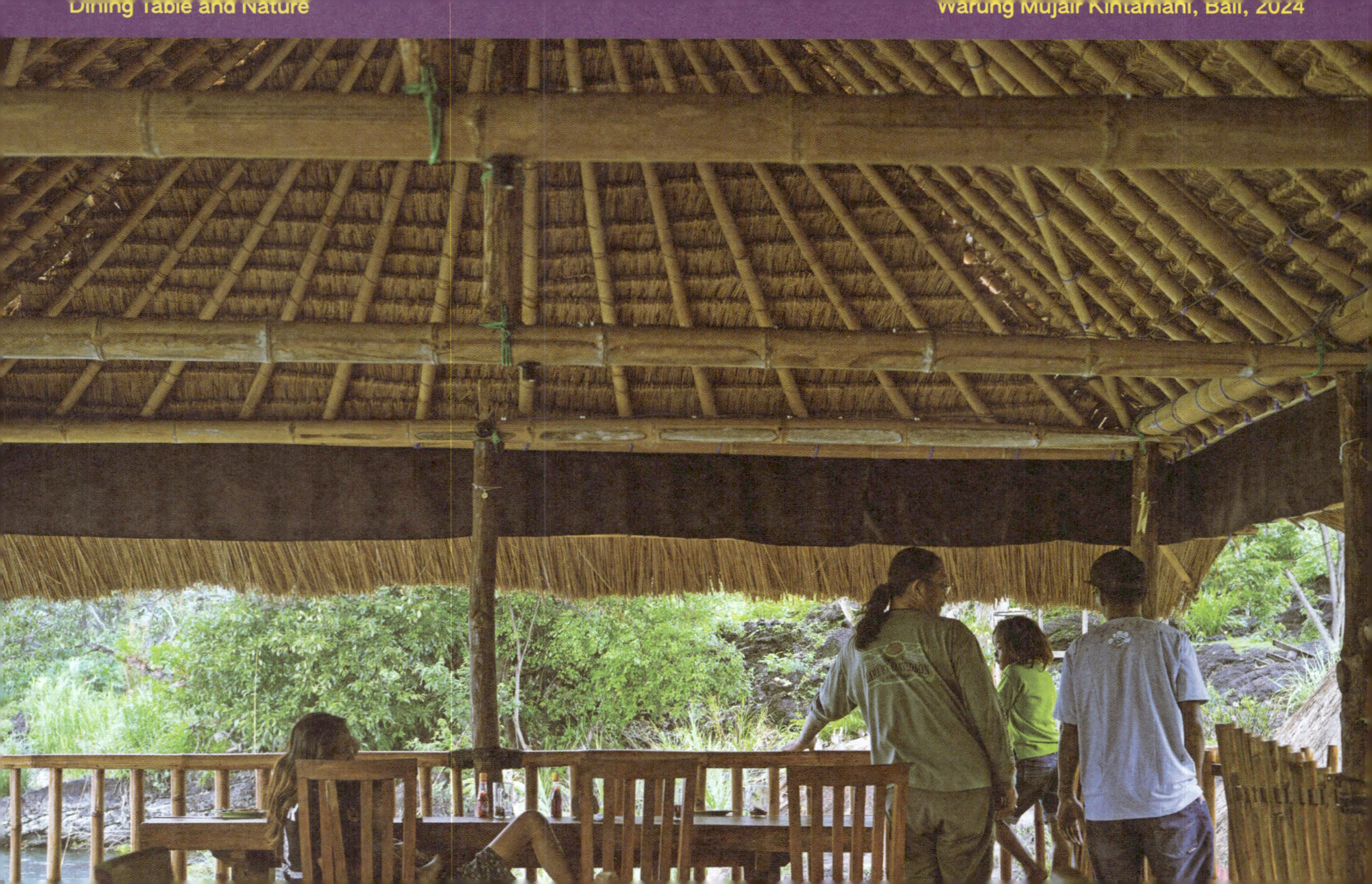

dining table and beyond

In Indonesia, dining often extends beyond conventional tables. It embodies fluidity in people's lives, adapting to limitations and making the most of available resources, even for dining. For many, dining experiences reflect socio-economic realities, with a significant percentage of the population experiencing varying levels of economic stability.

Access to formal dining set-ups — from proper tables and chairs to restaurant experiences — is still uneven. In rural areas and working-class neighborhoods, meals are often eaten on the floor, on the move, or outside near workplaces. Instead, dining becomes something mobile, shared, and improvised. It reflects how families prioritize practicality, with food prepared and consumed quickly between shifts, commutes, or daily tasks. Even in urban centers, street-side meals and plastic-stool warungs remain popular not just for convenience, but because they're affordable and familiar.

Dining in a leisure context is not always a priority, making eating out a perceived "little luxury," especially for families. A trip to a restaurant or fast-food outlet often marks a special occasion like payday, report cards, or birthdays, moments when the act of eating becomes a reward, a celebration, or a collective treat.

This perspective makes shared dining moments at the table even more special and irreplaceable, highlighting its significance in creating family bonds and memories.

You'll often see meals shared on makeshift surfaces like cardboard on a floor, a parked motorbike, or a repurposed bench at a construction site. For many, the idea of a "dining table" is less about furniture and more about wherever food can be gathered and shared. These settings, though improvised, carry the same weight: connection, survival, and care; however modest the meal may be.

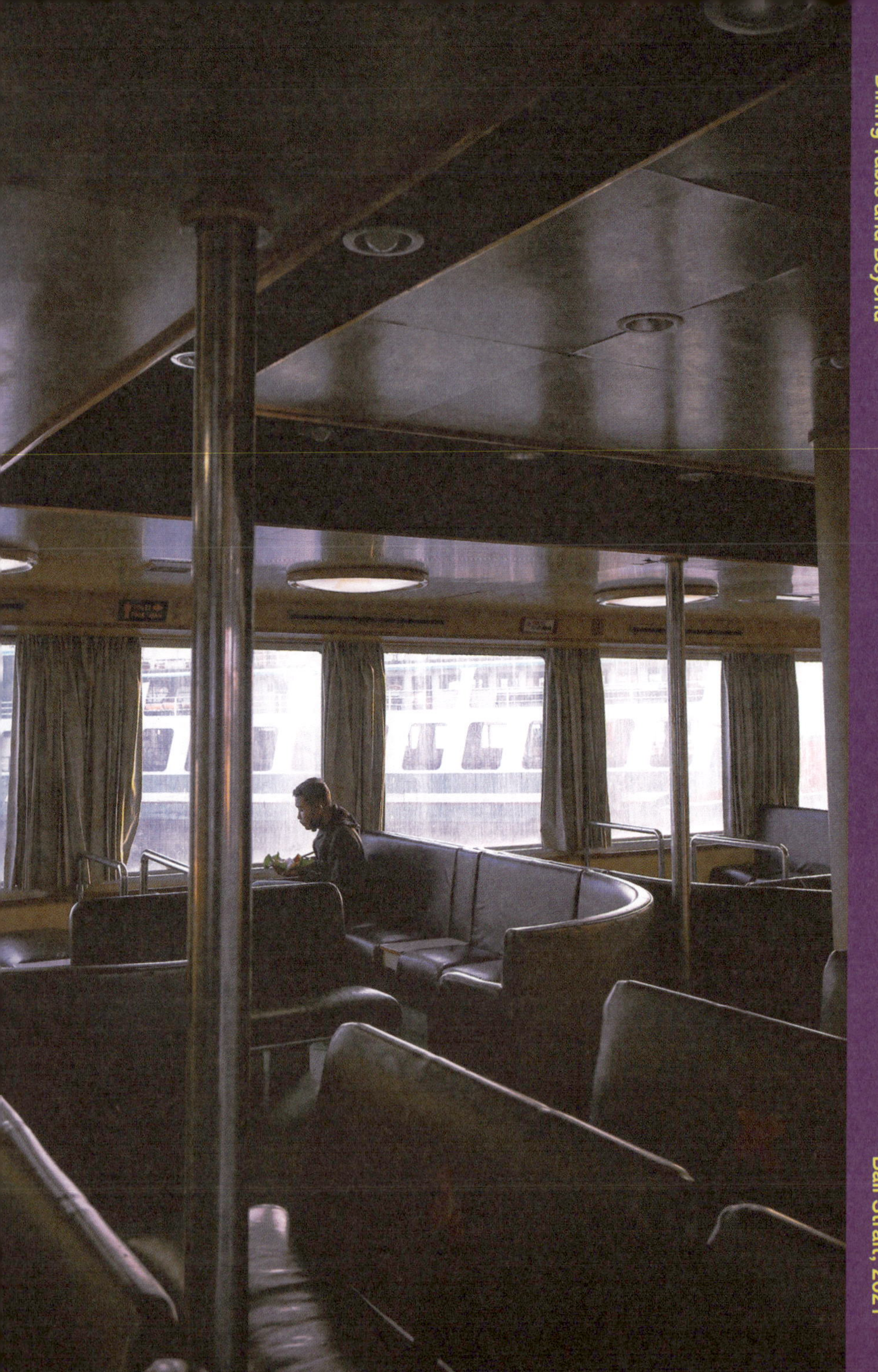

Bali Strait, 2021

Muara Karang, Jakarta, 2022

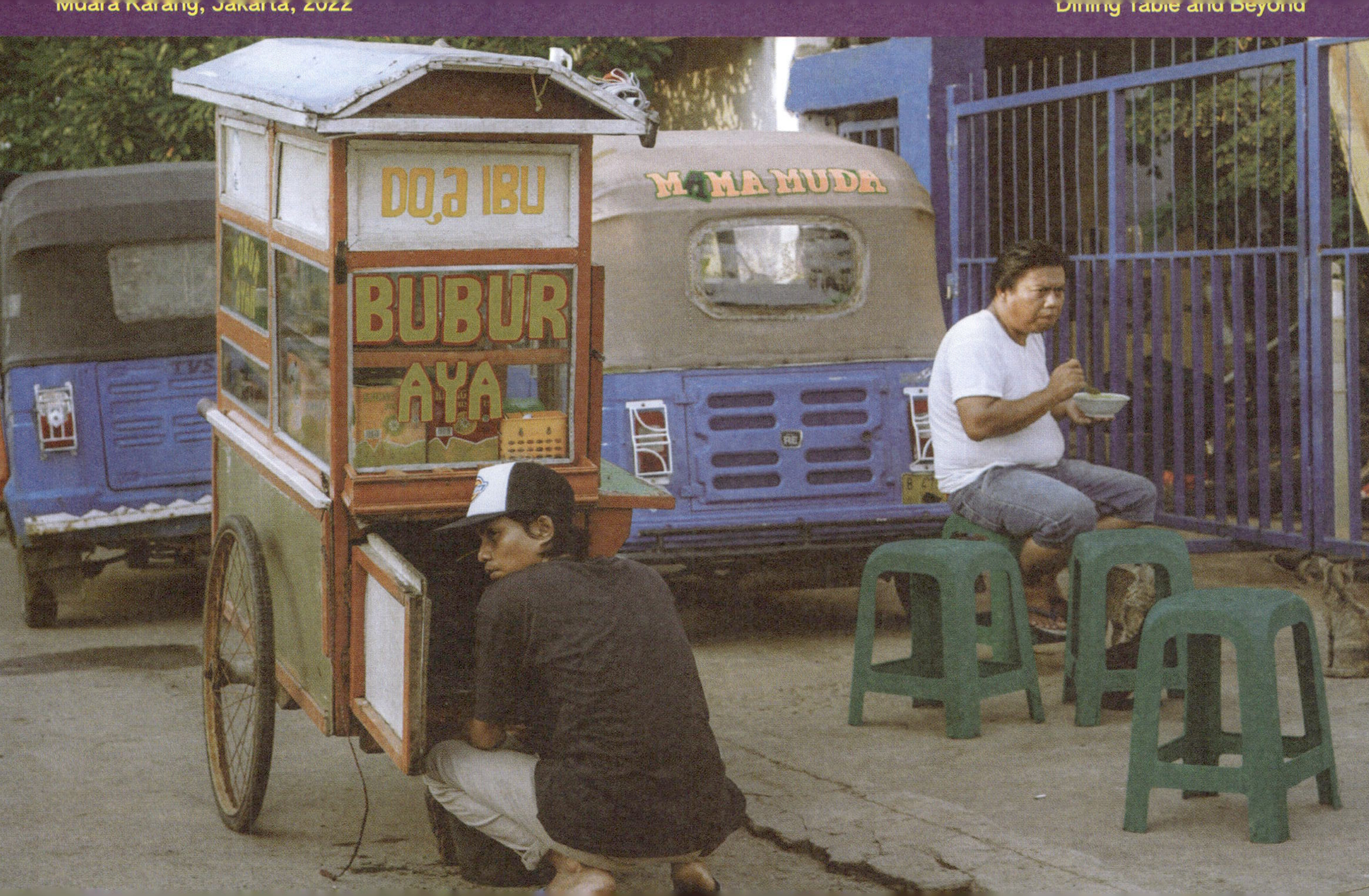

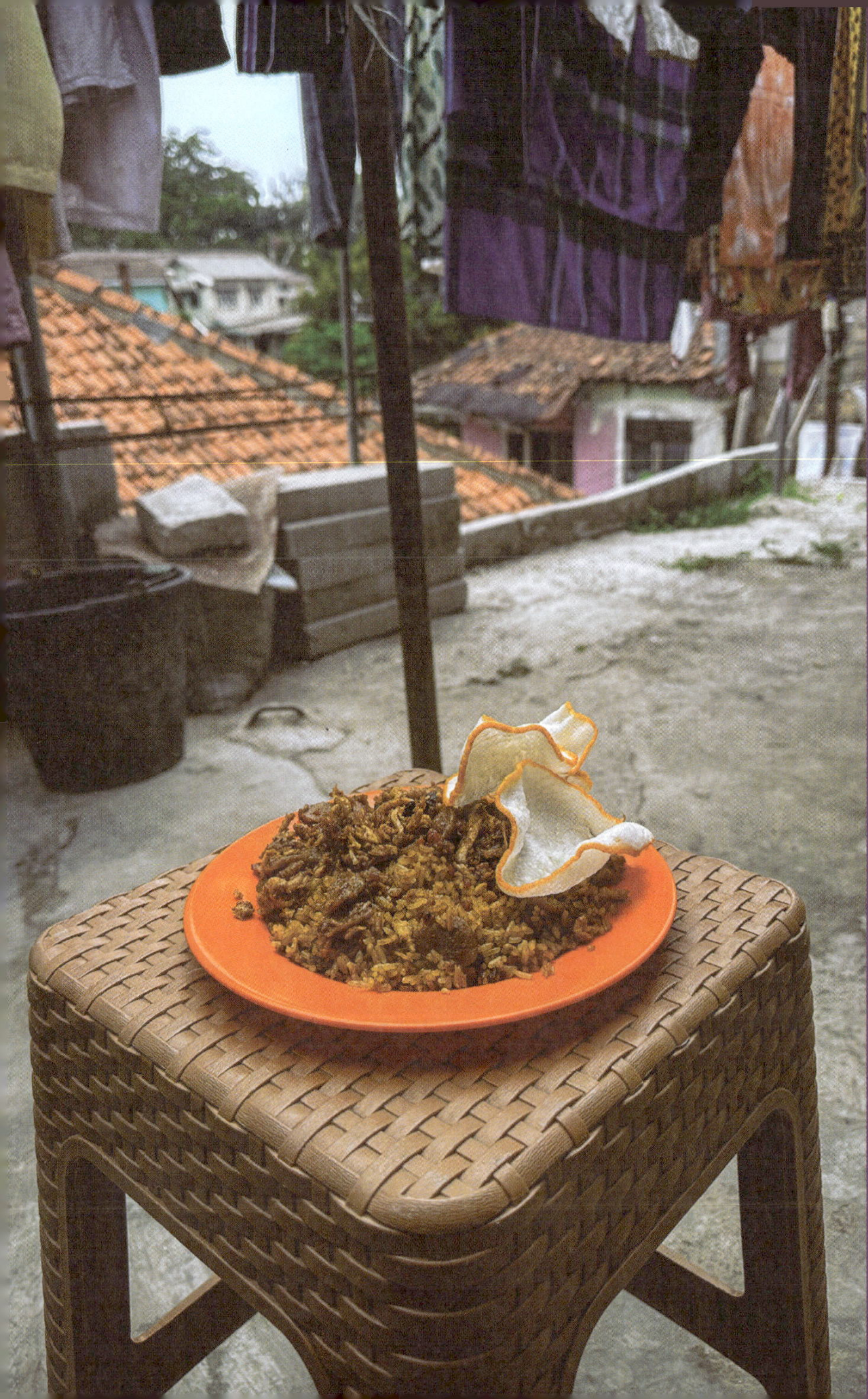

Nasi Goreng Aban Liem, Bogor, 2023

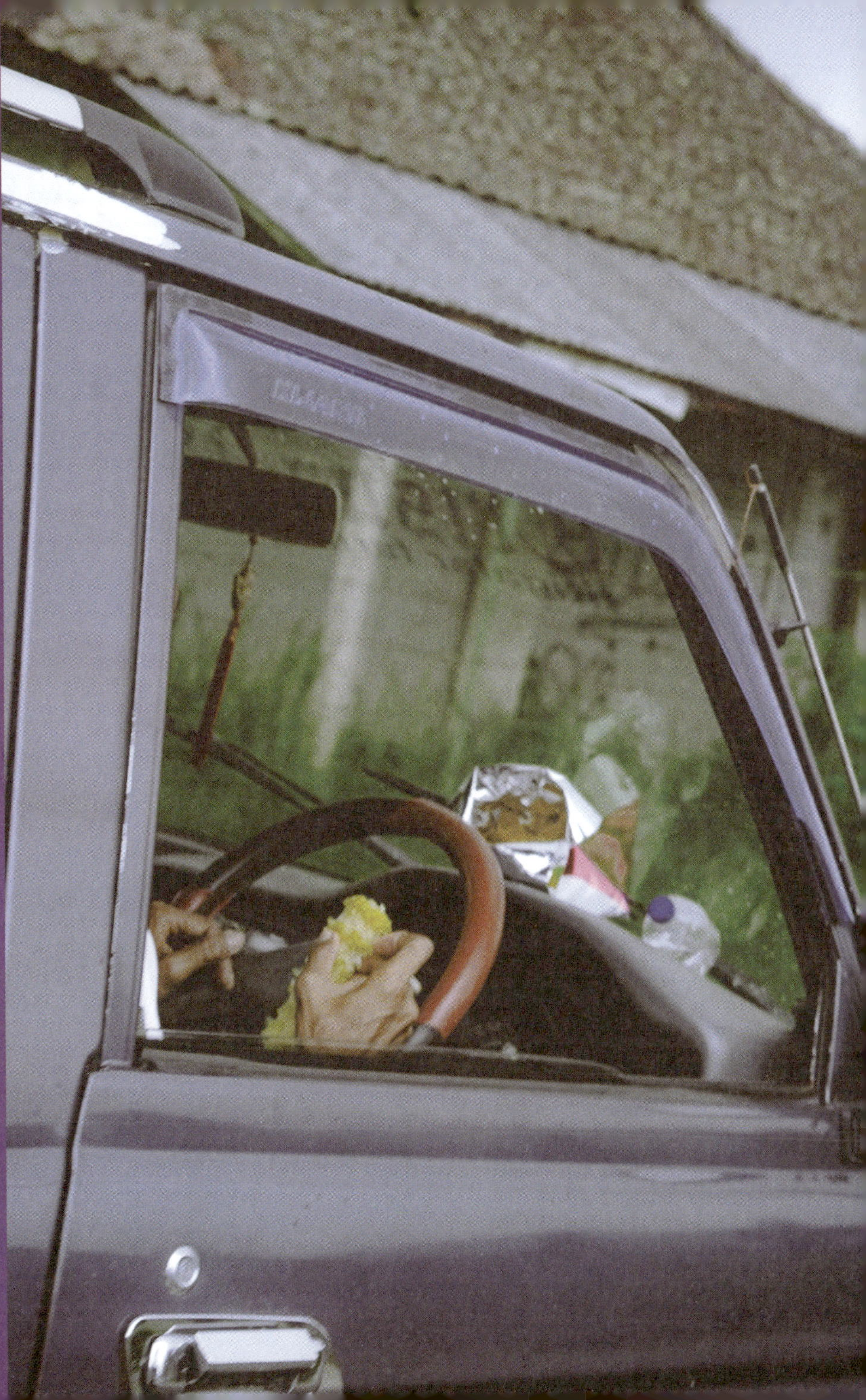

Bali, 2024

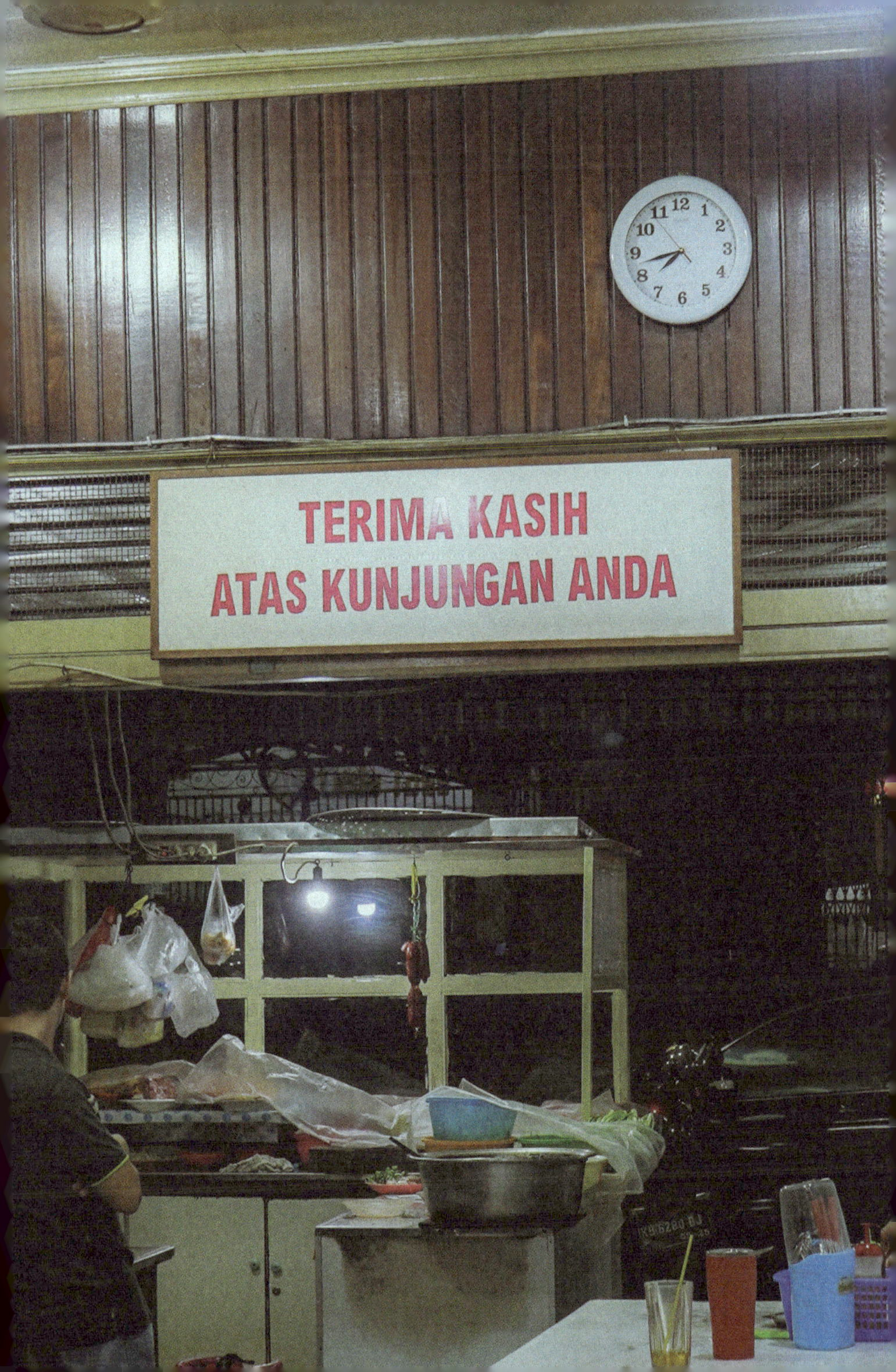
TERIMA KASIH
ATAS KUNJUNGAN ANDA

everything on the dining table

Sometimes we overlook the priceless nature of moments spent at the dining table, moments that cannot be recreated. Even when it feels like a routine lunch with ordinary food, these occasions can hold deeper significance. When differences arise at the table, whether in clashes of cultures or harmonious blends of human and natural elements, they can lead to something beautiful.

Rather than being feared, these differences should be embraced and celebrated. We often reserve celebrations for special occasions, yet they can be found in everyday simplicity, even when the table itself may be empty. If we are fortunate, these moments occur at the dining table, surrounded by loved ones.

Even as I write all of this, I'm reminded of the reality that not everyone has the privilege to eat on a dining table. That something sounds so simple: sitting down for a meal, with a plate on a surface and time to share it. It humbles me. It breaks me a little too. It's wild, almost tenderly cruel, how easily we forget how rare and sacred that moment can be.

Dining tables hold the weight of unsaid things, the comfort of familiar routines, and the presence of those we care about. Not every meal is a celebration, but every gathering is a chance to feel less alone. In the passing of dishes, in the silence between bites, in the refills of tea. Something real and human is exchanged. And often, that's enough.

Sometimes, in our search for grandeur, we overlook the beauty of these irreplaceable moments.

Dining tables are the symbol of how precious simplicity is.

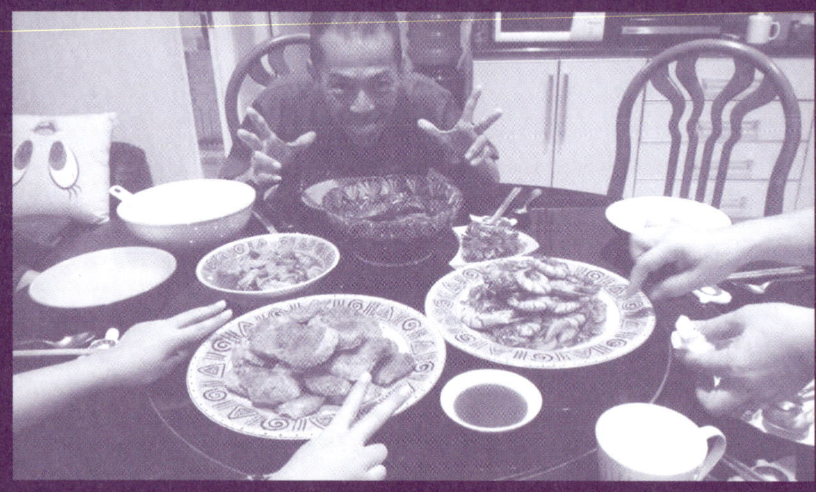

Home in Jakarta, 2015

ABOUT THE AUTHOR

Valensia Harumi Edgina is an artist and writer whose work explores how food rituals shape identity, memory, and belonging—particularly in contemporary Indonesia. Her practice spans photography, videography, storytelling, and cultural projects that document how Indonesians eat, gather, and live across time and place.

With a background in law and a deep connection to her Chinese-Indonesian heritage, Val's work often reflects themes of hybridity, cultural equity, and the ways food anchors identity and community. Beyond the page, she works in the hospitality industry, curates dining and music experiences, and performs as a DJ—using different formats to explore how food connects people across spaces, sounds, and memories. She is also the co-founder of Lazy Susan, an initiative exploring Indonesian food culture through art and community.

www.valedgina.com

Printed in Indonesia

First Edition, 2024
ISBN 978-623-96567-3-7
Xpatial Occasion Publishing

All photos by Valensia Harumi Edgina
Cover and Book Design by Hary 'Munir' Septiandry
Editorial Consultant by Alyandra Katya

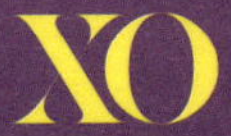

Meja Makan Indonesia

Valensia Harumi Edgina

9 786239 656737